M

D0548495

FROM THE LIBRARY OF

Margaret J Beattie ~

BIMBASHI McPHERSON
A LIFE IN EGYPT

BIMBASHI McPHERSON
A LIFE IN EGYPT

EDITED BY BARRY CARMAN AND JOHN McPHERSON

BRITISH BROADCASTING CORPORATION

To
The Land and People of Egypt,
the inspiration of the Letters, and
The Kinsmen who valued them.

Published by the
British Broadcasting Corporation
35 Marylebone High Street
London W1M 4AA

ISBN 0 563 20134 7

First published 1983
© Barry Carman and John McPherson 1983

Set in 11 on 12pt APS Baskerville

Printed in Great Britain by
Spottiswoode Ballantyne Ltd
Colchester and London

Contents

PART FOUR
FREE AS THE SEA 1925–1946

Preface

The author of this book, which has been distilled from some twenty-five volumes of his correspondence covering a long and various life in Egypt, was one of the most singular and captivating personages it has been my fortune to encounter. Our paths crossed in Cairo and I was honoured to be the recipient of what must have been the last complimentary copy of his 'Moulids Of Egypt', an account of the fairs and *fêtes votives* of the Egyptian delta, an invaluable work despite vagaries of chaotic printing, which gave one a superb first hand glimpse of the low life of Egypt. My own copy, which I laid under heavy tribute when I needed colour for my Alexandria Quartet, now reposes piously in the University Archive at Illinois. It is starred and underlined and cross-hatched in a way which makes clear the extent of my debt. My lack of Arabic was a terrible handicap. But with the help of this little classic I was able to make ends meet sufficiently for my purpose. Now comes a much greater work, also a classic, which fills in the gulf which yawns between the massive and beautiful book by Lane – his 'Modern Egyptians' – and the present. There have been many books of political analysis and of gossip but nothing (that I have seen) which bears the authentic stamp of first hand knowledge as this one does.

Of McPherson himself it is hard to write in a way that does justice to his many-sided personality. But one saw him, as somebody said, 'ambling about Cairo on a white mule lost in thought and looking like God the Father.' He gave off the most extraordinary scent of human grace. Had he wandered into Tibet he would at once have been recognised as a lama of superior attainments. He was of medium height and slightly built with a small and beautiful head which housed eyes of extraordinary luminosity and smiling kindness. He had a way of sitting passively in the oriental manner which was as eloquent as a whole speech. The Egyptians loved him and thought of him as some sort of seer, though his sense of humour and witty turns of phrase made him seem more approachable than the ordinary holy man. He carried out his modest functions with a delightful good grace and warmth which won all hearts. And of course the amazing thing was that as well as all this we had to do with a fine scholar, accomplished linguist, as well as a *bon viveur* and man of action! It is baffling to recount in this way but the readers of this book will see how many-sided their author is.

His long life covered a whole period of transition as well as two wars; when he arrived in Cairo the population was only 400,000. When he died it was over two million and still growing. Something of these great

changes reflect themselves in his observations. The book which has been
edited with exemplary piety and scrupulous care is that rare thing, a real
classic about Modern Egypt—a scholar's treasure and a readers delight!

LAWRENCE DURRELL

Editorial Note

Editorially, the family letters of Joseph McPherson are as full of hazards as the golf links he constructed in the desert (see p. 108). They are luxuriant with topical and historical allusions, quotations in several languages, ancient and modern, private family jokes and code-words, digested Biblical and literary allusions, et cetera.

To avoid serried ranks of footnotes, many of these allusions have been omitted. There remains a profusion of material requiring explanation, and to provide it has been a fascinating and time-consuming exercise (see on p. 193 the 'Arabic' word, on which much time was spent, which turned out to be Cockney).

McPherson's punctuation followed his own rules, and his use of capital letters has a seventeenth-century style of casual abundance. We have left much of this undisturbed.

Editors' explanations, interpolations, etc, are shown by square brackets.

Arabic transliteration: This was a particular problem and we appeal to the forbearance and curiosity of Egyptians and other speakers of Arabic. McPherson's letters are a museum of changing transliteration practices over forty-five years, plus his own highly individualistic variations. He frequently wrote the word or phrase in Arabic script (omitted in this book) followed by its English transliteration and translation; the object was to add interest and colour to his narrative. So here, casually put down in personal letters, are displayed a beginner's blunders (e.g. *fi'l do-el-kamr* on p. 29), forms taken from the first (nineteenth century) grammars and vocabularies he studied (e.g. *fattah, arabieh*) and attempts to convey dialects and uneducated speech. As an extra individual touch, he occasionally uses the Scottish *ch* sound (as in loch), where another would write *kh* (e.g. *bacheel, bacheer*).

We sought expert advice on this matter, but made our own decisions on what to rationalise (in the interests of avoiding irritation), and what to leave as examples of period and personal style – so any errors of judgment are our own, and not our advisors'.

In McPherson's own book *The Moulids of Egypt*, he dealt with the problem thus: 'The author has not found it practicable to standardise completely the English spelling of Arabic words. Many of the terms and names were transcribed from verbal accounts where the pronunciation differed from place to place and time to time. The difficulty will be appreciated by anyone with a knowledge of the variations in Egyptian colloquial.'

A Note on the Family Letters

Joseph McPherson, my great-uncle, was a figure in my childhood who at infrequent intervals appeared at home, thrust sweets and sixpences into the hands of my sisters and myself, played strenuous practical jokes, could give a spirited rendering on the piano of 'Polly Wolly Doodle', and spent long hours with my father drinking beer and talking of Coptic, Armenian, and Melkite churches, and such incomprehensible matters. The impression that remains with me of Uncle Quack, as he was known to us children, was that he was something of a mystery but fun, definitely fun.

His letters in twenty-six bound volumes came into my hands on the death of my father in 1955. Uncle Quack's letters had always been something of a joke among the younger generations: none of us had ever read them and they seemed to take up an inordinate amount of space wherever we moved. It was only in the mid-70s that I began to peruse and study them, and appreciate what an extraordinary mass of documentation of a vanished era they provided.

The letters were never intended for publication, but for a private family archive. They were written during his forty-five years in Egypt to various members of his family in England. In his own preface he explained: 'The genesis and preservation of the following letters is the natural outcome of the spirit of clannishness and the indissoluble bonds that exist between my brothers and their families and myself. When first I left England for the East I thought it would be a source of pleasure to the "Folks at Home", if from time to time I sent them an account of my wanderings, observations, mode of life, etc, and it was not until my holiday visit to England in the summer of 1904 that I found the various "Family Letters" that had been despatched to different members of the Clan at Home had been typed by my brother Dougal, and even then the idea of binding them into volumes did not occur to me, nor perhaps at once to him'.

In fact, Dougal, my grandfather, undertook the task of collating the letters, later helped in the task by my father, Campbell. The recipients of the letters ranged over three generations: his brothers and their wives, their children and their children's spouses and their grandchildren. From the earliest days he wrote to both old and young, and often fitted his themes to his addressees, e.g. to a brother a description of a ceremonial occasion; to a sister-in-law an account of his housekeeping; to a young nephew the story of a rough-house; to a young niece an enjoyable shudder-provoking recital of the insect and reptile life of Egypt. All

John McPherson, great-nephew of Joseph, aged 9 months, in the arms of his Bedouin nurse, Zenna, in Alexandria, 1926

letters, however, were for family circulation and then collection into proper sequence.

Later the typed letters were bound into volumes, and photographs and sketches inserted. In the binding of each volume was a wallet, in which he put all sorts of ephemera: menus, invitations, postcards, Egyptian nationalist tracts which he had confiscated during the 1919 Revolution, and documentation relating to various episodes he narrates, e.g. the safe conduct from the Turkish sub-governor which he used to get himself out of a tight corner when crossing the Taurus Mountains in 1909.

Until quite recently I had thought the original hand-written letters lost or destroyed, until they turned up unexpectedly in the possession of his last surviving niece, Gladys, who died several months later in her ninety-first year. They were written, often scribbled, on all manner of paper; notepaper from the Turf Club in Cairo, from Shepheard's Hotel, and from the Khedivial Mail Steamship Company; on leaves from Field Service notebooks and the backs of Intelligence Report forms – in short anything that came to hand during his travels in peace and war. I marvel at the application of my grandfather and father in their 'editorial' task.

The bound volumes of letters have survived various hazards: in my great-uncle's lifetime they were hurriedly packed and hidden when Rommel's Afrika Korps threatened Cairo; while in storage they have been attacked by insects and deluged by a burst water-pipe.

This book based on the family letters is presented with Joseph McPherson's own modest introduction for his family readers:

'Amongst their many defects they have one merit, which is certainly rare in writings on the East, they describe people and things at first hand, not from notes supplied by other people who are often interested in adding some political or social colouring, nor from books. This has been carried even further than I should have wished, for my somewhat unsettled life has deterred me from bringing my books from England, and from obtaining works of reference, so that even quotations are from memory and remain unchecked.

May Allah grant all readers patience and the spirit of indulgence'.

JOHN McPHERSON

Acknowledgements

'*Bimbashi*' *McPherson – A Life in Egypt* sprang from the trilogy of radio programmes with the same title, based on Joseph McPherson's letters. The producer of the programmes was Alan Haydock, to whom we owe a debt of gratitude. His enthusiasm for the material made him a prime mover in the writing and publication of this book. We thank him for his encouragement and sage counsel throughout.

We are much indebted to Peter Mansfield for casting his authoritative eye over the manuscript; to John Kerry for meticulous reading and constructive criticism during the writing; also to friends (of John McPherson) from St Mary's College, Newcastle upon Tyne, particularly Andrew Knowles, who made valuable suggestions for an earlier draft.

We thank the staff of the Central Reference Library of the BBC (most particularly its classicist Michel Petheram), and of the Arabic, Turkish, Persian and Southern European Sections of the BBC External Services, and the BBC Monitoring Section, for sustained assistance over a long period; also the staff of the libraries of the Royal Geographical Society, and the School of Oriental and African Studies.

Other institutions which helped included the Centre for Middle Eastern Studies, St Antony's College, Oxford; the Imperial War Museum; Fitzwilliam Museum; the Australian War Memorial, Canberra; and the Ministry of Defence (Army Historical Branch).

For advice on Arabic transliteration we are obliged to Peter Colvin of the School of Oriental and African Studies, and A. L. Gammal of the Polytechnic of Central London.

Many people responded with great kindness to requests for information, sometimes on general background, sometimes on minute points of detail. They included Mary Embleton of St Antony's College, Oxford, who generously shared the results of her research into British Officialdom in Egypt; Brigadier D. V. Henchley, Keble College, Oxford; John Parker, History Dept., York University; the late Sir William Morris; Jeremy Coote, Wolfson College, Oxford (who explained 'Bakurëmi'); Prof. V. L. Ménage and Humphrey Fisher, School of Oriental and African Studies; Louis Allen, Dept. of French, University of Durham; Miranda Mackintosh; Ventura Varo; Jan Morris; Sir John Richmond; John Julius Norwich; Lady Anne Hill; Lawrence Durrell; Major-General Abdel Aziz Safwat (who recalled the police organisation and the control of drug trafficking under Russell Pasha); the Governing Body of Christ Church, Oxford; also members of the French, Italian, and Spanish Institutes in London, and the Cultural Section, Turkish Embassy, London.

In Cairo, we were afforded valuable assistance by the British Council, and by Sherard Cowper-Coles of the British Embassy.

We thank Pat McPherson who has sustained and supported her husband's obsession with the Family Letters over twenty-five years; also members of the McPherson 'clan', particularly Joseph McPherson's great-nieces, Hilary and Christine, for their help in reconstructing family history.

For wide-ranging logistical and psychological support we thank Edna Oppenheimer; and for most valuable working accommodation and facilities, Elena and William Graves, and Sasha Magasiner.

Finally, we were gratified to find in our editor, Victoria Huxley, an ally who combined enthusiasm with serenity.

THE McPHERSON FAMILY TREE

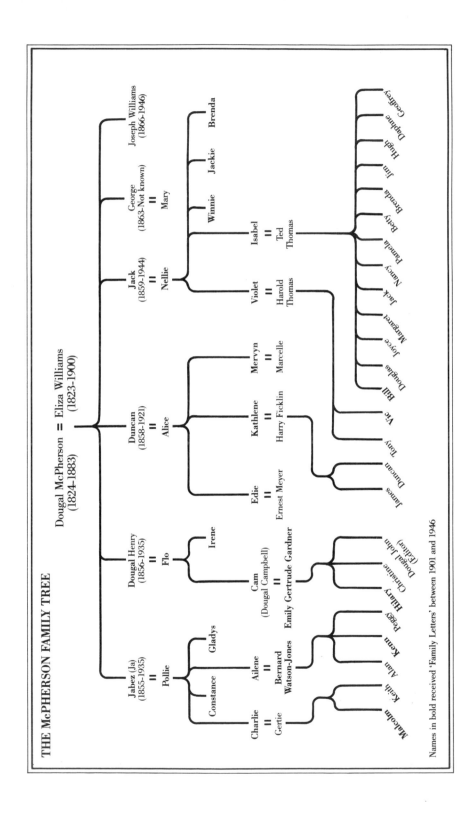

Dougal McPherson = Eliza Williams
(1824-1883) (1823-1900)

Names in bold received 'Family Letters' between 1901 and 1946

Prologue

In the traffic-frenzied streets of Cairo during the Second World War there was often to be seen a straightbacked old Englishman serenely riding a white donkey, with his syce striding alongside. As he passed, an Egyptian might say: 'That is he who taught me science at the Khedivieh School in 1901' or 'That is he who commanded me at the Battle of Gaza in 1917' or 'That is he who imprisoned me during the 1919 revolution', or 'That is he who knows more than any other *Ifrangi* of our Islamic religious feasts'.

This veteran who represented in his own person much of the history of the British presence in Egypt was Joseph Williams McPherson (Bimbashi, retd.), often called in his social circle simply 'The Bimbashi' (Turkish for 'Major'), a living reminder of past days when many Britons entering Egyptian Government service assumed the exotic titles of the Ottoman Empire. He had arrived in Egypt in November 1901, in the high noon of British imperialism, and he lived there until he died, aged eighty, in 1946. Few other Britons had such a long experience of Egypt; none recorded it as minutely as he did in his family letters written to his brothers and other relations in England.

Joseph McPherson was born in Somerset in 1866, the youngest of six sons in a Highland Scottish family which had migrated southwards. His parents were Covenanting Christians of exceptional fervour. His mother once wrote that she had named her first-born son Jabez, after the Biblical Jabez whose mother 'bare him in sorrow', because she too bore him in sorrow, 'knowing my child would be born in sin, like others, and would continue in sin, unless saved in the Lord with an everlasting salvation'. However, despite the bleakness of her creed, she seems to have been exceptionally sweet-natured, and Joseph was intensely devoted to her; the family believed that no woman ever replaced her in his affections, and that this was one reason why he never married.

His father had been an estate manager to the Duke of Gordon and other great landowners in Scotland; after coming to England he obtained a post as supervisor in a lunatic asylum outside Bristol, where he discovered within himself a rare and effective understanding of the mentally ill. His relationship with his youngest son, however, was painfully unsympathetic. In old age, Joseph recalled with still fresh feeling 'the austere and morbid twist of father's religion', and wrote:

He was a man of inflexible righteousness and missed his vocation as monk or missionary or martyr . . . But he should never have had boys, certainly not me to scowl at habitually . . . He was a comely person enough, judging from a painting of him in tartans and sword, in front of Huntly Castle; and from the obvious admiration of the women folk, in spite of sometimes brutal coldness, and 'hirsute stigmata of Victorian side

Some of the 'band of brothers' at
The Rookery: Joseph, Jack,
George,'In the Golden Age'

Dougal, the brother who was the
first curator of the family letters

Mother – Eliza Williams McPherson
'Salve Sancta Parens!'

Father – Dougal McPherson
'A man of inflexible righteousness'

whiskers'. In fact, I gather in spite of his reticence about himself and his family that he left Scotland as a Joseph fleeing from a great wickedness and a Mrs Potiphar in the person of the Marchioness of B——.

Father could be courtly and debonair, even to me, as I discovered when, in my thirteenth year, we toured about Scotland; and much more so later, when I spent a fortnight with him and a few of his patients at Lorne Hall, Torquay, and he took me boating and fishing and bathing. He treated me as a guest or as a *patient*. So impressed was I, that a sort of emotional wave convinced me that we had misunderstood one another, and a realisation of his great qualities urged me to a sort of hero worship. But on our return, when my intended good works displeased him, and I laid my homage at his feet, only to be kicked metaphorically into the vertical, I gave up the attempts I had always made or at least intended to please him, and ingratiate myself with him, which had been so unsuccessful, and, I fear, rather studied to annoy him, this time with the greatest success. And I vowed I would never have children of my own.

Nevertheless, because of his mother's 'gentle affection', and the comradeship of his older brothers, his was – he declared – a happy childhood. The family home was a Jacobean house called The Rookery, part of the asylum domain, but set in large grounds with an orchard and private graveyard and ancient trees, and surrounded by fields and woods. All his life Joseph McPherson looked back on it as an enchanted playground, the 'Little Kingdom' of the band of brothers.

Elizabeth, Duchess of Gordon, godmother to all the McPherson brothers except Joseph. Deeply religious, she was probably an important influence on Joseph's father

Left: Joseph McPherson, aged 24, 1890, 'Oxford Days End'. *Right:* Very Rev. H. G. Liddell, Dean of Christ Church, father of the Alice who inspired Lewis Carroll. He gave McPherson a reference stating that, 'he fully justified our choice by his industry and good conduct'

He was educated at Clifton College in Bristol, where he was well-grounded in Latin, Greek and several modern languages and literatures. In 1883 he won a scholarship to the Royal College of Science in Dublin, and four years later another scholarship to Christ Church, Oxford, where he gained a First Class degree in Natural Sciences. At Oxford he was successful athletically and socially; he was much involved in strenuous undergraduate pranks, and, through high living with aristocratic friends, ran up large debts which his brothers paid. At the same time he was devoutly religious, having converted to Catholicism while in Ireland. After Oxford, he was for a while secretary to the 4th Baron Camoys, then proceeded to a career in education as science master at the Merchant Venturers School in Bristol, and at Clifton College, and other schools of repute. He was also a Senior Extension Lecturer for Oxford University. It was a career of minor distinction, and some promise, but somehow unfocused. Indeed, as he wrote, his thoughts were elsewhere:

Since my boyhood it had been my dream to live in Cairo, and, from that centre, to see and know as much as possible of the places, peoples and languages all round the Mediterranean, but particularly those in the Valley of the Nile.

When he was thirty-five, his mother died. He recalled, years later:

Mother's death left a deeper shadow and more terrible void than even my worst forebodings, and nothing in England seemed to rouse much enthusiasm. The old longing for the 'storied shores of the Mediterranean', which had been repressed while Mother was still alive and anchored me at home, returned now unrestrained.

> At this time he heard that a delegate from the Egyptian government, a Mr Houghton, was in England, 'collecting a few Oxford men' for service in the Egyptian administration.

Mr Houghton was not to be found at the address given, nor at his home, and time was almost or quite up. His sister, however, kindly told me that he was interested in one of the St Leger runners, and was not likely to miss Doncaster, then opening. I post-hasted hither, ran him down on the course, was hospitably entertained at his quarters in the evening, and instantly fixed up with a post, with practically no written or verbal particulars, except to whom and at what date I should present myself.

> The post was with the Department of Public Instruction, and from 1901 until 1914 he worked in Cairo and Alexandria as teacher, lecturer and educational administrator. During the Great War he served as a Red Cross Officer at Gallipoli, and as an officer in the Camel Transport Corps in the Sinai campaign, and was present at the Battles of Romani and Gaza. In 1918 he was appointed Acting Mamur Zapt, or Head of Secret Police in Cairo ('the lurid gulf in my life'), and for several years combated crime, corruption, and the irresistible rise of Egyptian nationalism. When he retired in 1924, he stayed on in Egypt, to which he had given his heart when he first arrived, and wrote a comprehensive work on Islamic religious festivals.
>
> Joseph McPherson, though a noted identity in Anglo-Egyptian society, was not famous, and never achieved the eminence in any of his careers which his abilities seem to have warranted. On his own testimony, the cause was an innate lack of ambition. In old age he looked back to an occasion when he was a boy of sixteen. Challenged brutally by his father to decide what to do with his life, he had escaped from the argument 'horribly perturbed', and to ease his mind, read some verse – Keats's *Endymion*.

I was electrified when I came to the words:

> 'I can see
> Nought earthly worth my compassing.'

Keats had given expression to my thoughts and feelings. I felt that I was up against a stupendous proposition, that must be thought out – for on its acceptance or rejection hung one's life in this world – and perhaps in the next. So I thought and dreamed and read and reasoned, and furtively asked questions of those I thought might guide me; and I marshalled careers that might lead up to all earthly attractions and goals into the light of that luminous thesis of Keats, and all faded, and I was compelled to know and feel that I agreed with Keats. At intervals throughout my life I have reconsidered this problem and paraded wealth, power, titles, eminence of all kinds, but always with the same negative result.

At the same time, he insisted that life 'offers *a mine of treasures* worth enjoying, and intended for our enjoyment'.

In the forty-five years of his life in Egypt, he wrote – to his brothers and their families – over three thousand pages of letters, nearly a million words. The letters were intended to inform and entertain the 'folks at home', and to become part of a family archive. The descriptions of the plain facts of his life included traveller's adventures, battlefield despatches, tales of mystery and detection, episodes dramatic and humorous and exotic, sidelights on historical events – the letters of a born storyteller, a brilliant reporter, and a continuously surprising personality.

McPherson's originality is displayed early in the letters when he describes a visit to the Grand Mufti, the arbiter of religious law in Egypt. They went riding together, the Mufti on a mule, McPherson on a donkey, continuing to discuss doctrinal matters. On coming to a narrow defile, with room for only one animal at a time, the difficult question of precedence arose, each insisting that the other go first. 'I settled the point', wrote McPherson, 'by riding in front but sitting in the reversed position so as to face the Sheikh.' *Riding Forward, Facing Backward* could well be the motto of McPherson's life. For here, displayed in the family letters, is a personality of many contradictions and paradoxes: part hedonist, part lay-monk; open to new experiences, yet stiff with prejudices; warmly responsive to Egyptians but scornful of their political aspirations; a solitary who loved good company; the most convinced of Catholics with a deep interest in Islam; alternately, furiously energetic or abandoned to languor; the most civilised of men, with a streak of bluff insensitivity and a penchant for violence. He was, perhaps, something of an actor, a self-dramatiser, who would play with some swagger any part life assigned him, whether as traveller, warrior, inquisitor, or 'Old Swan'.

When he died in his eighty-first year, a friend wrote in a letter; 'Ah . . . so the Wild One is gone'. Another friend lamented the passing of the 'Wild Egyptian'. At first glance, this is an unexpected term for a man who spent most of his working life as an educationalist, and much of his retirement as a student of religious ritual and mysticism. But the family letters support the epitaph, not only by the bravura episodes they contain, but also by the pervading sense of McPherson as a maverick (what his Scottish forebears might have called a 'gae'n aboot body'), someone who is always in some way a stranger. His own self-analysis was precise:

I think it is my fundamental nature to love vagabondage and liberty, to dread any sort of tie, as much as animals you have known which though

affectionate enough and loving human company and sympathy, shrink
at being picked up and the freedom of their movement threatened even
by the friends they love best.

Egypt at the beginning of the twentieth century, when McPherson
arrived there, was the most ambiguous of British possessions. It was neither
colony nor protectorate; in fact it was not a part of the British Empire at
all. Nominally, it was an autonomous province of the Ottoman Empire,
with a Head of State, the Khedive, who owed allegiance to the Sultan at
Istanbul. It had its own parliament, government, army and civil
administration; yet for nearly twenty years, since 1882, the British had
run the country, and the real ruler was Evelyn Baring, Lord Cromer, the
British Agent and Consul General, and the most masterful of imperial pro-
consuls.

Egypt had been acquired in an action to re-establish 'law and order'. In
the 1870s the country had become virtually bankrupt, because of the vast
debts owed by the Khedive Ismail (the 'magnificent') to European banks.
He was induced to abdicate, and Britain and France imposed financial
controls, exercised by commissioners, on his successor the Khedive Tewfik.
A nationalist revolt against the Khedive and his foreign guardians
erupted in the Egyptian army, led by the Minister of War, Colonel Arabi.
Europeans were killed during riots in Alexandria, the British intervened
with naval and military forces, and in August 1882 a British army under
Sir Garnet Wolseley defeated Arabi's troops at the Battle of Tel-el-Kebir.

The expressed wish of the British government was to evacuate its forces
from Egypt 'as soon as the state of the country and the organisation of
proper means for the maintenance of the Khedive's authority will permit'.

Nevertheless, further thoughts about the responsibilities of power and
imperial self-interest prevailed. British officials were installed in key
positions in all departments of the administration; the Commander-in-
Chief of the Egyptian army was British, and so were many of his officers. A
garrison of six thousand British troops was stationed in Egypt; their
barracks dominated Cairo. The apparatus of control was complete, and in
1901 the country was quiet and largely acquiescient.

As for Egypt's status, the imperial statesman, Lord Milner put the
matter candidly in his book *England in Egypt*: 'It was a veiled Protectorate
which we could not avow ourselves, and therefore could not call upon
others to recognise. It was a veiled Protectorate of uncertain extent and
indefinite duration.' As such, Egypt provided, in much the same way as
the territories of the Empire, career opportunities for young Britons like
Joseph McPherson.

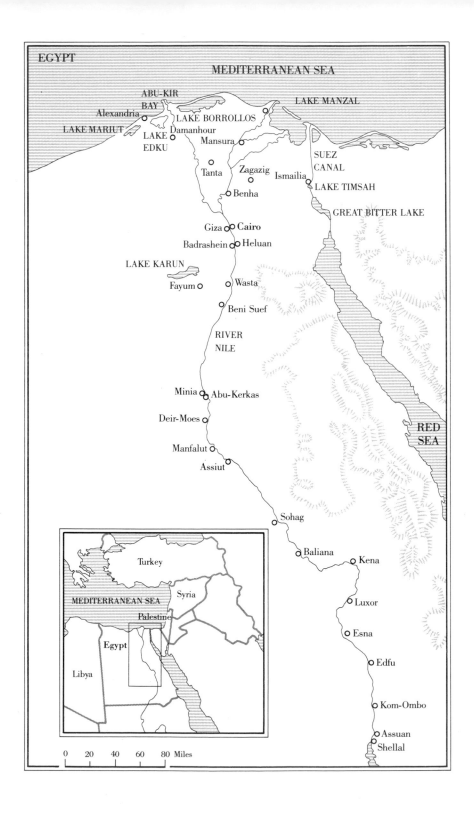

PART ONE

A MINE OF TREASURES
1901-1914

EDITORIAL NOTE

In the period 1901–1914, Joseph McPherson wrote one hundred family letters, some of great length. In this copious flood of words, certain themes and subjects stand out, and are here presented as chapters. When an excerpt only from a letter is quoted, the recipient and the date are indicated, but the salutations ('Dear Dougal', 'Dear Pollie', etc.,) and the signature ('Yours affectionately, Joe.') are omitted.

1

At First Sight

Egypt possesses high natural attractions, in the peculiar charms of its Oriental climate, the singularly clear atmosphere, the wonderful colouring and effects of light and shade, the exuberant fertility of the cultivated districts contrasted with the solemn, awe-inspiring desert, and the manners, customs, and appearance of a most interesting and most diversified population.

BAEDEKER'S *Egypt – A Handbook for Travellers*, 1902

Joseph McPherson arrived in Alexandria from Marseilles on the paquebot *Le Congo* on the morning of 1 October 1901, and immediately dashed off a first impression to his eldest brother, Ja:

I think I shall like the Egyptians, they are a fine, good-tempered, rather noble-looking lot, they appear to belong to a vastly higher type of humanity than the French for instance.

At thirty-five, he was a good deal older than the usual British recruit to the Egyptian educational service, and more accomplished. He was a practised lecturer in science and mathematics, a classical scholar and linguist, a notable games-player and horseman. His presence was striking: a spare athletic figure, ramrod-straight; a strong bony face, with a forceful nose and chin and large, intent, hazel eyes. In personality, he was admirably suited to respond to the Egyptians – a cordial and vivacious people.

His first posting was to the Khedivieh School, which he described as 'a sort of Eton of Egypt', a school for the sons of well-to-do families. It was housed together with the Department of Public Instruction, itself a part of the Ministry of the Interior, in a vast old palace in Cairo.

To Dougal   *Cairo, 5 October 1901*
On Wednesday I was formally presented at the Ministry – with military etiquette, and was assigned to teach in the buildings of the Ministry in connection with the Khedivieh School. They allotted to me the most advanced Chemistry and Mathematics (the latter a little to my disgust as I shall have to rub up my Higher Algebra and Geometry).

Joseph McPherson at the Khedivieh
School correcting students' exercises

To Duncan   *Cairo, 9 October 1901*
The boys (and men) are marshalled into their places by officers and the
professors, as they call us, have no muddling about like in English schools.
There is quite a big staff of servants and officers to look after everything
beyond the actual lecturing. I have to wear a tarboosh as do all the
professors and students, by order of the Sultan our Suzerain. On entering
and leaving a class the students all rise and salute in military style. I have
not had to complain of anyone's conduct as yet. The first complaint to the
Head means a long drill for the offender, a second means imprisonment,
sometimes on bread and water. The chaps as a rule are much keener on
learning than in England and therefore give much less trouble; but on
the other hand it is hard to explain things and to make oneself heard.
Turkish coffee is served free in the middle of the morning and afternoon,
and lunch is provided midday for a nominal sum.

   We have a luxurious room for the English masters with couches and so
on, and unlimited smoking, and officers in attendance and another
secluded room where we can sleep if we want to. There is also a common
room for all professors, French, Arabic, etc.

   During the last few years the English side has grown enormously at the
expense of the French; in fact we have collared nearly all the best rooms
and best posts from the French side.

   I have four lessons in Chemistry to give. The lecture room and lab. are
fitted – like everywhere else – most lavishly; but nothing is labelled in
English. My chief assistant (Smashman) is a Syrian and knows no
English but fortunately knows a little French and German. My second

assistant (Mahommed) knows not a word of any European language. The pupils know a little French and English beside Arabic. My other twelve lessons are advanced Mathematics . . .. Most of the students are very nice chaps (and differ in very few respects from English fellows).

McPherson immediately set about learning Arabic. He was to master it so completely that in future years he could pass for an Arab or Egyptian.

The leading authority on education in Egypt during the British presence, Humphrey Bowman, wrote in his book *Middle-East Window* of the British teachers in this period: 'There was little or no friendly intercourse between them and their pupils; as soon as their work was over, the English masters escaped on their bicycles to the sporting club at Gezira, there to indulge in their own games of golf or tennis or squash racquets, or to sit and gossip at the Turf Club over tea or a whisky and soda with their English friends.'

McPherson was an exception: he entered with zest into Egyptian society, gaining an entrée through his students and their friends. Among the many new acquaintances mentioned in his early letters were the young sons of the Colonel Arabi who had been defeated by Sir Garnet Wolseley at the Battle of Tel-el-Kebir in 1882, and who, after long exile in Ceylon, had been permitted to return to Egypt and live as a quiet pensioner. Particular student friends were Ibrahim Zaky and Hamid Mahmud. Forty years later, when he wrote a book about the Moulids, or religious festivals, of Egypt he paid tribute to them in his introduction for their friendship. By then Zaky was a distinguished doctor, and Hamid Mahmud the Minister of Hygiene in the government.

In his descriptions of his new life, he writes as if falling under an enchantment; and indeed McPherson gave his heart to Egypt at first sight, and for life.

To Jack   *Cairo, 28 October 1901*
It is the evening of the 15th day of the month (Ragab) in the year of the prophet 1319   and therefore it is the night of the full moon and though it is the 5th hour of the evening (10.30 p.m.) I can write with perfect ease *'fi'l-do el-kamr'* (by the light of the moon)[1] whilst we lie in our felucca under the palm trees of the Gezira. Zaky, at whose house I dined and who arranged this moonlight sail on the Nile has been very much afraid when the strong Southern breeze rushed us past the piers of the bridge of the Qasr el-Nil (one of the extravagances of Ismail Pasha) against the tremendous rush of the Nile, but now he is happy as a bird and is chattering in a way which makes it impossible to write a sane and orthodox letter. He is telling me now that it is fortunate that I write not on a *mendil abiud* (white handkerchief), else the *do-el-kamr* (moonlight) would shred it in small pieces; and he has explained to me the generation of the Kangaroo water rats which Allah forms from the mud of the Nile –

---

[1] Arabic speakers are referred to the Note on Transliteration on p. 9.

he himself has seen several half-rat and half Nile-mud and so I have set him to seek for one.

The moonlight is marvellous – the sky gleams with blue, the land with red, the water with silver, and it is easy to read even the points of Arabic writing. The river spreads before me like the sea and we tacked up against the stream until we could see the Pyramid of Sakkara and were it only a holiday tomorrow we would leave the felucca and ride on donkeys to the Tombs of the sacred Bulls. The boat we are in is of a rough native structure but I think I never realised the beauty of line and curve so much as in our triangular sail and slender masts and spars.

I left the above to follow with Zaky a party of the Zikr – religious fanatics who carry mysterious lanterns and invoke Allah perpetually. Our pursuit of the Zikr brought us to an Egyptian Lokanda and there in spite of a long dinner some hours ago we have made the quaintest of Arab suppers. The food was excellent but each course was brought with a couple of spoons or forks and a single plate for the two and nearly a gallon of Tamarind wine was served in one huge tankard.

I had these two sheets of Club paper in my pocket and these only so (to Zaky's intense satisfaction) I will conclude this section and we will take advantage of the mighty stream to make our way back.

To Dougal   *Cairo, 10.30 p.m., 14 November 1901*
Today has been by no means a lazy day although I have no work on Thursdays. I worked at Arabic all the morning as the exam in conversation, reading manuscript, translation etc. is on the 15th of next month.

This afternoon at 2, I took a horse and rode to Giza to a football match in which I was not playing but where I was asked to attend in order to write a report for the Khedivieh Magazine. Our men won six goals to nil which makes my work as reporter much easier. Mahmud Sidky and another chap were also riding so I rode part way with them but on leaving them I missed my way and got into an interminable orange grove. It was all very well plucking oranges in all stages of ripeness and good fun jumping the ditches, but suddenly the sun disappeared and night came on at once. The beauty of the young night was quite beyond description and surpassed anything I have ever seen in that direction. Half round the horizon there was a blaze of red fire against which the orange and acacia and palm trees were silhouetted as one sees them sometimes at a firework display. The whole moon was brightly visible although only a day or two old and near it were Venus, Saturn and Jupiter, looking like balls of living white fire, which one half expected to see fall like the stars from a rocket.

> He now began what was to become a practice: to intersperse his frequent bulletins to his family with a sustained set-piece of description of some experience he rated particularly interesting or significant.

Dear Duncan and all *Cairo, 23 November 1901*

I have just returned from one of the most delightful and about the most original little holidays I have ever had.

One of my pupils Mahmud Sidky Mahmud called for me on Thursday morning with his brother Hamid Mahmud, and his cousin Ibrahim Zaky; and with an *Arabieh* (carriage) to take us to the station; whence we trained to Toukh which is about forty miles from here and rather in the Damietta direction. At Toukh we were met by a dog-cart with a galloping Arab horse in the shafts; they gave me the reins and we had a lively drive of about five miles to his house where the father Mahommed effendi Mahmud made us very much at home. We rode buffaloes down to the threshing floor and I took a turn at driving a pair of *Gamooze* (buffaloes) over the cut corn on a curious implement whose wheels consisted of about a hundred circular knives. We then adjourned to the orange fields and after picking and eating as many as we could we had a fight with them and then went shooting. My first shot happened to be successful and I brought down a Hoopoe with a crest like a peacock's tail in miniature. One or two other fellows arrived and after fooling about brook-jumping and riding, boxing with some of the farm men, etc., we settled down to coffee, etc., in the garden and on the arrival of the eldest brother Mahommed with the second brother Ahmed Aziz (one of the best forwards in the Khedivieh football team) we settled down to a long and elaborate dinner which to my surprise was *à la française* and accompanied by excellent claret, etc., and followed by Cognac.

During dinner in addition to the singing of grasshoppers and frogs (and gekhoes) the howling of wolves came through the open window, so we went out at about 11 into the moonlight and rode down to a spot where a dead donkey had been placed with a view to attracting jackals and hyenas. It was rather eerie work lying amongst the *dourah* (Indian Corn) with a small rifle at hand and an enormous revolver in case of an encounter at close quarters, and young Hamid who was nearest to me was whispering the weird tales that these chaps (with their vivid imagination and their instinctive facility for lying) puzzle strangers with, for it is impossible to tell how much is or may be sober fact. Moreover the Arabic words for wolf, bear and hyena (*dyb*) are so much alike that the difference can hardly be written in English, or appreciated on the instant by an Englishman. However nothing more formidable than jackals fell to our rifles and an owl which Aziz brought down by a ripping shot. On our way to the *dourah* field we had one exciting chase after a wolf and as the horses were too hot to stand about we had sent them back by the fellahin.

At about 2 a.m. we took a beeline for home, jumping streams and climbing trees, etc., on the way; and after a game of *Wizier wa torah* ['Heads or Tails', a coin-tossing game] and a glass of Scotch Whisky and Schweppes Soda we retired. I shared a double-bedded room with

Mahmud (Sidky) and Hamid (Mahmud); the room like the rest of the
house being fortified like a mediaeval castle (almost) with iron bars and
bolts and with revolvers by each bed; – for this is a lawless district
(probably there was not another European within twenty or thirty
miles), no homes except the mud huts of the fellahin for several miles and
although the chief of a noted band of sixty thieves who is the terror of the
district took bread and salt with us all in Mahommed's garden during the
evening and was therefore to be regarded rather as a protection than the
reverse, yet there are minor bands who are reputed to do a little killing in
addition to their plundering, just for the fun of the thing. A pack of house
dogs (like wolves in appearance) were roaming round the place and as
these occasionally answered the distant cry of a wolf or jackal and roused
the owls and other night birds; as the grasshoppers and frogs kept going
and as in spite of the spotless whiteness of my bed it was not wholly free
from fleas and a mosquito had somehow found its way inside the
namuseyeh, I did not expect much sleep, but I was mistaken for in spite of
all I slept like a top until about 9.30 a.m. when Zaky and Aziz charged in
with pillows.

After an excellent breakfast and a gallop down to the orange fields, we
went on foot to the cotton fields. About forty fellahin (mostly boys and
girls) were kept at their work by a huge Arab with a long whip which he
used very conscientiously. He was introduced to me, a ceremony which
on his part was full of oriental politeness and hyperbole. He insisted on
kissing my hand and when I complimented him on his great reputed
strength he at once replied that he owed his strength to my existence and
were I not – he would be less than nothing. I bid him '*El Sala'am Alekum*'
and we made for the *dourah* fields catching locusts and other strange
things on the way and in a clearing amongst the corn we made a fire and
cooked the young corn (and also ate it raw) and a woman wearing the
borkah and *kassaba* milked a couple of buffaloes for us and little maidens
from the farm made us popped corn.

It was a gloriously hot morning, so coming to a good wide stream we
stripped and had a most enjoyable swim, and on the way home I spotted a
hornets' nest and fired both barrels of my fowling piece into it.
Thousands of *dabours* swarmed out and we had an exciting chase for
nearly two miles, this time however being the hunted parties; we escaped
stings but some Arabs who were unusually interested in our movements
got it rather hot I fancy.

A lunch consisting of soup, curried fowl and quail, fish stuffed with
crab, mutton and salad, beef with egg plants, asparagus etc., macaroni,
figs, pears, grapes, Camembert, claret and cognac, etc., etc., awaited us.
We had hardly finished our café and cognac when an officer of the
Khedive (who had an estate of 4,000 acres adjoining Mahommed's) was
announced. He had been the guest of a certain Hassan bey Tenineh
whose son Ahmed Aziz Hassan Tenineh had been at dinner with us on

the previous evening and he had come with a request that we should visit Hassan bey. He had brought for me a pure-blood Arab stallion belonging to the Khedive and the lot of us mounted on horses (and some on donkeys) set out for the eight miles across country to Hassan bey's. I can't say I much enjoyed this ride; my mount was too lively for my lunch and could not bear the rein and I do not like as yet the Arab saddle with its high pommels and the great stirrups like coal scuttles placed back immoderately. This horse had no leather about it; the reins which were rather complicated appeared to be of silk, the stirrups were similarly supported, and it was covered with tissue of silk and gold, with chains of silver coins and a glittering star and crescent in silver over the face. It was a most superb horse and had a wonderful motion; in Tenineh's courtyard it literally and absolutely danced in time to Arab music and it played about like a great cat, and though terribly high-spirited it appeared not to have an atom of vice. Tenineh had prepared an imposing reception and I was presented to all the Sheikhs of the district. *Suffragis* (stewards) brought round coffee and then some sweet drink and then there was a banquet of fruit – I don't know how the devil we ate it after such a lunch; I wished George had been there. Then servants poured water and perfumes over our hands and dried them with care and then I had to brace myself to the final exchange of oriental compliments – a task which was made doubly hard by Mahmud Mahommed (junior) who made profane remarks in French (he having twice visited Paris) which none of the company understood. I rode the same horse back, with more comfort; and had an excellent tea at sunset at which amongst other guests there was present Ali effendi Baba as I named him – the reputed leader of the band of robbers. We had to curtail a delightful evening in order to catch the last train. I drove myself, Mahmud (Sidky) Aziz and young Tenineh; and Zaky and Hamid came on donkeys – servants took back the animals and revolvers and all of us proceeded to Cairo – the journey reminding me of a return from a football match in England. Zaky had borrowed my yachting cap and he would wear that and my white *galabieh*, as he called it (my nightshirt), on the platform at Toukh and in the train. The porters etc. were pelted with oranges and figs and there was much singing and sundry absurd native games played. When at last we reached Cairo they all squeezed into an *Arabieh* and saw me to my rooms, but as they did not come in I have settled down to this attempt at an account of a weekend with Egyptian scholars and their friends.

It is nearly 3 a.m. (Saturday) and I begin a fresh week's work tomorrow so I had better turn in and I don't think anything short of a scorpion or a vampire bat will disturb my night's repose.

Love to all at Clifton and Birmingham
Yours affectionately
JOE

With a boyish enthusiasm, remarkable in a man in his mid-thirties, McPherson was interested in everything – language, religion, customs, antiquities, the swarming cosmopolitan life of the cities, the timeless ways of the fellahin, and the mysteries and silences of the desert. In the early years of the century, Cairo's population was only 400,000 (when McPherson died, in 1946, it was two million), and the desert was never far from the city's heart. He delighted in breakneck rides over the Mokhattams, the bare hills that overlook Cairo. And he did not rest until he found himself a house in the desert fifteen miles from the city, a little chalet near Mataria, or Heliopolis.

To Nellie   *Heliopolis, 2 May 1902*
My usual morning's programme is to turn out about 5 a.m. or 5.30, put on a pair of footer shorts and have a gallop in the desert. I usually ride the horse (in the mornings) bare-backed-and-chested and often barefooted. I get in for a cold bath and breakfast and don't dress unless I have to go to Cairo or somewhere important. I either use the horse or my bike to Cairo but my servant Aly insists on my turning out spick and span and he spends hours over my leggings and boots and over the horse and occasionally when I do not gallop across the desert to Cairo, but take the road and the town, he runs on foot in front of the horse. He would do so every day if I would let him – it is a kind of instinct with a true syce (groom) – and he runs with wonderful speed and grace and clears a course through the thickest part of the town with his voice and his wand.

If I do not ride the horse to Cairo, I almost always take it out about sunset usually in the desert or though Heliopolis which practically adjoins this place. Heliopolis is full of fascination; there is an obelisk over 4000 years old (very like Cleopatra's needle) standing on the ruins of the temple of the Sun-God Ra; and close by is the spot where the Phoenix springs to life every hundred years from its own ashes. Heliopolis is the place referred to in the Bible as On. Here Joseph took his wife – the daughter of Pa-ta-pa-Ra, priest of On. The place is full of memories of Alexander the Great and Strabo who were here long ago; and there is a Sycamore tree under which Our Lady rested during the flight into Egypt and a well close by the tree which sprang into existence so she might have water to wash Jesus and there is a tiny Chapel erected in the garden. The Virgin's tree and fountain are treated with the greatest veneration by the natives, especially by the Moslems who as a rule have vastly more respect for the Virgin Mary and for Christ than Christians have.

McPherson had a particular interest in religious creeds and rituals. He was regularly at Mass, not only in the Catholic communion, but also in the Eastern churches, e.g. Melkite, Armenian and Maronite, which, while having differing liturgies, acknowledged the supremacy of Rome. In the first year, he was a guest at several spectacular weddings, Moslem, Armenian, Greek and Coptic, and noted with pleasure that at one of them 'out of 500 guests I believe I was the only Englishman there'. Egyptian friends took him to religious occasions to which non-Moslems were rarely admitted:

To Duncan   *23 October 1901*

I had arranged to spend the weekend with Zaky. He called for me at 8 a.m. and we drove to his house at Bab el-Louk. We drove later to the big mosque Sidna Hussein at the hour of prayer, and whilst he was praying I sat down on the holy carpet near the *Mihrab* (which points to Mecca) and had a rest. For some reason however they suspected us and accused Zaky of being a Copt. They examined our wrists for the tattooed cross and finally Zaky was taken before the Sheikh and I believe stripped and then made to go through all the formulas and declarations of the Moslem faith. Meanwhile I was a prisoner – all the doors blocked and a crowd of Moslems round. I was careful not to speak a word of any sort and made myself comfortable on the carpet and amused myself staring at them. Finally Zaky's father arrived and we were let go and took the train to an extraordinary spot in the desert: a city of tombs. We visited another mosque which was very full, mainly of mourners, but had no special fun there. One friendly Moslem held my forehead for an uncomfortably long time whilst he read many verses of the Koran for the good of my soul.

We visited the mausoleum of Zaky's people and sat smoking with his Dad in a room above the vaults until train time when we returned to Bab el-Louk to lunch.

To Ja   *6 p.m., 11 December 1901*

I spent Monday evening at Zaky's house and heard much Koran sung by the *Fikhy*. These holy men seemed to have no more objection than my host to my presence, but I gathered from some *sotto voce* remarks between the *sura* (verses) that they had their doubts whether I was really following them in the Koran which was open before me, and they were preparing a trap for me. As a matter of fact I not infrequently lost my place especially as coffee and cigarettes and sweets were constantly brought in, so I asked Zaky (in English) to give me the tip by rattling his coffee cup if they deliberately went wrong.

I had just thought out a pretty fair selection of Eastern curses when the cup rattled, on which I sprang from the Divan and denounced them so effectively in the name of Allah and the Prophet for perverting the 'Relevation' that they fairly squirmed and grovelled, and I was afraid Zaky's father was going to take the matter up against them *au sérieux*. However, he was very delighted at his holy men being sat on when we subsequently explained the affair, and Zaky nearly gave the whole show away at the time by the fearful faces he made in suppressing a laugh.

To Campbell   *Ramadan 30, 1319. 9 January 1902*
On Wednesday after *Fatur* (the meal breaking the Ramadan fast) we reascended the nearest spur of the Mokhattams armed with knuckledusters and Ramadan lanterns. Arabi by a half-appointment met me and took us into the minaret whence the scene was fascinating. Every minaret of Cairo was illuminated and the muezzin at about 6.30 when we went could be distinctly heard and in some cases seen. We stumbled upon a group of the Zikr after leaving the Keyed Bey Mosque with an enormous lantern and all of them contorting themselves and uttering the one word 'Allah'. Shortly after we found a little group of Hasheesh smokers, all more or less under the influence. I am making a second attempt at sending some Hasheesh cigarettes to Charlie, the first lot with the Hasheesh pipe etc. having been destroyed by the customs people, for Hasheesh is under a terrible ban here. Under its sway people assume sometimes an apparently second nature suggestive of *Dr Jekyll and Mr Hyde*. They even commit most cold-blooded murders under the impression they they are acting very cleverly and well. These people we met were only *'Magnun'* (idiotic) and sang and danced in a weird way, and all of them seemed absolutely unconscious of our presence. It requires many months steady smoking to induce the proper Hasheesh condition (after which one pipe or cigarette is enough to temporarily overturn the reason of the smoker) so that Charlie must not blame the few Hasheesh cigarettes for any vagaries he may commit.

Thursday I went with Sabry to his place where I had often been invited and never gone. After a chat in French to his Father who was half-dead from keeping Ramadan, Sabry announced that the carriage was waiting to take us round to see the illuminations, etc., in honour of the Khedive. He and his younger brother and I thereupon drove across the Nile and round the Gezira where native bands were playing and countless thousands of lamps were suspended. The ships and *dahabiehs* (river boats) were also all illuminated. We then drove to the Abdin Palace where fireworks were commencing and saw the Khedive drive off to the Opera and followed through the magnificently decorated and illuminated streets to the Piazza dell'Opera. Sabry had tickets for the Ezbekieh Gardens where an unique kind of Gala was proceeding. We stayed there until midnight listening to Native and European singing, watching Turkish sword-dancing and sham fighting and innumerable shows. The fireworks were particularly fine and the whole gardens most lavishly lit up and furnished with tents, etc. Fruits and Ruhbat Laqaom were passed around gratis and boats in the lake were free.

To Dougal   *23 May 1902*
I witnessed a very curious ceremony some weeks ago, the performers being Persians, followers of Hosein the grandson (I believe) of the Prophet and therefore sectarians and not acknowledged by the Moslems,

as on the slaughter of Hosein and his brother, the Caliphate was diverted. However, the Moslems tolerate this ceremony and allow the Mosque Sidna Hosein (the one in which I had a rough time) to be used for the first part of the ceremony. The Persians bewail the 'martyrdom' of Hosein and proceeding through the streets, in the glare of flaming torches and with their bodies in some cases half-naked they slash themselves with their sharp curved swords. When they passed us their heads were gashed in all directions, they were blinded with blood and their bodies and clothes dripping and they left the streets slippery behind them. The police under British direction with Mansfield bey at their head were securing them an uninterrupted course and driving back the surging crowd with whips and the flat of their swords. The horse belonging to one of the police received an accidental sword slash and did some havoc in the crowd in consequence.

We have had a warm spell with strong winds of the Khamsin type but not in the usual Khamsin direction.

I suppose it gets monotonous after a time, but I quite enjoyed the ten days toasting, though the dust storms were not nice. The South Khamsin blew two days whilst the Arabic exam was on, the shade temperature varying from 102 to $107\frac{1}{2}$ in the day and I had a lovely ride home one of these days on my bike with the wind right behind me. I coasted along the desert track with my feet up and my helmet fastened on and it was most exhilarating, just like being blown out of the mouth of a furnace.

The following day (of the exam) I arranged to spend at the old home under the Mokhattams where Aziz and Mahmud and Hamid live and I thought I would ride there by the desert and mountain route. It was a weird and fascinating ride; first a gallop over the desert as far as the warmth of the day would allow and amongst the tombs of the Mamelukes which looked like a city of Mosques, and then over the hills away behind the Citadel. I had no idea what a rough ride it would be; the horse luckily is sure-footed as an Exmoor stag-hunter; and it took the up-slopes at a gallop when too steep to get up any other way, but an entirely new and unexpected danger arose when I was crossing a fairly elevated ridge – an enormous bird swooped down on us and so frightened the horse that I had some difficulty in keeping him on the narrow track; it came straight for us until a metre or two off kicked up a great fuss with its wings and then flew off. The same thing happened in a similar place later on and when bye-and-bye I met Aziz who had ridden over to meet me (and luckily did not quite miss me), he said it is a little way these birds (Eagles he calls them) have of making a bid for a cheap and copious dinner. If this is true they are intelligent beasts, aren't they?

19 October 1902

To Dougal   *Ministry of Public Instruction, Dasl el Gamameez*

For several nights there had been a sound apparently of music and

The Geiushi Mosque on the Summit of the Mokhattam Hills

dancing not far from my rooms, and last evening at about 9.30 I was just debating in my mind whether I should go and investigate it or not, when Zaky settled the point by coming in and telling me that there was a particularly big assembling of the Zikr in Boulac, and begging me to come with him to see them.

The Zikr are a fanatical Moslem party who get the name from the repeated mention of the word 'Allah' and usually they are content with sitting round a lantern and repeating this word innumerable times and swinging their heads and bodies in time. The British régime is supposed to have suppressed the excesses to which they used to go.

When we reached the isolated spot in Boulac where the Zikr had met we found a space about the size of a tennis court, lying between native houses and decorated with flags and partly filled with benches and carpets. The Zikr were seated in a circle on the floor and singing repeatedly 'La illah illa Allah' (there is no god but God) when we arrived, and many Sheikhs and others (no Europeans) were seated or standing round.

A nice old Sheikh gave us seats and cushions and coffee in an excellent place, and suddenly one of the Zikr sprang from the ground into the middle of the circle and commenced to utter loud gasps in time to the words of the others; gradually the others rose and soon all were gasping desperately; then some native instruments of music were brought (mostly drums and flutes and tambourines) and the time was quickened until all the party were gasping in earnest, most of them were swaying their bodies and several spun like tops and others contorted themselves horribly, then several sang in loud tones and the others followed suit, and the uproar was deafening. A *Ghafir,* a kind of native policeman, came and we feared for a moment that he would try to stop the Zikr, but on the contrary he was quickly drawn into the circle, and swung and bawled with the rest. For a moment or two the noise stopped and subsided from sheer exhaustion, but a few rushed forward and danced wildly and with wonderful skill. Then one made an impassioned and, as it were, inspired address, which he punctuated by stabbing himself with a sharp Sudanese spear, and as soon as one spear was thoroughly embedded he seemed to forget its existence and another was given him until he was bristling with steel.

Then again the dancing and music and whistling became general until one man burst from the ranks in a wild intoxication and spun with such a complicated and rapid twist that he appeared to have many heads and legs, and gave me the impression of being entirely removed from the ground. I had made room on my bench for a boy of about sixteen who had danced and contorted himself until he was on the point of fainting, and who wore (like Zaky and I) a tarboosh, and who seemed to belong to a much better class than the rest, and he told me that this dancer was 'wrapped in God', could eat fire, broken glass or scorpions and that he could teach others words mainly from the Koran by which they could do the same with impunity and which rendered them invulnerable to all poisons and deadly beasts. I have heard this so often that I thought it was a pity not to humour this gentleman's taste for a pungent diet (and to see how far it is true), so I told a boy to bring some hot charcoal – unfortunately there were no scorpions available – but the dancer anticipated me and began to shriek for fire. He thrust burning candles into his mouth and crushed the hot charcoal and then a blazing mass of thorns was given him. He threw up his flowing garments, clapped the blazing mass against his side to which the thorns fixed it and dropping his robe he proceeded with his dance; as he spun the thin robe swelled out and was literally filled with flames and he had the appearance of a Chinese lantern which was taking fire inside. Then with a movement like lightning he removed the blazing thorns and struck another of the Zikr across the face with them – an attention which seemed to please the other Zikr. The boy I had been talking to suddenly sprang from my side and appeared to go perfectly mad amongst the Zikr; then seizing a torch, he held the blazing end in his mouth, as we blow tobacco smoke. After that the frenzy became general, fire was blazing everywhere, clothes were to a great extent rejected, and half-naked men with knives and spears sticking in their throats, mouths, faces and chests and abdomens were dancing and shouting 'Allah' with the rest. Two more *Ghafirs* came, but one of them was evidently of the sect and fell in with the rest whilst the other disappeared.

Shortly after midnight food and drink were brought from the adjoining houses in immense quantities, and we were invited to sup with the Zikr. We took some coffee and grapes only and departed. As I turned in at about 1.30 the invocation of Allah was recommenced and I went to sleep to the sound of *La illah illa Allah.*

As we left we were invited to come again tonight which they say is to be the last night of the meeting of the Zikr, and now as I write on my balcony, with the pyramids standing out clear between me and the setting sun, I can hear the sound of the *Tamba* (native drum) recommencing and the Zikr's voices blending with those of the Muezzin in *La illah illa Allah.*

McPherson had a remarkable rapport with all classes of Egyptians. With his students (at 'the Eton of Egypt') he might have been expected to get on good terms, relating them in some way to English public school boys. But he was at his ease also in the humble and crowded home of his servant Hagazy when 'pretty little brothers and sisters, absolutely naked, crawled over me like tame kittens and puppies' and he was welcome at the homes of some of the most distinguished of Egyptians. One was the Grand Qadi (the supreme judge) of Egypt, the Sheikh Mohammed Bikheet.

The Guest of the Skeikh Mohammed
To Ja   Bikheet at Matieh, Madariet d'Assiut. August 1902
This man is one of the most remarkable and admirable characters that I have met in my life, he only loves the work, the prayer and the instruction of his friends and of his co-religionists. Notwithstanding his work as a judge he instructs the young Sheikhs gratis during six or seven hours of each day, excepting in the month of August. He eats little and seldom, is always gay, and likes to see his guests eat much and often. He is one of the most learned men in the world, notwithstanding which, he understands neither the language nor the customs of Europeans, and he is always ready to dispense his enormous riches amongst others.

With the Qadi and his family and friends he spent a long and remarkable holiday, cruising on the Nile, exploring the antiquities and the villages of Upper Egypt.

Another friend was the Grand Mufti, who took precedence over the Grand Qadi on religious matters. McPherson described a visit with a friend one Ramadan.

To Isabel   *21 November 1903*
I propounded to him a question which was rending my servant Hagazy's soul; whether he has broken his fast by swallowing some of my cigarette smoke accidentally. His reply strangely coincided with my argument to Hagazy: 'Tell the boy', he said 'that if swallowing smoke is the breaking of one's fast then the smelling of food is more so. Yet if he smells the best of

food throughout Ramadan, he will die of starvation before the feast of Bairam, and he will die because he has not broken his fast; and here,' he said, 'is a *suffragi* (steward) who would rather thrust out his eyes than break his fast, bringing your excellencies' coffee, lacoum, and lighted Narghilehs.'

The Mufti then accompanied us some distance on a magnificent mule. My companion Jones dropped behind with a relative of the Mufti's who talked French, and I rode on with the Mufti who loves to talk Arabic though he is said to be the best scholar of occidental languages in Egypt. We came to a narrow path between a row of palms and a stream and the difficult question of precedence arose. He would not ride in front of me with his back to me, so I settled the point as I have often done before by riding in front but sitting in the reversed position so as to face the Sheikh. (For some reason the fellahin look upon this mode of riding with superstitious horror and one clodhopper said as I passed '*Harem aleh illi yirkib kede* – Sin upon him who rides so', but he got such a wigging from the Mufti that he simply grovelled in terror and ejaculated '*Harem aleya maskeen* – Sin is on me the miserable one').

> Early in his life in Egypt, the letters begin to show, not only the wide range of his interests, but also certain contradictions in his nature. Very occasionally, he wrote a letter with strict instructions that it should not be circulated around the family. Such a letter might contain rather wide-eyed observations of manners and morals in Cairo:

To Jack   *1902*
Many of the lady visitors to Cairo are pretty hot and one wonders sometimes whether they are attracted most by the antiquities or the iniquities of Egypt. On Xmas night, when Hamid and I rode out to the Sphinx we saw in the moonlight in the sand hollow a colossal bedouin and from beneath him appeared a little feminine attire, so little that it would not have betrayed its wearer, but that a little voice said in English: 'Mind tomorrow night'. When we called for our bikes at the Mena House Hotel a little gentleman was looking for his wife and fearing she would catch a cold through her stupid habit of wandering 'alone' in the moonlight. You know how frightfully rigorously the Moslem ladies are kept, but in spite of Eunuchs and all sorts of precautions they often bribe their custodians and escape to keep assignations in apartments which are kept up for the purpose – usually over fashionable shops. The pimps who keep these 'private houses' either accommodate the (amateur) friends of these ladies or more often procure boys for them. Perhaps the most characteristic and worst vice of Cairo is this traffic in boys as no handsome European boy of poor circumstances is not liable to be tempted to become the lover of one of these women, for the Egyptian ladies as a rule prefer European youths and men to Arabs. (And the vice

is not limited to Moslem women only but is I believe more common amongst European residents than is generally supposed.)

A few nights after my arrival in Cairo I lost my way in an after dinner stroll and after vainly trying to get directions from Arabs, I met a gentlemanly well-dressed chap who spoke Spanish and a little French and Italian (he was half-Spanish, half-Greek). He politely conducted me back to the Hotel Bristol, and on the way and more particularly over a café cognac, he told me that he had a 'lover' who paid him well, but although she was nearly seventy, she was very *exigeante* and compelled him to consummate the act every night. He was barely sixteen and sometimes he said it half killed him but she would never let him go until he succeeded.

One such letter, which he delayed in posting for some time, perhaps suggests why he preferred Egyptian to British company ... it was less likely to lead to 'wildness'. Incidentally, his companion mentioned, Bowden Smith, – a teacher colleague at this time – was shortly to become the Private Secretary to Sir Eldon Gorst, Financial Advisor to the Egyptian Government.

Dear Jack   *May, 1902*
I've just had a hell of a night. You would have enjoyed it in your unregenerate days and so would have Ja and perchance Duncan and mayhaps Dougal (which last is a bit of an old sphinx).

This letter is an isolated narrative for very very limited circulation and if you think advisable for immediate destruction. If you don't destroy it you might let it lodge finally with Ja.

Now it came about in this wise. A month or two ago, an English chap named Edgar dined with me at the club and after a bottle of port by the old-fashioned coal fire for it was a chilly evening, we sallied forth on what Edgar called a gin-crawl. We called at one or two noted German beer-houses and Edgar had an invitation for the two of us to a dance at the 'Princes Club' but as neither of us were keen on dancing long, he took me to a queer house which was ostensibly a café, but in which we were served in an inner very sumptuous apartment by nymphs who did not consider the weather sufficiently rigorous to justify the wearing of apparel – which is a vanity of modern convention. Now, as you rightly judge, I am leading a perfectly Godly, righteous and sober life and only tolerated a brief sojourn in a spirit of exploration, and so after a cognac all around we declined a very pressing invitation to remain and Edgar paid for the cognacs at the rate of a franc apiece – four piastres – which is of course four times the price. However Madame demanded three francs apiece and Edgar refusing she ordered the Arab porter to lock the outer door. We got rather savage and after ordering the door to be opened in vain, we tackled the porter who made a very feeble resistance and would

The Verandah of Shepheard's Hotel

have delivered the key but that suddenly a Greek bully appeared with a murderous cudgel and went for Edgar with it. I managed to keep him off and then tried arguing and persuasion with Madame in French and threats for the bully and the porter in Arabic. Finally I persuaded the porter to give me the key and we got away without further payment and without losing any of our belongings except Edgar's hat which Madame hid somewhere. I put the case before young Arabi (Arabi Pasha's son) and others and they all agreed that we had got off rather well and that to attack Madame by the law would be worse than useless: so we developed a private reprisal which we just put into effect. Edgar and I dined at the club tonight as the guests of Bowden Smith, a young Eton chap who was keen on helping us to revenge, and a young officer of the Seaforth Highlanders and another chap were with us. We had four revolvers between the five and knuckle dusters galore – all well concealed. We spent some time in the house and fairly sampled the wares and on Edgar's asking what we owed and Madame saying '*ce que vous voulez bien me donner, messieurs*' he proffered a small piastre (just one penny farthing). Edgar selected this coin from a good handful of gold and Madame expressed a preference for the latter, which was not gratified. Madame had not appeared to recollect Edgar and me but on our attempting to retire we found the door already locked and an extra bully on the spot. These latter however and the porter seemed little disposed to detain us, and I think we might have retired quietly but that Bowden Smith proposed smashing the lock with a revolver shot. His first shot was so successful that the key was no longer capable of opening it and suddenly the bully of the last occasion whacked the Seaforth man over the head and fled upstairs. We followed and caught him and left him the sadder and wiser man and then found that Madame had locked the door at the foot of the stairs up which we had pursued the Greek. That soon lay across the floor but the outer door was much harder to tackle. I let the other chaps deal with that and I found I could employ my time pleasantly and profitably by revolver practice at the bottles on the top shelf. As a rule I think it is a dreadful sight to see good drink wasted, but somehow there was a pure joy tonight in seeing those magnums and those glass spirit barrels popping and the contents coming down in a cataract.

Finally the outer door yielded to the combined exertions of our party inside and a *Shawish* (military policeman) and two *Ghafirs* (nightwatchmen) outside. These officials very sensibly took our part, not only because of the liberal backsheesh which Bowden Smith and some of the others proffered but because as they explained they knew the 'Madame'. She had quite lost her wonderful politeness and *sang froid* and was an inarticulate, raging, foaming devil. We talked things over at Flash's Bierhalle and decided that the only risk which might accrue would be a private revenge by Madame, so to avoid the risk of being followed and our places of abode being noted by her emissaries we took *Arabiehs to* the Gezira, passed back into Old Cairo by the ferry and finally retired by different routes.

I have not retired yet as I am writing this at the Club, but am quite confident that if any attempt was made at pursuit (which was hardly possible) it will have long since been abandoned.

It is nearly 4 a.m. and time that all sober and discreet citizens were in bed, so I will set the good example and retire straightway.

Good Night, yours affectionately,
JOE

P.S. May 21 1902

Dear Jack
The above is just as I wrote it on the night of the incident a couple of months ago or more. I almost decided not to send it at the time, but as I indicated in my last letter to Ja, I will commit it to your discretion.

We have none of us seen or heard any more of Madame and the affair is almost entirely unknown here but to ourselves. Bowden Smith is particularly anxious to keep it dark partly as his uncle Colonel Bowden Smith is in Cairo. I am just about to write a respectable letter to Dougal.

Above all, the letters of these early years are a catalogue of his felicities: sailing on the floodwaters of the Nile far upstream 'the country like a vast sea, dotted with islands crowned with groves of palm trees'; riding an Arab horse 'of the purest blood, soft and affectionate as a gazelle but fiery and free as a stag'; admiring the beauty of a Bedouin girl, 'it is a property seemingly of self-luminosity of eyes and skin just after sunset – the rich light of the sun seems to have been absorbed and as evening comes on to radiate out'; discussing with a Coptic priest 'the heresies of Arius and Nestorius and Eutyches and the merits or demerits of Donatism'; taking part in a sea-battle against smugglers off Aboukir when 'the whole side of the felucca blazed out instantly in defiance, the shots splashing in the water'; observing that 'on the dark evenings of Ramadan nearly all the youngsters in the native parts of Cairo run about with lanterns and very often in the quaintest costumes. Strings of little red imps holding onto one another's tails swarm past one, or a procession of gigantic cats appears, all carrying coloured lanterns and usually throwing fireworks'; noting that at sunset 'colours begin to burn like red fire behind a purple curtain, and sometimes the curved shadow of the earth forms a dark segment of a circle in the eastern sky'; and sailing home in a felucca singing Gounod's *Dites la jeune fille*:

> '*Où voulez-vous aller,*
> *La voile ouvre son aile. . . .*'

It is no wonder that he wrote at the end of one letter describing a full day:

One learns and sees so much without making any personal effort in a few hours as in some countries one might do in as many months. That is the beauty of Egypt – you can be as idle as you like, but you can't wholly waste your time unless you cultivate exclusively the insular British set.

2

At Work

Never since the heroic days of Greece has the world
had such a sweet, just, boyish master.

GEORGE SANTAYANA (on a type of British Empire
administrator) in *Soliloquies in England* (1922)

'The PI (Ministry of Public Instruction) was then considered to be the
lowest of the low, classed perhaps with, but only just before, the
Scavenging Department,' wrote Ronald Storrs,[1] Oriental Secretary to the
British Consul General, 'The result, and probably the reason, of this
absurdity was that none ever remained in the PI who could manage to get
transferred anywhere else. It was indeed recruited from London as a
testing ground: a limbo from which ambitious entrants might –
             '"rise on stepping stones
Of their dead selves to higher things."'
Indeed compared with other departments of the Anglo-Egyptian
administration such as Finance, which had revolutionised the economy of
the country, or Public Works with its great achievements in irrigation and
engineering, Education was unimpressive, starved for funds and limited in
aims and achievements.

McPherson gave no indication of being aware of this, and did not try to
transfer to the 'higher things' in Finance or Public Works. Perhaps it was
because his work was at a fairly high level in the Ministry, and at what he
called 'swell' schools, and, as a scientist, he was sometimes co-opted for
other tasks by the Egyptian government. More likely it was because the
life suited him: he had little ambition in the usual sense, the pay was
adequate for his needs, the job left him plenty of leisure to enjoy and
explore Egypt, and the long leaves of absence allowed him to return to
England every two years, and to go on his 'vagabondage' around the
Mediterranean. He enjoyed the games-playing and training young
athletes for championship contests. And he had an obvious rapport with
his students. The famous tribute by George Santayana, the American
philosopher, to a type of British Empire administrator, 'sweet, just, boyish'
is not totally applicable to McPherson. His 'sweetness' was extremely
variable, his justice could be harsh (as his later career was to show) but his
boyishness was perennial. In his classroom there was between master and
pupils a meeting of young minds as the following description of a mutually
enjoyable class in the Khedivieh School shows:

[1] In his Preface to Bowman's *Middle-East Window*.

Joseph McPherson with a colleague at the Khedivieh School. 'A common room with unlimited smoking'

To Edie, *Christmas Night, 1902*

On Monday I had no work of my own but was called upon to take a class in (English) conversation for one of our senior men, who was mixed up in a law case and detained in the mixed Tribunal. On entering the lecture room I was surprised and pleased to recognise amongst the students who rose to salute Achmed Aziz, Sadiq and nearly all the others who took part in our full moon ramble in the mountains, and also Aly bey Tolba, son of one of the Pashas who helped Arabi [leader of 1882 rebellion] and who died in exile in Ceylon. I found that the mode of conducting the class in no way differed from that in vogue in the days of St Augustine, and of Plato and of Euclid – a theme was proposed and discussed by the students under the presidency of the teacher who sat practically in the midst. The theme they were expecting was 'Integrity', so I told them briefly in Arabic the tale of Pasqual the Primer Asistente of Seville in the days of Dom Pedro[1] which they seemed to like very much and then after they had told me parts of it in their own words in English and some similar tales, I gave them the yarn of the Thieves who were driven out of their house by their guilty consciences when the Donkey and the Dog and Cat and the Cock sang outside the window[2]. They all seemed in a very

[1] Pedro the Cruel (1334–1369), King of Castile, while hunting in the mountains, sheltered in the house of a farmer, Juan Pascual. The king, incognito, was impressed by Pascual's opinions on government and justice, and appointed him governor of Seville. There Pascual was famous for his dispensing of justice, even when the offender was the king himself. Known as *El Montañés* (The Mountaineer), he is the hero of various classic Spanish plays and tales.

[2] *The Town-Musicians of Bremen* by The Brothers Grimm.

Christmassy and merry frame of mind and were delighted with the yarn which you of course know, and then I called on Sadiq for a tale illustrative of the theme. Sadiq's tale delivered in a mixture of French, English and Arabic (English as far as he was able) was as follows:

SADIQ'S TALE: 'THE SILVER SLIPPER'

There was once a very honest man who wished to convince himself that dishonesty brought no profit with it, so he paid his licence to the Mudir [Governor] of his province, and joined a band of robbers, but so many officials had to be appeased by backsheesh that nothing remained to him but one of his *shipship* (slippers) which was ornamented in silver. 'Verily', said he, 'the dishonesty of others bringeth no profit to the honest man' – and this, Sir, is the first moral conclusion. The robbers said, 'Go forth and show that you are worthy to be one of us', and he went and placed the slipper in the path of a rich Fellah who was leading two valuable oxen. The Fellah muttered to himself: 'One odd slipper availeth nothing', and as he passed along the winding road the 'honest man' picked up the slipper, ran across the fields and placed it again in the road. The Fellah saw it and said: 'Truly this is the fellow of the other which I was fool to leave, now will I leave my oxen here and go back for the first', which he did; and whilst he was thus seeking, the 'honest man' untied the oxen and led them back to the robbers from whom he received great honour and thus it ends.

Of course I demurred to the moral of this story and all the class murmured against Sadiq and several boys volunteered an illustration of how truth and honesty prevail. Amongst them was Ameen Uzain but he is reputed to be a very wicked boy and to frequent Hasheesh dens and other awful places and some say he was secretly married two years ago – so I would not risk a tale from him; but Aziz is a blunt straightforward chap, a rattling footballer and a good shot and rider and no one has ever whispered a word against his *bona fides* as an exponent of Integrity. So Aziz saluted and began:

AZIZ'S TALE: 'THE CREAM-POT'

Near our house behind the mosque of Saida Zenab a tailor stitches stitches, and he loveth cream. One day amongst these he must go forth and he went but lest the apprentice should become hungry and steal cream which he left, he said; 'Look *ya Walad* (boy), that which appeareth as cream to your ignorance is not so in truth but a very deadly poison, touch it not or ye die', and he went forth and the *walad*, the little *Sabee* (apprentice), said to himself, 'By the mother of the Prophet, there is no poison, but lying only, mixed with the cream, verily it is even as cream and honey; but to eat cream aright asks *dhura* (maize) bread and jam of *mishmish* (apricots) and he also went forth with the best scissors of his sahib, and he came to the man who maketh the stone to turn and asked him 'Can you grind me this scissor?' and the man said 'No, I am busy and the scissor moreover is very sharp'. 'Then,' said the *Sabee*, 'give me five piastres and grind it for yourself when it blunteth.' And he returned and with him *dhura* bread and jam and *mishmish* and cigarettes of a small piastre, and he had but just eaten the cream and the *dhura* bread and the jam of *mishmish* and but just drunken the cigarettes and had given thanks to Allah, when his Sahib returned and said '*Salaam Alekum*' and the *walad* replied '*Alekum Salaam*'; but when the Sahib saw that the cream was gone he was *zalan keteer* (angry very) and began to *beshatim* (abuse) the *walad* with words, and he said 'Now may Allah torture you and make it truly poison to your inward parts; did I not tell you that if you were to eat it you would die?' and the *walad* wept and said '*Ya sahibee* (Oh my master), when you had gone I found that your best scissors was lost and I sought and sought it and when at last it was certainly not to be found I feared greatly and said 'By the life of my master's moustache, he will be so *zalan* that I shall not be able to bear it, by my God it is better to die and so I ate the poisoned cream'. Thus it ends.

I had great difficulty to keep from laughing at this audacious yarn and so I think had all the class but I told Aziz that he was no more to be trusted to tell a story than the *Sabee* was to be left with cream and that I predicted the same gallows for both of them, but Aziz with a distressed look of injured innocence rose and saluted and said: 'The wrong, Sir, is with the *Sabee* not with me; if he had observed integrity that would have been sweeter to him than many ships full of cream and *mishmish* in his stomach and I would have told a far more beautiful history.'

I told Aziz in very bad Turkish which hardly anyone understood but himself that he was a humbug and that I would pay him out on the first opportunity.

Another tale was told which however was by so unskilful a narrator that it was difficult to tell in what language it was supposed to be or whether the moral was good or bad. But in the midst of it an officer reminded me that we had gone beyond the period of the lesson. There was a general request however from the boys that we should go on, especially as lunch interval for boys who are bound to fast is rather a farce and several other youths, mostly senior boys, asked to be admitted. I consented to go on for half-an-hour until 12, the time of my own lunch, and our party was augmented by most of the football team (who play no football in Ramadan) including Sabry; and also came along young Saleh el-Din. We took some of the other moral topics from the list which the monitor had, but the spirit of mischief and inversion seemed to have affected even the newcomers, as witness by the following tale by Lutfy Goma on Thrift:

LUTFY GOMA'S TALE: 'THE LITRE OF HONEY'

Little Fatimy Kaj was better instructed by his father in Thrift than in common sense and once he took with him the money of a litre of Greek honey and the *sultaniya* (basin) to carry it in: but the basin held only 980 cubic centimetres so he turned it *foqiana Tahtana* (upside down) and poured the remaining 20 centimetres into the ridge at the bottom (on which the *sultaniya* rests when it sits aright). *Bade zalik* (Following this) he backs him to the house and his *Baba* (father) demands him, 'Is that all the honey you have brought for such money?' The boy laughs cleverly and says 'No, this is but 20 centimetres of it, behold the rest', and thus he turns the *sultaniya* upright again. (imitating the action with his tarboosh).

HAMID'S TALE: 'THE SHADOW OF THE CHEESE'

Sir, said Hamid, Aziz's brother, who had crept in somehow, I know a man who is so *bacheel* (miserly) that years ago he bought some cheese and sealed it with a cork and red candle in a bottle and when he eats his dinner of brown bread he holds it in the shadow of the cheese, and he keeps it locked up that his children shall not learn to want such comforts whilst they are young. And one day he caught his eldest son holding his bread near the keyhole of the *dulab* (cupboard) and he said, 'Why, my son, do you set your little brothers such an ill example of extravagant luxury?'.

Amongst the newcomers was Tsabet Tharwat, monitor of the top section and practically captain of the school and an excellent all-round chap and he seemed to want to speak so we extended time a little for his tale which was in fairly good English and much as follows: – (every one of the boys listening with great respect and attention even when he attacked them).

TSABET THARWAT'S TALE:
(THE VALUE OF EDUCATION) 'THE DONKEY'S AGE'

Sir, I do not say it to grieve them but because it is true – these boys are nothing but rubbish boys, their brains are *muqlub* (topsy-turvey) like the honey pot, their education is yet but as the shadow of the cheese, they have much to learn and to be educated in many sciences. How great is the value of education (which we Egyptians have only now begun to realise) I will try to indicate by my tale. There met a dog with a *Talab* – in English it is called Renard – and they disputed about the age of a donkey who was eating berseem near them and in the end they asked the donkey, 'show us your teeth that we may know how many years you have', but the donkey replied 'My age is not written in my mouth but in my heel, if you are well instructed you may read it there.' The dog was ashamed and said, 'But I cannot read', and the Renard reproached him and said 'Ignorant son of a Fellah, shame upon you that you cannot read. I have been to school and will read it to you.' But as he went near to read the donkey's age, he received a terrible kick which smashed up all his face, and the dog said, 'Thank God that he blessed me with a wise and good father, who neither sent me to school nor allowed the Sheikhs to teach me these foolish letters'.

I condemned Tsabet and Aziz and Sadiq and Lutfy Goma to write their tales in Arabic as a punishment and bring them to me after the Bairam and told them that I should set myself to write them in English and should send them to England as a punishment to myself for listening to such 'Rubbish boys' and to let the people of England know what indeed is 'the wisdom of the Egyptians'. I added 'Now I know why Thoth the Egyptian God of learning is represented as a monkey.' Then I dismissed them, but before they departed they crowded round with invitations to all sorts of places in Egypt, wanted my address for sending Xmas cards and Bairam cakes etc., and all wished me a Very Happy Christmas. I wished them, '*K'l aam w'entum bacheer* – on your year and you be blessing' to which they all rejoined '*w'hadratkum bi'saha w'salaama* – and on you good health and God's peace'.

That same evening I had *Fatur* at Aziz's house and on the table amongst many things was cream and *mishmish*. Aziz suddenly burst out laughing and then got up and fled. I pursued him through a palm grove and he caught his foot in the *tawnis* (rope) of the *saqqieh* (water wheel) and came a rare cropper. I asked him 'What are you looking for on the ground, Aziz, the moral of your story?' and he replied in a dolorous voice – 'Yes, and I have found it at last and shall wear it on my nose through the Bairam'.

Generally, he judged that the family would be less interested in education than in the exotic pageant of Egyptian life, but once, answering a direct question from a young niece, he wrote:

To Kathlene   *August, 1902*
I have never defined my 'post' here in Egypt because it is impossible to render into English the Arabic words by which it is described in the 'Code' to which I have to subscribe, which are something to the effect that 'it behoves me to assist the Ministry of Public Instruction in any educational work with which the Ministry entrusts me'. I am *not* a

schoolmaster, my work mainly being that of 'Educational advisor to the Government', which involves some teaching and examining and a good deal of Report writing with suggestions as regards programmes of study, examinations, etc.

And once when invigilating at an examination, he described the scene:

To Dougal   *30 June 1903*
As I am writing on Exam scrap paper, with 360 exam. candidates in front of me, a little crowd of examiners and superintendents about and an enormous staff of *ferasheen* (servants) sharpening pencils, distributing blotting paper etc., the beginning of this letter will be somewhat Scholastic.

In addition to innumerable native schools '*Kutabs*', where little but the Koran is learnt, and the great Moslem University 'Al-Azhar' of 15,000 students or more, there are schools here under the Jesuits and other Catholic Missions; American Mission, German, Greek and French schools (though strange to say not a single Protestant, or English school in Egypt) and a regular system of government schools of which the Khedivieh is the swell one. There are two great Government Diploma exams: (*Shadadah ibtadieh*) Primary Certificate, and (*Shadadah thanueah*) Secondary Certificate. The 2nd exams which take place at the end of a course varying from 7 to 14 years are all over for this year, and the Primary exams (at the end of a course of from 4–8 years) begin to-day. It is really a fine sight the exam at the Khedivieh Centre, about 3000 boys in tarbooshes occupying 3 football grounds, all of which are awned over in bright colours, and the discipline and arrangements are so perfect that out of 3000 boys frightfully keen on passing the exam by any means, there is not one hundredth part of the cheating and the muddle that accompanies an exam of a couple of hundred boys at Wakefield or any other English school I know. There is absolute silence and order from start to finish.

In 1904, he was transferred to the Ras el-Tin School in Alexandria and three years later to the Agricultural College at Giza, outside Cairo. He kept some letters of farewell from his Alexandria students, of which the following is the most eloquent:

My Dear Teacher   *Ras el-Tin School, Alexandria, 19 January 1907*
I cannot put in words the sorrow and sadness I have for your departure. I wept bitterly and all your pupils began to have a retrospect of your kindness, goodness and ability of teaching. See Sir! Mr Cadman gives us mathematics. I say freely he is to you as the duplicate ratio of 1 : 10000. Mr Colonson came to give us chemistry, and to prove and show to the class his cleverness, he said he will make next time Electrolysis of water

English staff of the School of Agriculture, Giza, 1908

mixed with sulphuric acid not (he said) of water only as you give it to us. Mr Cadman cannot know how to teach, and I am growing weak and weak in mathematics for there is no teacher who is well experienced and has quick inspection like you. Both the two mentioned teachers do not taste well in my mouth. I have written your name in one of my last essays in the composition exercise book. It was headed a 'Retrospect'. Every hour I remember you, and when I have a pleasant time and think of you, I become extremely sad. I heard that you were in the school on Friday but unfortunately I did not have the pleasure of seeing you. I hope that your salary is increased and that you are going well with *your shares*.[1] All the class gives you their best compliments. It would be a very good year if you stayed among us.

With all good wishes,
I remain, yours obediently,
MAIIMOUD SAMY

The Agricultural College rated a couple of mentions in letters, for mixed reasons:

To Mervyn   *Agricultural College, Giza 27 January 1907*
On Tuesday I came to Cairo, went to the Ministry and then came on and took possession here. I took a couple of days off to run up and bring my piano here and a few special things and am now comfortably installed.

[1] McPherson was a keen speculator on the Bourse at Alexandria, but not lucky. In later years he had a room in his house papered with worthless share certificates.

There are five other fellows here – all but one very nice men – and I at once paid my £6 entrance fee to the mess. . . We live like fighting cocks here, to a great extent on the produce of our own farm which is over 100 acres. I am going to introduce improvements in our model dairy in the Devon and Cornwall direction, though we have now an unlimited supply of lovely milk, butter, eggs, etc., – the cream only not coming up to the Bude standard.

Of the other five men in the mess, one a Cantab. looks after the farm, a younger chap McCall assisting, the third is a vet. and entomologist and botanist, the fourth an engineer, the fifth agricultural chemist, and I occupy the chair of physics.

The school buildings are magnificent, the laboratories being at least equal to anything I have seen in Europe, I have a fine private research place fixed up as a study and another comfortable well-furnished room with shelves, writing table, easy chairs, and etc., in the school my hours are 17 per week when in full work.

To Mervyn   *Agricultural College, Giza. 7 February 1907*
This afternoon I was referee in a football match between our students and the Military School. The first half the visitors scored one goal to nil and the game proceeded without incident until in the second half our men scored. Then the game which had been keen and rough throughout became keener than ever. Presently one of our men, Pengelly (of English parents and Levantine birth) the captain, was kicked badly on the leg. He neither appealed to me nor waited for the whistle but struck the kicker with his fist. Then one of the Military side struck him and I ordered the three off the field. Before they could obey however, the spectators broke in, including probably a hundred military students, whose officers so far from restraining them are reported to have ordered them to use their belts. I had my hands so full trying to restore order that I did not see the arrival of the director, Dr MacKenzie, and the first I saw of him was a bleeding tattered object. He had been attacked with sticks and fists – one of our students, a Greek named Philadelphis, had felled one of his attackers with a huge stone and Pennington our 'vet', a very big man, had helped to relieve the pressure. We got order at last somehow and the officers got their men into line who were sullenly marched off whilst we kept our fellows away. MacKenzie wanted to get at one of his aggressors, but had he or Pennington or I once hit out as we were sorely tempted to do the place would have been a shambles in a few seconds, and our chances and those of our team would have been remote as we were overwhelmingly outnumbered. There is a good deal of evidence that the Military chaps came in force with the deliberate intention of a fight, and the fool Pengelly precipitated it. I recognised an old Khedivieh pupil in one spectator who was led off dripping with blood from head to foot and managed to get the name of the brute who had

Football team, coached by McPherson, of the School of Agriculture, Giza, 1908

broken his head with a chair. The Director's face was a pretty sight and his gold watch chain and part of his waistcoat are quite lost and I think, his hat.

What no one understands is how I have escaped without a blow or a scratch – seeing that I was referee and had given a goal against the military side which they disputed and was in the thick of the affair trying to turn the original combatants off the field.

We had a rather similar affair a few weeks ago at Ras el-Tin when a team of British officers and soldiers played our boys, and a little Moslem boy looking on, suddenly rushed in mad with excitement and kicked a Tommy furiously. He tried to catch the boy but was at once surrounded and overpowered by the pupils. As there were about 400 pupils nearly all Moslems and not fifteen English including the team we were a bit apprehensive for a bit but soon got order.

Today I did not anticipate a row as the bulk of both teams were natives and Moslems themselves.

I shall be sorry if this little incident stops play, as I have had some very enjoyable football since I came to Giza and want some more – but I do not want to referee.

An assignment outside the Department of Public Instruction came in 1905, when he was appointed by the Egyptian Survey Department to one of the research commissions which were to study the total eclipse of the sun in August of that year. His task was to make magnetic observations during the eclipse from Ghartas, deep in the Sudan. Accompanied by his lively young servant Saleh, he completed the last stage of the journey on the upper Nile by paddle steamer, and then felucca. They set up their tent and 'observatory' by an ancient temple. McPherson was aware of a good deal of hostility from the local inhabitants who believed that he had come to do the sun an injury. On the day of the eclipse the hostility came to a climax.

To Isabel   *Helwan, 5 September 1905*
The morning of the 30th the manner of the natives was rather strange. No milk, butter, eggs, or other provisions were supplied and in applying we were refused and found ourselves boycotted. My provision chest however contained 'condensed milk', tinned butter and other unheard-of things and when at breakfast my tent was thrown open presumably for air, the crowd of sullen savages were electrified to see me breakfasting rather better than usual with a jug of hot milk, rice pudding yellow with eggs, fish, fruit, etc. This was not merely an object lesson, I knew I should have little chance of a meal until after dark and as a matter of fact I did not move from the Magnetometer from 10.30 to 6.30 and noted about 400 readings of the scale, besides vernier and azimuth readings etc. Just as I had taken an absolute set of declination readings, with Torsion, Azimuth, etc., and was taking each minute a reading of the scale, the temperature which had been previous days steady at about $41°$ ($106°F$) – a very pleasant temperature – ran up tremendously and shoals of burning sand were dashed over me and the instrument by violent gusts of wind, not however seriously complicating calculations on the readings. I noticed the natives concealing saws and other weapons under their scanty garments, so Saleh ostentatiously loaded the revolver and touched up our knives and spears and made a bogus cannon of the case in which the legs of the Magnetometer had been. He repeated his oft-told yarn that so far from having come to injure the sun I had brought a wonderful remedy to cure it without which it would never recover, but very few understood Arabic. Whilst I kept at the telescope of the Magnetometer and the *Sai* (Chain-man), Abdel Ghranem, announced the minutes, Saleh was watching for the beginning of the eclipse with special glasses and announced it at 3.16.

The Berberines did not notice it for some time and some of them were inclined to mock at our anticipations and preparations, but presently a weird half light replaced the invariable brightness of the sunshine, faces and objects took a yellowish shade and suddenly all the village was aware that the infernal dragon was devouring the sun. Where the temple walls were broken the rising Nile had protected the gaps and we had moved some of the mighty blocks of stone that served as steps up to the gate, but suddenly a frenzied mob surged up the front more in terror than in anger. Nearly naked women and men and quite naked children! Our native guard of police had disappeared and the Omda (the Mayor of the district) had left command and was not to be seen. Only the Sheikh el-Balad (chief local magistrate) retained any idea of protecting us and when I appealed to him, he rained, in deadly terror himself, frantic blows on the heads and bodies of the villagers with a stout club. The *Sai* lost his head and I had to take the chronometer from him, but Saleh as all through the day was a little brick. He was ready and keen on firing at them and stabbed their hands as they tried to climb up with one of their native blades and they knew we meant business so with the help of Sheikh Ismail's gentle persuasion they disappeared from the door and did not even come in line of the bogus cannon till long after the eclipse.

The lamps were lit and Abdel Ghranem tried to work the reflector to illuminate the scale but his hand trembled so that the whole point of my mission would have failed through my not being able to see the scale during totality if Saleh had not kept cool. With the dark lens in his eye he noted the beginning and end of totality and timed it ($121\frac{1}{2}$ seconds) with the stop watch, keeping a full light on the scale from a distance of 3 metres. The *Sai* managed to call the quarter minutes and I noted down the movements of the needle stealing two 8-second intervals to admire the marvellous light of the Corona flaming round the jet black moon. At my second observation exactly at 4.24 as the *Sai* was yelling the minutes and Saleh announced his stopping of the watch at the end of totality I saw a point of blood-red fire burst out like a volcano from the side of the disc, the stars went out and the great shadow sped away at a thousand miles per hour into space and I got in my reading a second or so after totality was thus ended.

We had been vaguely sub-conscious of a horrible shrieking and battering of drums and instruments and howls of objurgation and entreaty to the devouring demon and of the firing of many guns, and a litter of dust and stone fragments in and about the instrument and a whitish mark on the side of the wall indicated that someone had failed to shoot the moon and had got a bullet slantingly into the temple gate. This shrieking changed at once to the unearthly *zaghout* (a trilling by the tongue) of the women in sign of rejoicing. The eclipse was all over at 5.33, but I was busy till dark, and a little inclined then to go off in the felucca which the Omda's brother had in readiness, so the Omda rode off in the dark to a distant post and telegraph office, glad to make amends for the poor show he had made at the eclipse. Saleh found him in my bed at 6 his head still enveloped in blankets and in answer to Saleh's expostulation that he had not even seen the eclipse he said, 'No, but I heard it and the horrible hissing made me shudder'. All the villagers whom I questioned swore to the hissing the only point on which their evidence was consistent and even Saleh stoutly supports them in this to this day.

When I woke the next morning about 9, everything but my tent and its contents and breakfast was packed in the felucca and a large party waited to salute me. I kept them waiting until I had breakfasted and written out my notes etc., and a report to the Mudir, commending the Omda and the Sheikhs el-Balad and some of the Ghafirs and the people generally and thanking him and them all, giving a digest of the roll call I had kept of the guard and complaining of Hadji Hassan who had expected good money for bad eggs and milk and who had incited the other villagers to boycott us. I read this aloud for the benefit of those who could follow, and then the Sheikhs produced presents of milk and curds and eggs, horns of Gazelles and great beasts of the Sudan, *Hajabat* (Talismans), a hippopotamus whip, and a native drum (*Tabla baladi*) like I took home, gourd drinking vessels and green beads from some prehistoric shores. But for that I believe we should have gone away and forgotten my reserve store chest which Saleh had buried with a lump of iron, and now he sought it by means of a magnetic needle which he passed over the level sand. He had all along taken the thing in a Swiss Family Robinson spirit and had refused to light the breakfast fire or a cigarette except by a burning lens, and now when his little needle dipped and pointed to a spot in the sand like all the rest, from which however he proceeded to extract and distribute as I described tinned peaches and sardines, biscuits, kippered herrings and many bottles of jam and beer, they looked rather frightened at him, which did not diminish their appreciation of the gifts.

> After the interruption of the Great War, McPherson never returned to his educational and scientific work, and rarely referred to it. But when he occupied the post of Mamur Zapt, or Head of Secret Police, in Cairo, he had an acrid reminder, at a trial of a number of Egyptian nationalist conspirators accused of planting bombs.

One of the accused, Dr Mansur, I think, who was finally hung, who was proved to have prepared the bombs, with an ignition arrangement of chlorate of potash and sugar, and a tube of sulphuric acid, was asked by the President of the Court Martial who had taught him this. Confronting me who was in court officially, he replied 'Bimbashi McPherson, the Mamur Zapt'. Sensation in court! Returning his look I recognised him faintly, as a gentlemanly pupil whom I had taught Chemistry at the Khedivieh School, when I first came out. Feeling as Head of the Special Section and a sort of chief inquisitor, that a cynical role was the best for the occasion, I remarked: 'It is very gratifying to me to learn that my poor attempts at teaching were not thrown away, that one diligent pupil anyway did not forget what he was taught'.

3

At Home

A servant is either friend or foe.

J. W. McP.

For all his love of travelling, Joseph McPherson was a home-maker and a home-body. He had need of a place where he could be idle, and in the letters, one favourite image of himself – the daredevil horseman on a breakneck gallop across the desert – is matched by another – the dreamer asleep in his garden in a bed of thyme. He was not over-sociable, and never shared a house, as many British officials did. But he was hospitable. His luncheon parties were famous to the end of his days, and he established the tradition early in his little chalet near Heliopolis.

To Ja   *23 May 1903*
The Qadi and two of his sons came in to lunch in my garden. The younger boy was tremendously delighted with the *Mergiheh* (swing in the garden) and with climbing the apricot trees. The Massieh family (the landlords) have gone to Italy and left me a parting injunction to eat as much of the fruit as possible. I can't do much more in that direction than I've done the last month. I doubt if my average falls below 35 or 40 apricots per day besides guavas and plums and I am certain Hagazy's [his servant] average is easily in 3 figures. These apricots are nothing like so fine as the Rookery ones were. They grow however on trees big as the biggest pear or apple trees in England. The garden is a most sensible one, beauty and utility combined to perfection. My dining room balcony is connected with an alley of vine-trellissing about 50 yards long (grapes not quite ripe yet). The next side of the garden has a row of acacia trees whose fern-like leaves are almost hidden at present by glorious blue flowers. The most vulnerable side is protected by a row of prickly figs like gigantic cacti, covered now with great yellow blossoms and unripe fruit and millions of needles; outside of the prickly figs is a spiked fence hidden by clematis, which together with jasmin and tuberoses buries the garden house and half covers the chalet. There was a squall of wind yesterday, with the result that the little avenue between me and the obelisk is soft with flowers (mostly acacia) and with mulberries. The latter are just black ripe. . . .If it were not for the natural resources of the place, it would be rather difficult to run a house, for there are practically no shops. An

In the garden of the chalet at Heliopolis

old woman brings a cow to the gate and milks until Hagazy says '*bas*' (enough), vegetables etc., generally seem to appear when wanted and are abundant in the garden and there is a spasmodic meat supply.

Last evening Mahmud Sidky and his brother Hamid Mahmud paid me a visit from Toukh and consented to stay to dinner and Emilio Anastasia happened to come about the same time. There was no time to borrow a cook, so Hagazy seized a little black boy to help him, wrung the necks of a few pigeons and managed to raise a little scrappy looking meat, about a pound. About an hour and a half after the following meal was served and eaten half in Arabic and half in *Ifrangi* (European) style. Soup – of meat, tomatoes, lentils, and all manner of things. Stuffed *badingans* – eggplants (olives, pickles etc., on the table). Roast pigeons, salad of tomatoes, onions, nasturtium flowers, etc., potatoes cooked in their jackets in the ashes, and chestnuts. Stewed apricots, rice pudding and custard. Dessert – apricots, guavas, mulberries, biscuits, Turkish coffee. Iced Chianti and Lemonade, Sherbet of Barley, honey, etc. At the time of the dessert the little black boy brought a *tisht* (native wash basin of copper) and water in a copper jug, and soap, and towels to each in turn, and then lit the *Sheesha* (Narghileh) with *Tombac* (Persian tobacco), in case anyone preferred it to cigarettes, which he proceeded to roll up for us.

His home life provided much material for the family letters, and he appreciated how exotically the routine of Egyptian housekeeping would read in the English provinces, as in this letter to a young niece, whom he is

An excursion into the desert outside Cairo, 31 December, 1908,
with McPherson exceptionally relaxed on his donkey

instructing in Natural History, and also providing with an agreeable
frisson. (Incidentally, this letter is a prime example of the 'editing' of the
family letters. McPherson's original was handwritten, complete with
sketches. After his niece Constance had read it, it was typed out by his
brother Dougal, who left suitable areas blank. When McPherson came
home on leave, he redrew the sketches; it was then circulated around the
family, and finally collated with his other letters.)

Dear Con   *July 28th 1902.*
We are not making pickles as you would suppose from the operations in
the Kitchen. We are merely bottling off Scorpions, Centipedes, & Bourse
with a few hornets & a hairy spider or two to give a flavour to the whole,
& the only thing seriously lacking is a snake.
  The Bourse is a domestic animal (very like a Lizard) which lays eggs in
salt, &
sometimes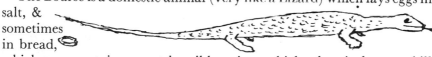
in bread,
which eggs contain a most horrible poison which when it does not kill
outright produces a disease something like leprosy (at least so they say).
They have a stupid habit of whisking off their tails when you catch them
or try to kill them in any way; out of five before me now only one has its
tail complete & that one we found in a biscuit tin & lowered gently into
the ice chest & froze it to death, I've got one egg in pickle also.
  On Wednesday Hagazy & I were busy in the store room nesting, we
found a bird's nest with young & two wasps nests between the windows &

the *Shamasi* (a kind of wooden Venetian blind). We were walking about in the straw bare-footed when suddenly Hagazy spotted a little Scorpion. He was a dear little soul but we pickled him. Hagazy had no pity for him as he had been stung twice & his elder brother got into bed with four Scorpions 'a gentleman & his lady & two boys' as Hagazy puts it & of course they killed his brother, – so he called it a son of a dog & cursed its father, the curse seems to have worked though it very nearly roosted on Hagazy's toe; for on Thursday night he very nearly trod on a great ugly devil at the foot of the balcony steps. We had a thorough hunt late at night round & in the house but found no more Scorpions. However we seized two Bourse & saw another, & in the corn room a Warena about the size of a big Weasel darted between my legs & escaped. Beetles etc. of all sorts were innumerable.

Today I had just had a nice siesta on the drawing room couch which I sit on or lie on every day & Hagazy was putting the cushions right, when he found Scorpion No. 3 – a plump little beggar – under one of them; he had also been having a nap there; he is united with is family in a bottle of spirit. Three others have been found this week within fifty yards of the garden.

I will enclose some sketches from life; some by me some by Omar of recent captures. The little gentleman sitting on his tail is a Lemur belonging to Colonel Mousally. He broke loose to see a great & memorable fight between Mousally's ten dogs 'of the one part' & my Wolf aided by a big dog called Koko 'of the other'. Z'b does not mind tackling five or six of the Mousally dogs, but he flees in dismay from the ten, so the artful brute made friends with Koko with whom he has had many a stout fight & who was the only dog in the district who would stand up to him, & the two deliberately walked into Mousally's garden & opened the attack. Unfortunately a Wolf's bite seems to be fatal, anyway to a dog for both dogs which Z'b bit before the fight could be stopped died of a kind of Tetanus. Koko lost a leg in the conflict & Z'b had to be stabbed three times before he gave up the attack, he will have the wounds all his life. I could not do much to stop the fight – for laughing at the Monkey (Lemur) who sat on the wall & clapped his hands & cheered on the combatants.

This house with its grounds (not quite an acre) is completely enclosed by a five foot wall & a ten feet spiked iron fence above, with two massive spiked iron gates twelve or fifteen feet high, so that all the domestic animals, rabbits & chickens & geese & wolf & mongoose roam about as they like & often the Horse with them & sometimes they call on me in the dining room or balcony & leave cards.

There are a lot of cats & foxes & wild dogs about; but except an occasional cat they never break in. We've had a Hyena in the immediate neighbourhood lately & the night watchmen borrow weapons from me; they are much disturbed as they are afraid to sleep. I had an exciting hunt a little while ago after a tiger cat, I spotted it when I was riding in the Khedive's cotton fields & chased it for miles & Z'b seemed very bent on the chase, but in the end it turned savagely at bay & fairly cowed the wolf who refused to tackle it. I had no weapon but a riding whip & the Horse was afraid & so finally it bested the lot of us & escaped. I was rather glad as it was a most beautiful animal.

Dear Con. *Sunday evening. July 27th, 1902.*
I expected a snake to turn up in due course but was hardly prepared to be wakened at 4 this morning to kill one; but such was the case; a little boy spotted it in the desert about 50 yards from the house. It was a kind of whip snake about four feet long most beautifully marked, he has a large pickle bottle to himself; I kept him alive until an hour ago.

I rode over to 6 o'clock mass at the Chapel of the Virgin & as I was twenty minutes early, I had a good look at the Sycamore which is said to have sheltered Jesus & his Mother. The hollow in the trunk where they hid from Herod's soldiers is perfectly concealed, the tree appearing perfectly sound until you examine it closely. I was afraid to risk climbing the tree but I knocked down a leaf or two with my whip which I enclose. I then had a drink in the spring which supplied the Holy family & which from being brackish became sweet. Riding home we were confronted by this beast (drawn like the others about life size). He stood on his hind legs & wanted to fight me and the Horse. I brought him home but did not pickle him as I found he was harmless & a most comical little beast. I don't know his name.

Wednesday, July 30th.
No more beasts worth potting until a few minutes ago when they caught a Warena next door & brought it to me on a rope as a present. It is tied up on the balcony. It is more like a crocodile than anything else I know but is also suggestive of the lizard, bourse,

toad & pig.

He bites like the devil but some say he is not poisonous, others that his bite is fatal. Hagazy is trying to find out his favourite diet, and is leading it about the garden like a dog. I am going (I think) to put it in the strong room whilst I am away at Assiut etc. to guard my *Shanta* containing stamps & other valuables. I have tied the *Shanta* also to a top window against which is built a bees' nest so that anyone who successfully manipulates the iron bars or the locks & escapes two other bees' nest in the lower windows, will on moving the *Shanta* pull the top nest in two & he'll probably get more than honey. The Warena can amuse himself catching bees & cockroaches etc. with his forked tongue.

The weather here which is answerable under Moses for all these beasts is from other points of view perfect. For two months the shade temperature has kept steadily between 80 & 100 & the sun temperature between 130 & 160. There is a fresh exhilarating feeling in the air here more like spring than summer & the gentlest breeze always blowing across my balcony. I have not felt the heat in the least (except to enjoy basking in it). I don't go out much in the day as a rule but yesterday I was riding from 11 to 3 in the sun (temperature 115°) & did not get uncomfortably warm nor spoil my linen collar.

Cairo itself is much more stuffy & at present is deserted in an absurd way owing to the Cholera, of which there are only a few odd cases out here.

I have acknowledged by postcard some welcome letters from Ja, Dougal & Campbell. Please thank them again.

> *Love to all,*
> *Yours affec.*
> JOE.

Such infestations of scorpions or spiders he dealt with, he said, by flooding the floor of each room in turn and sending in a couple of big geese to gobble up the escaping vermin.

Servants were a constant source of entertainment to McPherson. But unlike most British writers in Egypt, he did not treat them as comic figures.[1] Instead he saw them as mines of information providing him with a deeper understanding of Egypt. As with his students, it was a mutual exchange.

To Kathlene   *July 1903*

I hope some day to continue and then turn into English some rough Arabic notes I have made on native legends and tales of the crusades and of local heroes and saints such as Abu Zaid, Mitwally, Taid el-Haggag,

---

[1] It is instructive to compare McPherson's tone with Lord Edward Cecil's *The Leisure of an Egyptian Official* (1921). Cecil was a notable Financial Secretary in Egypt; but his book is an exercise in unclouded self-esteem and superciliousness (sometimes witty) towards the people he served.

Abu Khalil, Joseph McPherson's syce, in the chalet garden at Heliopolis

'When the energetic syce is not a-syceing, not a-syceing,
  He loves to lie a-basking in the sun, in the sun.
But he'd have you know that though it's most enticing, most enticing,
  He never basketh till his work is done, work is done.'

etc., nearly all of which I have got by word of mouth from Hagazy. He
pulls up short sometimes and objects to proceed until I tell him a tale and
I sometimes am surprised to find that my tale is not wholly new to him, so
many of our Nursery and similar tales having an Eastern origin. My last
tales however had better have been left untold for the more utterly
fantastic a yarn is, the more real it seems to be to Hagazy's mind. They
were: – (1st) the story of Raegner, the wolf child of Lok, and the witch of
Jothenheim and the battle of Raegnerok[1]. (2nd) the three piglets who
sought their fortune and the wolf who hoofed and poofed. (3rd) Little
Red-riding-hood.
    Two nights after the last named, I was dining at a house (luckily very
near my own) and as we sat under the orange and banana trees after
dinner I heard shots being fired at my place; on going to the house,
Hagazy who was in a mortal fright declared that Red-riding-hood's wolf
had come to the door and wanted to come in and eat him. He had driven
it off with a 'harba' (Sudanese spear) and then fired wildly into the bushes.
It was useless laughing at him, he stuck to his tale and still does and is only

[1] Norse myths relating to the final battle between the gods and the forces of evil, and the
destruction of the universe.

just beginning to get over his objection to staying in the house alone after
dark. I thought the whole thing was pure imagination and invention on
his part, but about a week after the alleged visit I was dining in the house
with all the doors open, and looking right through into the garden I saw
two red eyes in the background and could dimly make out the form of
some animal. I threw out some bones without any results except that the
eyes disappeared, but the next night I threw scraps from the door on the
other side and watched carefully. Suddenly a magnificent wolf came for
a moment out of the darkness, snatched the meat and disappeared. After
that it came most evenings at dinner time and I tried to tame it and after
about a fortnight it took food out of my hand provided I did not make the
slightest movement or look it in the face. It was a lovely brute, by no
means fat but perfectly sleek and in good condition and slightly brindled.
It ignores the dogs of the house and neighbourhood, but is mortally afraid
of Hagazy and he of it, and I don't think it will ever be quite tame with
me.

> The following year he engaged another servant, Saleh, who was to stay
> with him for several years; he first appears in a letter which McPherson
> wrote from his new appointment in Alexandria where he was engaged in
> settling in to a new house. This letter was to a sister-in-law who he knew
> would be interested in the details of homemaking:

To Nellie   *27 Ramadan 1322. 4 December 1904*
I celebrated the first hour of Ramadan by entering my new place, which
though not to be compared with my little home at Mataria, is to my taste
infinitely preferable to either of the hotels I tried or rooms which I
inspected and in the end ought to be cheaper. The big upstair room with
a small verandah is where I live, the dining and some little rooms
downstairs being as yet practically unfurnished. My upstair room is
gradually becoming comfortable and attractive looking and I doubt if
you lady economists could have made the £11 which I have expended on
all the house go much further, though you could have made the place
vastly more chic and less bizarre. Out of the £11; £2 went on a Pasteur's
filter for the kitchen, and about £1 on spirit stove, place, dinner and tea
services, washing things and an *usrieh* [chamber pot]. The remaining £8
expended on the bedroom have purchased a fine writing table, a chest of
6 drawers marble topped, a marble-topped washstand with cupboards
and a drawer and marble backpiece with shelves, a mirror, 6 cane chairs
and a lounge chair, reading lamp; clothes rack etc., etc. The case the bike
came in (covered with a fine praying carpet) which I thought I had lost
and which cost me 10/-, and the underwriter, £1, screens off my bath,
quilt, rugs etc., in which I curl up on the carpet at night: and this carpet
by the way is my *pièce de résistance*. I bought it for 40 francs (£1.12.0) from
an Armenian who sold it and left the district in a hurry for reasons best

known to himself and I am told it would fetch £8 or £10 in England. It is certainly a beauty and I am in no hurry to get either bedstead or mattress.

Furniture is supposed to be very dear here and most English people have theirs sent out from England. One only wants time and a tarboosh however to get things on good terms in the native bazaars and bargaining (which is so distasteful in England) is rather fun here. For example one walks through many bazaars and *machzans* and at last sees a writing table with locked drawers and everything to his mind, and entering inquires the price of other things: at last the proprietor asks the purchaser if he requires a *Maktab* (writing table), which the purchaser disclaims asking casually the price which is given @ £6. This so shocks the visitor that he staggers out ejaculating 'ya salaam', 'ya hafeez' and many other emphatic 'yas'. On repassing he is hailed by the proprietor who begs him to state what he would consider a fair price and 6/- is suggested which in its turn paralyses the bazaar keeper. However the visitor proffers a cigarette and the bazaar man brings Russian tea and the two talk about the visit to Alex. of the Greek fleet and about Ramadan. The visitor happens to spill some tea on the table and feels that he ought to take it off the sheikh's hands: the latter however assures him that its value is greatly enhanced by the incident but *ashan Khatrak* (for the sake of his regard for the visitor) he will let it go for £2. The visitor however 'has no use for a table of this sort' and goes away and makes purchases or the preliminary or intermediate *pourparlers* for such at other bazaars. However in the end the table changes hands at 4½ riyal (18/-), both parties being highly satisfied with the transaction.

My servant has further adorned the walls after his own fashion. The books are mostly upside down in my shelves, and he has hung a crucifix on the same nail as a hippopotamus whip, and a *sibba* (Moslem rosary) shares a nail with the enamelled metal 'ruksa' – official badge which I took with some difficulty from a cabby who refused to drive me home under 40 piastres (the proper fare being 6); the corner where I sleep bristles with weapons, including a Sudanese *harba* 10 feet long, knuckle dusters, many cartridges and the gun case, and Duncan's pistol with a bag of cartridge for it, when Saleh the servant is not carrying it in his *hazam*. Sailing Club burgees and Oxford and running trophies and so on complete the decorations.

As this letter will be little more than a description of my new home, I must give some account of Saleh on whom much depends and who so far has been a very successful speculation altho' obtained in a somewhat unconventional way. In my search for an all-round servant like Hagazy of Theodoros (neither of whom I cared to take the responsibility of bringing up from Cairo), I had all sorts of applicants about whose idiosyncrasies, qualifications, and disqualifications I might write sheets, which I will spare you, especially as I gave you an account of a parallel

experience at Mataria. I was still undecided over a choice of evils the day
I decided to move, but my bill has been so fearfully inflated by extras I
was anxious not to stay another night; and as I was reluctantly coming to
terms with an Armenian, I was interrupted by curses and sobs outside,
amongst the men who are building a new wing to the hotel. A youth of 14
or 15 whom I had often noticed on account of his superior dress and
manner and everything compared with the others, was trying to fight the
riees (foreman) who had struck him and thrown a basket of quick-lime in
his face, a favourite mode of coercion used by this gentleman. I told them
to stop the row and summoned the victim and questioned him and as a
result of his replies offered to take him on subject to proper guarantees
from his father, whom I visited at once with the boy. I finally appointed
him at 6 *riyal* (£1.4.5) per month, his father to supply his food and clothes
(the latter being a very big item comparatively). He looked a queer
object at first one eye half closed from the lime and his long eyelashes
matted with tears and mortar, his face disfigured by lime burns and he
limping with similar burns on his bare feet; but he looks smart enough
now and has a wonderful stock of quite costly clothes. The initial
difficulties of the house were quite a picnic to him and he works and
cooks so well that I have practically given up lunching in town and
having my dinner sent in from the hotel. His great joy is to shoot birds
with Duncan's pistol, which he does with wonderful skill, and to roast or
make soup of them for me; and his delight at coming on the lake Mariotis
with Hickling and me is beyond all bounds. He is useful as well as
ornamental on these occasions. He carries my gun and a bag containing
spirit lamp and provisions, and makes tea etc., in the punt. He digs up
worms and gets other and the proper bait and all necessary fishing tackle
and is willing to swim for a wounded *sarcelle* [teal] like a retriever, and he
knows the best spots on Prince Omar Toussoun's land and lake (where by
Toussoun's invitation I usually go now instead of Mex), as he has
poached over it all as long as he can remember.

The drawback to the kid is that he hates to be alone and follows me
about like a pet puppy. If I am reading in the garden he brings his
potatoes and peels them on the grass, or if I am writing in my room he
will bring a wild duck and a newspaper and pick the duck on the floor,
and he looks very grieved if he is driven away. As he professes to be
terrified at being alone long, after dark I have to keep very good hours
and if I go out to dinner or the theatre as I do about once in six days I send
him home (to his disgust) to his wife and family. He is a great favourite
with all my visitors, partly because most of them knew him as a caddie
and tennis ball hunter at the Sporting Club, partly because his temper
and manners are as sweet as his face, no matter what amount of devilry
may be lurking somewhere; partly because he is a most keen little
sportsman, and partly because he understands their tastes in whisky and
cigarettes and does the honours (if I am out) like a Pasha. He suits me,

amongst other reasons, because he buys everything at ridiculously low prices and seems absolutely honest; but as I have to keep him employed and to stop him chatting for a bit set him to write an account of his life. I will give you a summary of it as far as I can get it into chronological order and check its accuracy – as an example of the life of an ordinary Arab boy, who has never had any extraordinary experiences and has never been 20 miles from his home at Hadara, which is a couple of miles from here. If I have already bored you with the little beast as may very well be, all you have to do is to ignore the enclosed version of his autobiography, the (illustrated) fly leaf of which is his original work and which I hereby translate :–

'In the same of God the Clement and Merciful in Ramadan. We sent to you with haste the Koran in this marvellous night. What can make thee understand the value of this glorious night? It is more precious than a thousand months. It was hallowed by the arrival of the angel and of the spirit. These obey the commands of the eternal one and bear his laws concerning all things. Peace was in this night until the dawn.

Ahmed Saleh Habib
The Story of his life.

The Peace of God be on you and may God bring you honour. Ramadan is generous but God is more generous.

Yussef McPherson. For his honour these pictures.'

The autobiography of Saleh is largely a chronicle of mischief, mishaps and beatings. It begins:

God gave me to my father fifteen years ago but I can only remember seven or eight years. My father is an *Arab dam sada* (pure blood) and my mother for whom he paid much money was Circassian, so that I have no Fellah blood – Thank God.

The first thing I recollect was reading the Koran in a *Kutab* and because I stammered a little then, the *Khoga* (teacher) smote me with his *busa* (reed) and said he could not hear the word of the Prophet from halting lips. I told my father and he said this remark must bring us ill luck and the next day – a holiday because it was Friday – my uncle and I were shooting by the Malhaha (salt lake) and as he rammed in the *rhussh* (shot), the *zunad* fell on the *capsune* and fired the *barood*, [the hammer fell on the cartridge and fired the gunpowder] and the ramrod went through my uncle's throat and I left him tearing up the sand with his hands and ran to my father, and he cursed the *Khoga* and ran with me but uncle was sleeping, so the women wailed and we buried him and my father broke the gun on the threshold of the *Khoga's* house and I went to his school no more.

At 12 Saleh continues, he married a cousin who is *helu* (sweet) and he worked as a labourer in building houses and as a caddy on the golf course, from which he was sacked because it was believed mistakenly that he had stolen a brooch from a lady golfer. Then he returned to the building trade.

My uncle the *Riees* (foreman) of the labourers cursed me all day long and loved to throw lime in my face from which I suffer yet. One day he was extra violent and hurt me badly with the lime basket and I threw it back at him and then he roared like a mad *gamus* (water buffalo) and rushed at me with his *kurbag* (whip) when suddenly a voice from a window close by shouted; '*Ma tesqoot ya ghrabalawy ya mutasharid ibn' qurd*' (Stop your noise you vile thieving vagabond dirty son of an ape). Now, uncle is a great Sheikh who never works, but only beats and insults others and he was like one shot, and even when the *Khouaga* (foreign gentleman) added that he would come down and flog him like the dog he was, he only slunk off silent and all the men marvelled and were delighted and the *Khouaga* called me and questioned me and asked me when I had taken my money last which was luckily the day before. Then just as the minarets were lighting up for the first evening of Ramadan he came with me and drank coffee in our house and everything was arranged in a few minutes, father making himself responsible for me. Mother and my wife cried very much for I had never slept away from Hadara in my life, but he promised them I should have a day and a night at home about once a week and mother is very glad now and I do not want to leave him ever, even if he got angry and beat me (which he has never done) and I would even leave Hadara and go to his country with him if he wished. And this is all, with the peace of God, your Honours, and His Mercy and His blessing.

In spite of the beatings Saleh had received, he was a spirited youth, and would fly like a wildcat at anyone who slighted or insulted him McPherson had been warned before employing him of Saleh's hot temper, and had replied that it did not matter to him as long as he did not sulk. In fact, Saleh's pugnacity was akin to McPherson's own, and on one notable occasion they cooperated effectively in defending their joint interests.

To Jackie   *30 September 1905*
To finish up the holidays I went cruising about Aboukir Bay and shooting on Nelson Island with a fellow named Hickling, with Saleh also to carry guns and generally act as man Friday. We returned yesterday afternoon to Aboukir and Hickling returned to Alexandria, whilst I stayed on for a dance at a certain Countess Eynaud's and in the interval strolled along the beach and amongst the reeds and palms, Saleh carrying the gun in case of a stray shot. A certain wealthy Engineer named Alderson was entertaining hundreds of the Berkshire regiment and we watched the fireworks which were very effective in a felucca and

McPherson with Saleh, 1908

returned to the one hotel to dress. It was still early and I sat chatting and smoking in the hotel garden with the proprietor and some of his Greek friends, whilst Saleh still gun in hand watched five amusing half-drunk British Tommies who were singing and playing the fool. Suddenly one turned and told him to give up the gun and on his refusing struck him a murderous blow telling him he'd take the gun and brain him with it. Saleh stuck to his guns and I interfered explaining that it was my gun and he my servant. However three of them set on the boy one of them giving him a blow with his fist which would about break the skull of a European.

I broke this gentleman's nose straightway and managed to floor the other two who were too drunk to stand steadily, but as the remaining two came on and the first ruffian got up and made for me like a wild beast I fought my way for the door, which was then shut in my face. I then made for the front door but that and the windows were slammed against me by the frightened landlord whose only defence was that they had better make one corpse than two. Saleh who had broken away with the gun ran for the police who of course were not to be found and every soul in the hotel grounds disappeared and left me for twenty minutes at the lowest computation. I was sat on, jumped on, hit up and down, and all appeals to the landlord to open were in vain though I told him in his native Greek that he would be responsible for my murder if he did not open. Finally Saleh, two military police and a civil policeman and a crowd of Aboukirites came to the rescue and got the Tommies to the station and into a train which was to depart at 10. Before this was accomplished the whole village surged in and Pangiotis ventured out. Him I seized by the scruff and held forth to the crowd as a 'base cowardly son of a dog' with all the necessary extensions of this text and a dissertation on his conduct pointing my remarks with finger pressure and feints at his face with the other hand. His private defence was as above. I saw his face no more. His family and Greek waiters opposed no objection to my commandeering a cold dinner (as no proper dinner was forthcoming) and several bottles of beer, the whole of which Saleh and I demolished though he could hardly stop his howling. He had assisted in collecting helmets, tunics, one of my sleeves, my cap and his own (with a crowd of other boys) and two whisky bottles, one empty, the other nearly full and which (howling horribly all the time with pain and rage and one eye bunged up) he secreted in my shooting kit and which will serve for callers who are no whisky-judges and who have never heard of Craig's Piper's Blend.

The police returned to tell me that it was impossible to take the soldiers' numbers and that they were telephoning to Alexandria for a squad of police to arrest them on arrival at Sidi Gabr. To stop this public proceeding I undertook to get their numbers somehow and finding them in a drunken sleep in the 3rd class carriage I went in and took some of their numbers, but the ring-leader had lost his helmet and with one eye open was concealing the number on his tunic. I demanded his number which he refused with some emphasis inquiring who the ------ I was. I told him I was in the British Government service and in that of Egypt and must report him and so on. After much parleying in which he kept his number concealed, I told him in response to his abusive language that he was a cowardly scoundrel and a disgrace to the Army and his country. At this he went for me and forgot that he had been concealing his number and I read 5387. There was a bit of a rumpus and the crowd on the platform fled including the civil police armed as they were with clubs.

Subsequently at the Eynaud's dance, where I went more to find Commandant Pardo than for the festivities, I arranged with him to quiet the local and civil authorities and promised to report the affair at Army Headquarters, to which I went direct the next day (yesterday) wearing the remains of a new shooting suit of white Sudanese homespun – for the last time, for in addition to being covered with blood and dirt it was almost in rags.

The adjutant at once had four of the five men paraded and we identified them, but the main culprit had not been reported even for being late. We swore to there being a fifth in face of the denial of Non-Commissioned Officers in charge and finally the battalion was paraded before me and I spotted the man after several hundred had passed me. (They were then paraded before Saleh who fixed positively on the same man.) On being asked through the interpreter how he knew him he replied in the words of a song the soldiers had been singing ad nauseam at Aboukir: "I know him by ze bimble ze bimble ozze nose".

We have been there all day today at their trial giving written and verbal evidence. Private Ferris, No. 5387, Chaplain's Orderly, is to be tried by Court Martial in 3 days, and Private Taylor, Saleh's original aggressor also, the others to be sentenced by a regimental Court. As they are sure to get it hot enough I have explained that I have only reported the case in fulfilment of my promise to Commandant Pardo and the local police, and seeing that (miraculously) I am no more knocked about than I have been in a Rugby match I don't wish to pursue the case any further.

Saleh has quite enjoyed his day and Major Gamble sent him down to a good lunch, after which three cooks (Tommies) pelted him with raw meat. He in return collected stones, gravel and sand, came on them suddenly and gave them a hot time, one having his eye bunged up. The kid then fled, hotly pursued to the Colonel's quarters, where however he did not report it. The kid was not in the least awed by the Colonel or by the clatter of sword and glitter of uniform, kept a steady eye on the regiment and if one of them ground his teeth at him and hissed 'B------ B------', etc., Saleh gave him a friendly wink and showed him the tip of his tongue.

McPherson's need for a home of his own was bound up with his need for solitude (a servant, after all, was not intrusive company), as shown in a letter written when he had been at the Agricultural College for a year and forced to 'mess in' with the rest of the staff, until he managed to reoccupy his old chalet at Heliopolis:

To Violet   *Heliopolis, 3 January 1908*
I have now had nearly a year of mess life. . .Xmas Day, turkey and champagne came in, and snipe and blazing pudding and mince pies and

old port and dessert, and after dinner we and our guests sat round the yule log. . .and the night was so fine that some one said the fire was a farce – and so indeed it was, for as I sat over it I felt a cold and loneliness that the snows of Lebanon and the solitude of the desert could never imitate, and I vowed that never never never would I spend Xmas in a mess again – or endure another year of what to me has been a galling imprisonment.

Tonight as I sit in my little chalet without a soul in the house, for Saleh I had to send to Giza for letters to return in the morning. . .I cannot realise what loneliness is; the great desert stretching away almost for ever on two sides and the masses of palms and acacias and bamboos on the other – all are friends and companions; the music of the jackals and bull frogs and night-owls is far sweeter than Cartwright's grand piano and McColl's singing in the mess. . .I would infinitely rather another year take a handful of pistachio nuts out into the desert and make my Xmas dinner of them under an old pyramid.

4

An Ominous Crack

'I would impress upon the critics of the present regime that the task of one race controlling the destinies of another race of entirely different qualities is one of extreme delicacy and complexity . . . .'

SIR ELDON GORST, 1910

When Joseph McPherson arrived in 1901, British control in Egypt was not seriously challenged by any group. The nationalist movement was weak and the mass of the people – the fellahin – seemed to accept that British rule had improved their lot. The welfare of the fellahin had been one of the expressed aims of the British occupiers from the beginning, and Lord Cromer, the Consul-general, surveyed it with some pride in his report for 1901; 'The foundations on which the well-being and material prosperity of a civilised community should rest have been laid . . . The institution of slavery is virtually defunct. The *corvée* [forced labour for public works] has been practically abolished. The *curbash* [the use of the whip to compel obedience] is no longer employed as an instrument of government.' As well, the great engineering and irrigation works sponsored by the British – the dams and barrages and canals – had visibly made the life of the fellahin easier and the nation more prosperous.

The political calm, which lasted several more years, was shattered by the 'Denshawai Incident' – as important in Egypt in the emotional development of nationalism as the Amritsar massacre was in India.

Denshawai is a village in the Nile Delta. On 13 June 1906, a party of British officers were pigeon-shooting near the village and aroused the resentment of the villagers who attacked them with stones and sticks. One of the officers broke away and ran to a nearby army camp for help, but died of heat-stroke and his injuries on the way. An Egyptian fellah went to help him, but some British soldiers coming from the camp mistook him for an attacker and beat him to death.

Fifty-two villagers were arrested and tried; twenty-one were sentenced: four to be hanged, two to life sentences and six to seven years in prison, the rest to fifty lashes. The hangings and floggings were carried out on the site of the affray and the villagers were assembled and forced to watch.

In Egypt there was a convulsion of rage and anguish. The writer Qasim Amin, hitherto a supporter of the British occupation, wrote: 'Everyone I met had a broken heart and a lump in his throat. There was nervousness in every gesture – in their hand and their voice. Sadness was on every face,

The villagers from Denshawai condemned for the murder of a British Officer, 1906

but it was a peculiar sort of sadness. It was distracted and visibly subdued by superior force . . ..' The fellahin withdrew their tacit allegiance, and the struggling nationalist movement gained mass support overnight.

McPherson was abroad at the time, but soon after his return was made sharply aware of a new tension in the country:

To Mervyn   *Agricultural College, Giza. 27 January 1907*
In the holidays which followed Ramadan I had some good shooting and boating on the lake Mariotis, but one day we punctured the canoe on a sunken stake and had a very great difficulty in getting to land. The only oars used in these sporting canoes are short stout reeds and one after another of these broke owing to the energy with which Saleh and my English companion – Cadman – used them, and we were reduced to our last pair and still far from land and my bailing out could not keep pace with the inrush of water: so we almost decided to take to the water but found that beneath about five feet of water were three or four feet of the softest mud, and mud and water alike were full of clinging weeds. The last two reeds held out however and I succeeded by plugging and baling to keep the boat afloat until we just reached a bank on which we threw guns and all provisions, sufficient of which remained to give us a right good consoling meal.

The next day a very unpleasant and extraordinary incident occurred, a scoundrel attacking me with an ancient pistol when I was shooting in a lonely spot and I had to defend myself with my gun. One of us would have been bound to have been shot but that Saleh made a quick rear manoeuvre and tripped him on to his face.

He had a lot of pals dangerously near but they seemed to know that I should not have hesitated in using my buck-shot cartridges, and would not back him up.

I was very much pressed to prosecute but I did not want another Denshawai business and to be a marked man in every way, so my attacker was only summarily imprisoned for a week or two, disgraced and reported to the Mamour.

Shortly after that Saleh was attacked in the dark and was found unconscious with concussion of the brain from which he soon recovered, but we could not find that this had any connection with the other incident. We believe it was a Berberine who suspected Saleh of having made reflections on his personal beauty.

Nationalist agitation spread to the schools and colleges, where already feeling was running high. Before Cromer retired he had, in 1906, upgraded the Department of Public Instruction to a full Ministry of Education, and appointed a rising politician, Saad Zaghlul Pasha, as

Left: Lord Cromer, British Agent and Consul General, and effective ruler of Egypt from 1883 to 1907. *Right:* Sir Eldon Gorst, British Consul General from 1907 to 1911. His liberalising policies were halted by his death in office. He was succeeded by Kitchener. Described by a contemporary as 'a studious little man in round spectacles' he is here depicted in a cartoon by W. P. Starmer in *The Onlooker*

Minister. In his farewell address in 1907, Cromer singled Zaghlul out for praise, saying that he had a great future. (So, indeed, he had – as the leader of the nationalist movement and the unrelenting foe of the British presence.) The real power in education, however, still rested with the British Advisor, Dr Douglas Dunlop, an abrasive Scot, who was execrated by the nationalists because of his insistence on English and French as the main teaching languages, and his stern discouragement of Arabic.

Cromer's successor, Sir Eldon Gorst, prompted by the Liberal government in Britain, decided on a general change of course in an attempt to soothe the country's passions. He released the Denshawai prisoners, strengthened the powers of Egyptian local government, and increased the numbers of Egyptians in the administration. 'Egypt for the Egyptians', as the policy was popularly called, aroused strong resentment among British officials[1]. Apart from threatening their own positions, it led, they believed, to a lowering of standards in the administration. 'Re-Egyptianisation' had been applied to education as well as other departments. McPherson reported on a resulting complication:

To Dougal   *24 August 1909*

As you will know I had fully decided after my accident [he had been thrown from his horse and concussed] to come to England this summer, and this was recognised by the authorities at this end. My work at Giza was wound up at the end of April, but instead of leaving at once I accepted some examination supervision which promised to be an ideal way of forcing me to rest the brain. However, I was so well by then that I went on the Commission which examined the work and corrected Geometry and Arithmetic papers answered in Arabic. When we thought we had finished and were about to issue the Pass List the native Press opened a furious attack on us. In the Secondary Certificate (Government Diploma) examination, the Mathematics has in previous years been in French and English, but this year as a result of the nationalist importunity, the vulgate was used; natives prepared the candidates instead of Europeans. The very natural result of their teaching (?) was that the standard was greatly lowered and only about 30 obtained pass marks instead of the usual 60 to 70. The Commission which set the questions consisted however of two Englishmen, one Frenchman and one Egyptian and the native papers discovered a dastardly plot laid by the perfidious Englishmen and exposed it to all Egypt. The alleged plot was that the English majority on the Commission set questions off the Syllabus and impossible of solution in order to discredit native teaching by forcing bad results; and two rather stupid questions lent colour to this. When the first lists were put up in the old court of the palace of Darb el

---

[1] Though firm figures are elusive, it seems that Egypt, compared with other Empire territories, had a lavish complement of British officials. In 1919, there were 1,671 in the Egyptian Service for a population of 13 million, compared with less than 5,000 in India for a population of 300 million.

Gamameez where we were working, a surging furious mob of students and their friends stormed the place. The Chief Inspector, Boyd Carpenter, had to be smuggled out by a back way like St Paul and subsequent days we worked with the mighty old gates doubly barred and a discontented mob outside.

Stewart who was held responsible for the unsatisfactory questions broke down in health and took a boat to England and I who examined, but luckily did not set, the questions was between the devil (i.e. Zaghlul Pasha – the Minister of Education) and the deep sea (i.e. the committee of expert savants who set questions with impossible answers) and the storm of the press and people raged on.

I had luckily marked the questions in question most liberally, giving practically full marks for any attempt so that the candidates really scored on them as I pointed out to the Minister, but this did not save endless readjustments, cooking of marks, re-examining of sons of big bugs, fresh lists, endless statistics and waste of public money; and the difficulties of my getting away became more and more insurmountable. At last I gave up all ideas of doing so, went to conduct another exam. at Beni Sueff, had a pleasant time at Mitylene at the expense of the Government, got a touch of sunstroke and a temperature of 103 to 104 for two days incidentally and then helped Boyd Carpenter with the digestions of reports on the Exam. which had caused such a political outburst. This I did at Giza or in North's tent at the Pyramids from July 1 to August 8, only occasionally going to the Ministry when points connected with the press attack cropped up or when the Minister wanted me.

As for Gorst's policy, McPherson was terse: 'Egypt for the Egyptians – and ruin for all'.

A few months later, in February 1910, the Egyptian Prime Minister, Butros Ghali Pasha was assassinated in a Cairo street by a young nationalist. Butros Ghali was a target for nationalist rage on several counts. As Foreign Minister in 1899 he had signed a pact with Britain which established joint Anglo-Egyptian control over the Sudan (which traditionally Egypt regarded as its own sovereign territory); as Minister of Justice in 1906 he had presided over the tribunal which so harshly judged the Denshawai villagers; and he had recently favoured a proposal to extend the concession of the Suez Canal Company. Also he was a Copt. The young assassin was tried and found guilty by a court containing two Egyptian judges, and executed. But he had become a national hero, and in the streets students chanted:

Wardani! Wardani!
Illi 'atal al-Nusrani.'
(Wardani! Wardani! who slew the Nazarene.)

There had been some doubt whether the Consul-General, Sir Eldon Gorst, would approve the sentence of death or commute it, and some time between the sentence and its execution, McPherson wrote:

McPherson with a colleague on the day of the funeral of Butros **Ghali Pasha**. He is wearing a 'stambouline' frock-coat, 'the correct rig for state occasions'

To Dougal   *1910*
The murder of the Coptic Prime minister, Butros Pasha Ghali, was a cause for great jubilation, public and private, among the Moslems, and Wardani the assassin is the hero of the day. If his life is spared it will mean the loss of thousands of better ones and terror and bloodshed throughout the land. I called on the old Coptic priest of Mustarad where there are 1200 Moslems to 12 Copts, and he wept as we came away and said 'We shall all have our throats cut before you come again for the people feared and respected Cromer but this Lord Gorst is a laughing stock and neither he nor the British troops are respected nor feared in the least'.

I paid a mourning call on the Ghalis. Negib (the Wizier's son) was made Pasha and Under Secretary for State the day I called and the Ministers and others were there and we sat and smoked in silence according to the custom.

The funeral was an impressive sight but a disgraceful affair. I had to leave the procession to rescue Assad [his servant] who was defending himself with the carriage key from some roughs who had torn his headgear off because they said he looked like a Coptic priest. To relieve the brightness of the red and gold livery, he was wearing a black crepe handkerchief round his red *Mughrebi* which gave him a singular air of mourning. After scattering his attackers with the whip we drove to the Opera Square and watched the troops and priests and all the procession pass us and then driving onto the Coptic Cathedral I got a 'throne' near the front. When the gun carriage approached the cathedral the Moslem students and others tried to upset the coffin and many members of the Legation were roughly handled and lost their hats and only after ten minutes scrimmage and repeated charging by the police and soldiers with sticks did the mob allow the funeral to proceed.

The Bourse which was recovering is now worse than ever owing to the assassination and the return of another Liberal Government [i.e. in Britain] and owing to the intimidation in vogue which had caused honest men to leave the legislative council in fear of their lives.

Egypt however is as fascinating as ever and its perpetual sunshine as delightful.

Throughout the pre-war period, the letters indicate that his interest in politics was minimal. But when the upsurges of Egyptian nationalism forced him to pay attention, he was revealed – in spite of his great liking and quick sympathy for Egyptians – as a conventional Victorian imperialist, holding firmly that British 'paternal' rule must be for the good of the subject people, and scorning those who believed otherwise. But he did not allow the political situation to weigh heavily upon him. In the same letter as the one recounting the furore over the examinations, he abruptly abandoned the subject of Egyptian nationalism to relate matters that interested him more: 'a ride through the fields and desert', a night's sleep on 'my camp bed under the stars', a festival in honour of the 'High' Nile, i.e. the Nile at its highest flood, with fireworks, and cannon and 'a beautiful maiden on a decorated barge', and finally a visit to a friend – an Egyptian.

Dr Ibrahim Zaky fell in love with an English nurse (a Miss Barr, I think) at Qasr el-Ainy Hospital, and though he assures me it was a most platonic attachment, and that they are vowed to marry when the world is less cruel to them, Miss B. left hastily for England and Zaky was at once removed from Cairo Hospital to Mansura and as a punishment was made head (Hakimpasha) of the Mansura Hospital with double the salary he

Dr Ibrahim Zaky, c. 1910

had at Qasr el-Ainy – a common way of punishing an Egyptian official.
He had written most pressing letters for me to see him in his new post so
to Mansura I went, but had to change lines at Zagazig and wait some
hours there. I took Saleh to the hotel to lunch where in spite of his humble
attire he used his knife and fork and serviette in a way that put some of
the Beys to shame and amused those near us by the way he put the very
swagger waiter in his place. Zaky met us with a carriage and after tea
and a visit to all his patients which interested me infinitely he put me on a
jolly good horse and we rode over the old battlefield of the Crusaders, by
the prison of Louis of France and back by moonlight by the river. I have
many friends in Mansura and Zaky had them in to meet me and a merry
evening we had.

> Ten years later, when it was impossible for him to avert his attention, he
> would be at the head of armed troops breaking up nationalist
> demonstrations.

5

Vagabondage

The perfect traveller whom we are building up is a charming creature, with every advantage of heart and head but he is diffident, and diffidence will not succeed in the East. Unless I have a touch of the regal about me, a glint of outward armour, my exquisite qualities will be wasted, my tact and insight ignored. The East is a bit of a snob, in fact. It does require its sympathisers to be great as well as to be good, and I must do my best to oblige it in this little matter; so may I be mistaken for a king!

E. M. FORSTER: *Abinger Harvest – Salute to the Orient*

'Vagabondage' – McPherson's term for his extensive travels around the Mediterranean – provided much material for the family letters. To the stay-at-homes in the West Country and the Midlands went long travelogues designed to inform and entertain, like chapters in a personalised *Baedeker*, with verbal snapshots of, for instance, a portentous landfall: 'At half-past ten Gibraltar appeared dimly in the dark with the lights of the town along its foot – like a great shrouded corpse with thousands of candles glimmering before it'; or of a bowing encounter with the Wali (Governor) of Damascus in 1907.

To Gladys   *Baalbec, Syria, 29 August 1907*
The ceremony was remarkably like the coupling of two railway carriages. The Wali and I approached with backs horizontal, with accelerated pace, each being desirous of saving the other an unnecessary step. When the tops of our tarbooshes were parallel (like the buffers of railway carriages) and a small fraction of an inch apart, we stopped suddenly and hooked hands together, but in my satisfaction at our

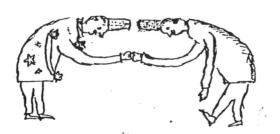

tarbooshes not having collided as I feared, I seized his hand, which is not the best of form, the true courtier keeping his fingers and hand about a thousandth of an inch from those of the Wali.

We then retired backwards and again I was unable to do the correct thing by touching the top of my boot as I retired, not being able to get lower than my knee. . .I was then ushered on to the State balcony with some superb Turks dazzling in stars and ribbons and other decorations, and then the bands greeted us with the Scutari March and some tens of thousands of people worshipped us for five minutes as those whom the Padishaw (Sultan), the Caliph of the Faithful, delighted to honour.

McPherson was not a serious Middle Eastern traveller in the line of Doughty and Gertrude Bell; rather he was a talented meanderer in the classical regions. On a couple of occasions his brother Ja came out from England and joined him on an excursion, but usually he journeyed alone ('alone and happy'), and equipped with his Keating's powder and a set of knuckledusters, laid himself open to interesting experiences. They duly arrived: an encounter with a bear in the mountains of Lebanon while stealing cones from the celebrated Cedars; rescuing a leper from drowning in the sea off Haifa; being arrested by Turkish soldiers for a night incursion into the Temple Mount in Jerusalem; becoming involved in an obscure vendetta in Corsica.

In 1909 he planned an experience: to ride across the Taurus Mountains in Southern Turkey through the pass known since ancient times as the Cilician Gates. 1909 was an awkward year for such a project. In 1908, the Young Turks, in a bloodless revolution, had forced the absolutist Sultan Abdul Hamid (the 'Damned') to accept a Constitution. In April 1909 a counter-revolutionary coup was launched and many Young Turk supporters were killed. At the same time, the Armenian community in Adana was attacked by rioters; thirty thousand Armenians died. It was widely believed that the massacres were initiated by the Sultan's partisans. When the counter-revolution failed, the Young Turks forced the Sultan to abdicate. During the upheavals, several European powers had sent naval vessels to anchor off the Turkish coast.

Grisly reminders of the recent horror were much in evidence when McPherson arrived in September 1909, and his blurry photographs show half-decomposed bodies by the River Cydnus. It was his first visit to Turkey, and the journey inspired him to his most sustained piece of travel writing; from stops along the way he wrote long letters to which he gave titles, like chapters in an adventure story. He arrived first at the port of Mersin, then travelled to Tarsus, where he bedded on the roof on an inn.

To Dougal   *September, 1909*

THE GARDEN OF AZRIEL

On the roof of 'La Fleur de Tarsus', the moon shone over a scene of beauty and peace and I was glad that I had had my bed prepared where I

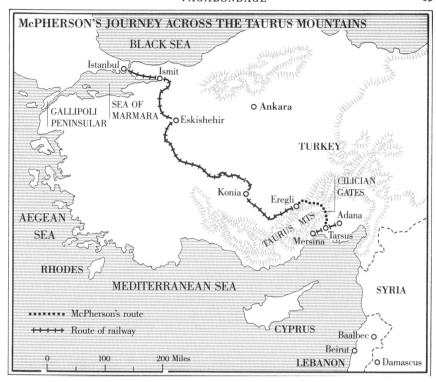

McPHERSON'S JOURNEY ACROSS THE TAURUS MOUNTAINS

BLACK SEA

Istanbul   Ismit

SEA OF
MARMARA   Eskishehir

GALLIPOLI
PENINSULAR

Ankara

TURKEY

Konia   Eregli

CILICIAN
GATES

AEGEAN
SEA

TAURUS MTS   Adana

Mersina   Tarsus

RHODES

MEDITERRANEAN SEA   SYRIA

•••••••• McPherson's route
┼┼┼┼ Route of railway

CYPRUS   Baalbec
Beirut

0   100   200 Miles   LEBANON   Damascus

was, rather than in the little cell allotted to me with a small and heavily barred window. Only occasionally there were subdued footsteps or voices in the streets of Tarsus and only the old clock of the Tekieh broke the stillness at intervals. Suddenly however I was roused by the light but rapid sound of footsteps in a neighbouring street, and heavier ones following, then voices, a scuffle and then a shriek which rent the night, then footsteps for a while and silence. Then groups of sleepers on the roof peered down shivering with apprehension and my landlord appeared half-dressed and pale-faced on the roof, just as a gang of soldiers commenced loud laughter and talking in the streets. I asked if someone had been waylaid and murdered, and he said, 'Most likely, but that's nothing new at Tarsus, we never know on going to bed whether we shall be burnt alive in the night, or when we go to market if we shall have our throats cut there. For God's sake take me with you to Egypt as groom or scullion or anything and they can have the hotel if they like. I am not an Armenian but I am a Christian. I have escaped several massacres and now they threaten to force me and many like me into military service. We are always being duped – when the New Regime [the Young Turks government] allowed us the use of weapons a few months ago we never saw the apparent boon was only a preliminary to conscription. . .'

Ja, back home in Birmingham with his wife Pollie, after some Mediterranean 'vagabondage' with McPherson

The city had settled down again to a nightmare of sleep, and occasionally a sob or a verse of a hymn came from over the houses and laughter and cheering from the soldiers who seemed to be holding a meeting. Before I could sleep again I had recalled my meeting of the refugees at the 'Fountain' of Alexandretta and their tales of fire and murder and flight through blood and bullets and I remembered the cellar 'Noury' showed, where he and his people hid until they could get a boat to Cyprus – and the tales of the captain of the crowds that came aboard and took tickets at any price to anywhere – and a wild weird impassioned sermon I heard in the Maronite church in Mersina where I was only admitted after repeating the sign of the Cross and where the intenseness of the faces of the congregation – all standing – and the tremendous vehemence of the preacher carried one back to the days of the catacombs.

[From Tarsus McPherson travelled to Adana by rail.]

The train had its terminus at Adana and passing from the station to the town I seemed to be once again in Pompeii – a ruin, not a city. 'Olim

Civitas, jam Macaber' (once a city, now a graveyard) was written in chalk on one of the blackened walls in Turkish characters, doubtless by some protégé of the Catholic Mission. What a dismally fascinating day I spent: talking to Christian survivors, sometimes, (thanks to my tarboosh) passing myself off as a Moslem on a group of murderers so as to get at their point of view. Race hatred seemed to be the motive more than religion, and fury at the boastful attitude of the Armenians under the supposed protection of the new regime, then they 'had their orders, and plunder is more honourable than work and a little blood many, many drunk'.

Taking a horse I rode through what normally would be an Eden of fruit and flowers and smiling crops and pleasant homesteads; but the hamlets were no more and in place of them *Macaber*, and the hamlets, where not destroyed, were being reaped in impunity by the slaughterers of those who sowed the seed. I had heard at Alexandretta of a 'brave fool' who advised the people of Adana to lay down their arms after the first conflict of last spring and here he was referred to again and again. One bellicose looking old Armenian, not like the common type but suggestive of an old Trojan (from whom by the way the Armenians pretend descent) said, 'Yes, he was an Englishman, and therefore understood little of the language and nothing of the nature of the Turks he lived with, and they cajoled him and no wonder, for they cajoled many of our own priests and bishops but he was brave and wrought miracles in the second massacre, leading alone or with his *kawass* (consular policeman) flocks of women and children to safety, whilst the Turks plied the hose (the fire engine being filled with petrol) over his head into the blazing houses: once he led eighty girls of the Catholic mission to the protection of the British flag and saved numberless helpless people from being thrown into the fire, until he himself was shot. His wife, too, was a heroine, and devoted her life to the wounded and starving – but God's curse on the '*Karagose*' (Punch and Judy) officers who came from the toy battleships which never fired a ball and filled their time with junketing with our murderers and curse on the Powers who mock us so, and on the blue-jackets who amused themselves with horses and women.' I pointed out that things would have been much worse if the battleships had not appeared, and he admitted that Smyrna, Mersina and the seaports had been protected by their moral influence, but assured me that a French Vice-Admiral was in Adana at the time of the great massacre and dared not open his mouth in expostulation.

When I returned to Mersina in the evening and dined with the Vice Consul, Mr Kenn, and told him what I had seen and heard, he informed me that it was the Consul of Mersina, Major Doughty Wylie,[1] who was

---

[1] Major Doughty Wylie, British Vice Consul at Konia, was awarded the CMG and the Turkish Order of Mejidieh for his courage. He was the close friend of Gertrude Bell, the Orientalist and traveller. At Gallipoli he was the Intelligence Officer to Sir Ian Hamilton, and was killed leading the charge on the fort at Sedd-el-Bahr, Cape Helles, in May 1915. He was posthumously awarded the VC.

Monte Carlo, 1908. 'The man that
broke the bank (more or less)'

supposed to have advised the Armenians to give up their arms as a tribute
of confidence and who had shown superhuman valour in rescuing the
victims of his error, if – as Kenn doubted – it was an error, for said he: 'In
the first place arms could not have availed them in the long run and in
the second Doughty Wylie could hardly be expected to foresee such
hellish treachery'. He confirmed what I had heard about the '*Karagose*'
officers and about the massacres being conducted under orders from
Stamboul – the last card of Abdul Hamid to throw discredit on the
Constitution in the eyes of Europe.

I only stayed one night in Mersina as I did not like the state of siege
which caused soldiers to pull up harmless pedestrians like myself and
impose a kind of curfew.

Returning to the hotel Zia Pasha, I found some fellow passengers of the
'*Ettore*' (Turks) off for a drive and went with them, bribing the patrol to
let the carriage pass. We saw some dancing Tsigani in a camp, and
visited some remarkable cafés outside the town. The following morning
(Tuesday, August 31), Mr Kenn, presented me to the Mutasarrif
(Lieutenant Governor of the Sanjak) who was very hospitable and told
me I could take as many mounted soldiers as I liked with me across the
Taurus and gave me a letter to the Kaimakan (Governor) of Tarsus
commanding him to give me what escort I required.

I took my luggage, except the most necessary articles in a boat to the
Russian ship and consigned them to Constantinople, and with the
remainder in a knapsack and a few tinned provisions returned to Tarsus.

Mr Kenn had introduced me to Dr Christie, head of the American
School at Tarsus, called St Paul's Institute, and his buggy with a pupil

driving was waiting at the station. He insisted on my visiting his place and Mrs Christie rivalled him in hospitality, laughed at the idea of there being a hotel in Tarsus and insisted on my putting up there. It was pleasant to have a comfortable bed and bedroom, a cold bath and such luxuries but I regretted the loss of my liberty, but their hospitality knew no bounds nor denial. There were about fifteen pupils remaining there 'all massacre orphans', all reduced to poverty and working for their education as painters, builders, cooks, waiters, etc. From these and the Christies I heard enough of the massacres to fill volumes. Their place had just escaped the fire and attack, and protected 4,000 refugees (Doughty Wylie protected at Adana 31,000). During this massacre the river Kydnos running blood and corpse-choked was the only water supply, and on my asking Mrs Christie how they managed, she said, 'Oh, we had too much else to think about to mind that, and besides we boiled it before drinking it'.

I revisited the tomb of Sardanapalus with Kovork Damlamian, a pupil teacher, whose friends had been slaughtered at Marash. He introduced me to a Turk who had a good horse and was willing to take me across the Taurus for four medjidies (about 14/-) which was less than the customary backsheesh, a golden lira to each soldier, and cheap enough for an eight day engagement of the horse and owner, going and returning. I was much tempted to dispense with the soldiers altogether in which case I could smuggle my forbidden camera over the mountains and Dr Christie subsequently told me he thought there was no less risk with the soldiers than with a simple guide and should himself prefer the latter.

I went to the Armenian churchyard and distributed fruit and sweets to the refugees encamped there, and I stuffed the St Paul's pupils pretty well with the same luxuries, but was neither asked nor attempted to commence giving money. Tens of thousands have been swallowed up and are still needed.

One of the pupils acting as groom rode out with me, I being mounted on a magnificent horse of the Doctor's called MacPherson, and he told me of the siege of Zeitoun some years ago from which he and his mother escaped with their lives, she to perish in the recent massacre at Kozoolik. One very handsome little chap, Nesib Aurganian, told me the strangest tale of all. He lived happily till last spring in a little village near Tarsus, when suddenly the whole Christian community was wiped out. He saw his parents murdered and all his brothers and relations, he alone being spared and carried off. Ignorant of the fate in store for him, he watched for an opportunity and bolted. He would have been caught but he had chosen a moment when he heard European voices and coming up with a carriage containing English or Americans he slipped in and was hidden by the occupants and handed over subsequently to Dr Christie.

Dr Christie, while befriending them, greatly blames the Armenians for giving colour by their braggadocio and foolish conduct to the reports

of an Armenian insurrection in contemplation, which made a pretext for
the massacres. He (and I also) saw the Mersina Customs full of
intercepted cartridges and arms all labelled to Armenian names, and
arms were distributed in Adana and the villages, and meetings held in
which much foolish boasting of coming independence irritated the
Turks. To properly appreciate the condition of these massacres one must
put oneself back in the Middle Ages, the days of the Cross and the
Crescent, and trace the history of Race Hatred and of Turkish policy, but
the two immediate causes were in my poor opinion: orders from the
heads of the Reactionaries, and the presumption of the Armenians
themselves misled by agitators.

THROUGH THE CILICIAN GATES

The more I thought of crossing the Taurus with a military escort, the less
I liked it, for although the *Zaptiehs* (or mounted soldiers) were to be
supplied free, each would expect a Turkish pound as an honorarium
besides keep of man and horse and a guide, and instead of being able to
practise bad Turkish on the latter and go my own way pretty much, I
should have him chattering to the soldiers, and all the horses causing dust
and discomfort. Finally I put the Mutasarrif's letter in my pocket as a
curiosity, not guessing how useful it would prove in an unexpected way,
for as you will see it probably saved my life in a tight corner.

Well, at daybreak on Friday September 3rd, Agha my guide brought
his horse, and my belongings were stowed in the *Heurtg* (pack saddle
bags) and I was anxious to start without disturbing the household. But
these good people were all up, a splendid breakfast was prepared, and
then Dr Christie read what he called the 'Traveller's Psalm' and had
prayers for my safe journey, and the 'massacre orphans' all wished me
God speed, and some of them accompanied me through the town. I
stopped at the Fruiterer's and a sweet shop, and sent them back with
mouths, bellies and pockets stuffed: bought a few pounds of lacoum,
burnt almonds and fig-stick for Agha and the same for myself to eat and
barter with on the mountain, and then filled every crevice with pears,
plums and pomegranates, though I found Mrs Christie, kind soul, had
already stuffed in 'cookies', jelly and home-made cakes. All of Agha's
money I had taken from him as a guarantee on engaging the horse, and
the bulk of mine was in a strap round my upper arm under the shirt: a
few pounds being left in my belt as a sop to the robbers if any fell upon us
as they always go for the belt first – so the Tarsus people say. I also
carried a purse of small money, of from a *metallic* ($\frac{1}{2}$d) to a *barghut* ($4\frac{1}{2}$d).

We struck right across country on no track at all, through olive and fig
groves, lovely woods and meadows and by the sparkling rapid Kydnos,
and rested after about 3 hours in a beautiful gorge full of trees, shrub and
fern and enjoyed the cold water of the river. Some boys were bathing

Armenian survivors camping in the churchyard at Tarsus

near us, one wearing an extraordinary air-tight *libas* (drawers) much blown up, so that he sat in the water and floated down stream with his body nearly or quite erect. I was inclined to lunch and sieste in the shade of the maples, but Agha was for pushing on to a Christian village with a well of pure cold water: so I perched myself on the horse again, and studied *Turkish Selftaught* by Prof. Hagopian, with grammar, phrases and vocabulary, and practised constructing sentences, and trying them on Agha. He was very chatty at first, but become thoughtful and preoccupied, and at last I accused him of having lost the way and not knowing the direction. 'No,' he assured me, 'I have been too often for that, though not for many months, but we ought to be in sight of the village and I can see no sign of it or life.' I made out some blackened ruins in the direction he was looking, and he said , 'Yes, that must be it but it looks forsaken, never mind there will be all the more water for us'.

By and by we reached the spot – utter desolation and no living beings, but a few children pasturing goats in what were once gardens and dwellings. These fled at our approach but were lured back, in vain for they were too stupid to give any information and were dismissed with some plums and sweets. 'Never mind,' said Agha, 'there is the well, and bucket and chain, and horse trough all right', and we unpacked, and whilst I opened a corn beef tin, he obtained a bucket of water, but hesitated to bring it. I saw and smelt the reason; it was a dull brick colour, and covered with fetid scum. If you have ever read the 'Pit and the Pendulum', you will gather what I saw when I peeped down that horrible well, it was too deep to see clearly, but where the water had sunk during the recent heat, women's clothes were clinging to the rough stone sides. I had some good red wine of Sharon, and I drank that undiluted with my lunch, and soon pushed on.

'There is another hamlet and a well, an hour and half from here,' said Agha, 'behind that hill you see to the North', so for the hill we made, but when we reached the little grove which sheltered a hamlet, the only person we saw was hanging in a sycamore tree, fleshless and gruesome. We watered the horse, and rode through the blazing heat for an hour or so more, till we reached a cool spring bubbling out of the mountainside, by the side of which, in the shade of a rock, I was soon asleep. Agha was too proud to get sticks and make a fire for tea, so I had more water and fruit, and rested until 4 o'clock, having ridden for $7\frac{1}{2}$ hours. There was a khan (inn) to be found in $1\frac{1}{2}$ hours, and we were now in a sort of track: and some horsemen of sorts, whom Agha seemed to know, came to the spring, and would have accompanied us, but that I was better mounted and made the horse gallop ahead, giving poor Agha a stiff run. He expostulated, but I told him, his company was enough for me, and mine would have to suffice him.

Just at sunset we reached the khan, a single wooden shed; and in it sat a haughty-looking, and magnificently-dressed youth, and an old sheikh, who scowled at us, and refrained from returning our salutations. That in the East is tantamount to saying – 'Let there be nothing between us, but wrath and implacable hatred'. So we scowled at them and passed on, till a few hundred yards beyond we reached a large stone shelter overgrown with creepers, capable of accommodating the beasts of a caravan, and with a flat roof as sleeping place for the men. Here we unpacked, and were greeted by a very fine athletic man, who was tending his dromedaries laden with tapestries and shawls and carved ebony and so on, from Bagdad, or Busrah, or Cashmere. He greeted us at once, and spread a rug by a blazing wood fire on which his dinner was preparing. I produced tea and a bottle of milk Mrs Christie had packed in, and Mustafa the cameleer insisted on making it for me and cooking my eggs, and we two and Agha dined together, mainly on Mustafa's stew of lentils, tomatoes, etc., for he was more eager to give than to receive. I was glad to be able to give him a cigar, smoke one myself, and curl up by his fire, for we were some thousand of feet up now, and the night was chilly. After 9 hours in the saddle on steep and rough tracks, I was sleepy enough, and was soon dozing pleasantly under the stars feeling most comfortable and contented, and the doze deepened into a dreamless sleep that lasted some hours.

Suddenly I awoke, and to my surprise saw Agha and two other men, who I think were of the riders who accosted us in the afternoon – Mustafa was sleeping some distance off by his beasts – and I at once perceived I was the subject of their conversation. Out of curiosity I tried to make out their jargon, and gathered that they were speculating on the amount of money I must have to carry me to Constantinople. One said, 'He won't have less than ten golden liras'. 'Please God', said the other stranger, 'he has fifteen, for that just divides into five apiece.' 'If there is a pound over', said the first speaker, 'that ought to go to Agha, or to the one who' – and as if to put any doubt of their intentions out of my mind, he drew his hand across his throat with a grin. They seemed to be going too fast for Agha, for he spoke up and said rather angrily 'All this talk is bombosh; it's all very well for you but there are many in Tarsus who know I am accompanying the *Khouaga* (gentleman)'. 'Hush', the others said, and then all their voices went quickly and earnestly, but in such low tones that I thought it would pay me better to think out some course of action than to attempt to follow. Could I trust Agha to remain staunch? Most certainly not. Could I make an ally of Mustafa? Possibly as a last resource, but probably he was already bought or coaxed over to neutrality at best. Could I get the horse and ride off unseen? Impossible to leave my present position unobserved. Could I bolt barefooted as I was to the nearest town? That was Tarsus, about 50 miles off.

These and many other questions I asked myself, but it seemed hopeless to find a satisfactory answer to any one of them, and I knew resistance would be useless in the end as they might have many allies, I none: the best I could hope for would be to stick the traitor Agha. Why the devil did I come to this beastly mountain, instead of going with my baggage to Chios and Rhodes and Stamboul? Why was I such a fool as to leave the *Zaptiehs* behind and come without an escort? And then I reflected that I had been in equally dangerous company, several times before, and had come out all right, but how? In the case most similar to this, in the Mosque of Omar at Jerusalem, my papers had produced an effect – why not try them again now with the necessary bluff? and the letter of the governor of the province? Following up this rather forlorn hope, I had thought out something of a scheme, when the elder of the two strangers got up, came round the fire, knelt on my rug and scrutinised my face. To me it seemed I had never seen such a horrible face, though I watched his hands more than his head, and tried to do so without betraying that I was awake. I had long since got my fingers into my knuckle-dusters and unsheathed a good Corsican dagger, but he gave me no occasion to use them. He saw that I was awake and started back, so I made as good a pretence as I could of just having roused up, and in spite of their

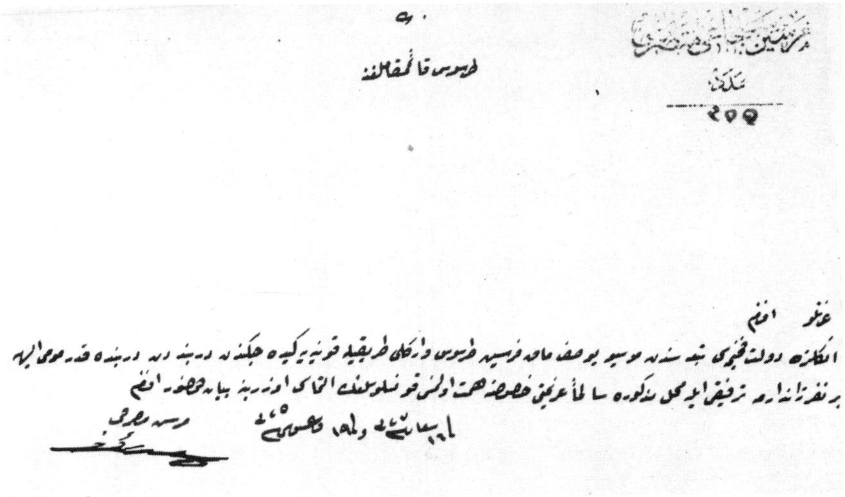

Office of Mutasarrif [Governor of Sanjak] of Mersin
Number 355

In the name of God
To the office of Kaimakam [Deputy Governor] of Tarsus

Honourable Sir,

Whereas Monsieur Yusuf Mak-Fersin, a subject of the puissant state of England, is due to go to Konya via Tarsus and Eregli, it is hereby declared, Sir, at the request of his Consulate, that care should be taken that he arrive safely at the abovementioned place and that he be accompanied by a gendarmerie private from pass to pass (i.e. across the mountains).

Dated the 16th of Sha'aban 1327 (Muslim lunar calendar) corresponding to the 19th of August 1325 (Muslim solar calendar).

The Mutasarrif of Mersin

The Mutasarrif's 'letter of safe conduct'

exhortations I got up and joined them at the fire, and passed round cigars, and some not very brilliant small talk ensued. Presently I hauled out my papers, British and Turkish passports, etc., and pretended to be hunting for something, and at last after displaying seals and stamps and parchments as much as I could, I discovered and opened the Mutasarrif's letter to the Kaimakan (or Governor) of Tarsus, and read it by the light of the fire. The Turks do not yield at once to their curiosity like the Egyptians, but this as I hoped was too much for them, and Agha asked me what I had been looking for and was now studying. I replied, 'Oh, it's the Mutasarrif's command to the Kaimakans of Eregli and Konia and Izmit to supply me with money and all that is necessary for my journey to the Sultan. I was afraid I had lost it, and if I had it would have been very awkward, I could not have paid you for the hire of the horse, nor even have returned you your guarantee money.' Agha gasped, 'But surely you have brought money with you!' 'Not a single lira,' said I, 'am I a fool to carry gold in this cursed mountain? All my money has gone by boat to Stamboul with my baggage, but of course I can draw as much as I like from the Kaimakan being on the special business of the Turkish Government, and when we reach Eregli you must take me at once to the Kaimakan so that I can pay you.' 'But', said Agha, 'I have seen you with a heavy purse.' 'True,' I replied, 'copper is heavy', passing him the purse, 'and if you can find a coin in it bigger than a *barghut* (this word means flea and is the name of a silver coin worth about $4\frac{1}{2}$d) you are welcome to it. No, keep the purse for the present, and pay any expenses we have on the journey out of it.'

Conversation now was more impossible than ever; they simply mused in silence and presently layed down, perhaps to sleep; and I, sure that I had made at least some impression, layed down too, firmly resolved not to close my eyes, and not to trust too much to the success of my scheme. Presently I saw the moon rise and light up the mountain above me, and then I noticed that it was well above the horizon, and realised with a start that I had been sound asleep. 'Bray a fool in the mortar',[1] thought I, 'this will never do' and I jumped up, and crossed to where Agha was and ordered him to saddle the horse at once, so that we might travel by moonlight instead of in the sun. He did not seem to me to be asleep, but he pretended he was deadly asleep, and raised all possible objection. At last I told him, 'Then sleep here till you rot', and went for the horse myself. Just then the imperious youth of the khan stalked up with a long whip and said, 'Get up Mustafa, you sleepy son of a hog, prepare the camels and let us get away by moonlight', at the same time I heard the distant tinkling of caravan bells on the mountain. I exchanged a few words with Mustafa, and he said, 'You are right in moving on, let nothing persuade you to

---

[1] Though thou shouldest bray a fool in a mortar among wheat with a pestle, yet will not his foolishness depart from him. Proverbs 27:22.

stay, and let your man walk so that you can see him or his shadow', and
he proceeded to help me pack the horse. Agha now wanted to get sticks to
make up the fire to prepare coffee etc., swore the horse must have a feed
and was not yet rested and generally made me feel as murderous as his
own ruffians. He realised that at last, and we took the road leaving our
late undesirable companions also preparing their horses. What a
wonderful caravan we met making for the coast, and what a welcome
one, all the produce of the East on magnificent dromedaries, and some of
these bore *takhtarawanat* (litters) containing veiled women, slaves very
likely. And after it were smaller parties and the mountain was busier
than I saw it at any other time, and no sign when I looked back of 'the
riders'. When Agha lagged behind and complained of tiredness and
injured feet, I made him mount the horse and walked myself, glad
enough to stretch my legs and warm my blood, for now the air came
straight off the snow, and blew in icy gusts through the Pass.

Now, in the moonlight, the mountain seemed to grow in height, and
the precipices and gorges in depth: great rock masses like witches
overhung the way, and the cliffs seemed to close in upon us. The moon
was in the zenith, and revealed as stupendous a lot of mountain scenery as
I should think could be found on God's earth. Ossa piled on Pelion,
bottomless abysses, glittering glaciers, multiple echoes, uncouth bridges
seemingly over space, a mountain track which appeared only to exist
where we were moving, forest growths on vertical bluffs, and we were
passing through the 'Cilician Gates', through which have struggled the
hosts of Cambyses and Alexander and many rulers of the world, and the
wealth of Mesopotamia and the Euphrates, and Bagdad; and suddenly a
great meteor swept across the strip of sky which the towering mountain
left open above us, and a turn of the way revealed water falling like a
spray of pearls from a height which the eye could hardly reach, to a
depth which tired it to penetrate.

[The journey continued for two more days, with more alarms and
adventures, until he reached Eregli, 'ready for another ride, but not
through the Garden of Azriel, nor the Cilician Gates'.]

THE MAULAVIS OF ICONIUM

Yesterday a few pleasant hours on the Bagdad Railways brought me
from Eregli to Karaman with its majestic old castles; and thence to
Iconium [Konia] the seat of the Seljuk Sultans, the ancient cradle of
Gnosticism, the objective of St Paul, the grave of Alladin and the
birthplace and capital of the cult of the Whirling Dervishes.

Half of my holiday is gone and I am still far from Stamboul and yet I
was bent on meeting Doughty Wylie at Iconium and of knowing more of
the 'brave fool' who played so dramatic a part in the tragedy of Adana:
so I drove direct to his house and sent in Kenn's card of introduction.

I found him reserved, almost frigid at first, but when I rose to go, his hospitality overcame his reserve and he could not hear of my going to the hotel and ushered me into dinner and it has only been with difficulty that I have come here tonight so as to be on the spot for the train tomorrow, which leaves before dawn. His frigidity thawed completely too and his wife was most pleasant, though both he and she are massacre invalids, he slowly recovering from his bullet wounds, and she from a terrible fever contracted in the impoverished wards of Adana. He is a strange mixture of the dreamer and man of war, he has seen service of a terrible description in India, and here in Iconium is surrounded with books of poetry and ethics, amongst which I noticed Montaigne's *Essays*, Martineau's *Types of Ethical Theory*, and translations of Persian Lyrics. He interested me in the 'Maulavis', the Whirling Dervishes, and undertook to introduce me to the Grand Chelabi (if, as he feared was not the case, he had returned to Iconium from a summons to the Sultan). The Grand Chelabi is the Head of the Dervishes of Asia (India), Egypt and all the World. His spiritual throne is here at Iconium, where the order rose probably from Gnosticism and Neo-Platonism and fused with Islam. He is a man of great learning and attainments, broad-minded and courtly, so I was much disappointed on going to the Tekieh (monastery) this morning to find he had not returned.

Other Maulavis were there but they made various excuses for not admitting me beyond the garden and ablutorium, but I was bent on knowing more of these strange visionaries. I have seen them of course at their rites in Egypt but regarded them from a very insular point of view as the most ridiculous of fanatics. Now they suggested to me more, the Lamas of Tibet and the followers of Gitama and the descendants of the philosophers. As they showed great repugnance to admitting me, I went with the *Kawass* (consular policeman) Doughty Wylie had sent to conduct me to the great Mosque of Selim the Conqueror and the tomb of Sultan Alladin and then returned to the Tekieh alone, divested myself of my boots and sat by the fountain deciphering the Koran texts carved in Farsi (Persian), Suluth[1] on the outer walls. At last an old Dervish opened a door of the Tekieh to pass in and I walked in too and he grumpily asked me 'at least not to slight the sacredness of the place by putting my hands behind my back', and on my submissively placing my right hand over the left on my breast he grudgingly showed me the holy places and the sacred tombs. But again I scandalised him by turning my face from one of these instead of retiring backwards, and he begged me to depart out of their coasts. I asked at least time to read the Farsi inscriptions over the *Qibleh* and the domes, and when he heard me read them half aloud his attitude suddenly and completely changed, and he said, 'Where, O my son, have you got the light, to read what is dark to many a poor Maulavi,

[1] Large decorative Arabic writing.

for Farsi is little known here and Arabic, the language of God's revelations to Man still less.' Then I talked to him in Arabic, with difficulty as he knew only the classical language, dead as ancient Greek and that from book study and but little from conversation, and he showed me beautiful old Korans and Dalils[1] illuminated by hand and led me by the hand into a kind of refectory where many books were. I was amazed to find Greek classics, Plato and an Arabic version of Aristotle, Spinoza and Geuliux and even Cambridge Press editions of the *Divani Shamsi Tabriz* in English and Persian, and regretted deeply that I could not see the library of the Grand Chelabi himself. Seeing my surprise at meeting with books printed in England, he said 'We are grateful to your great Universities for publishing such works as the *Divan* of Shamsi Tabriz, and doing us honour and justice at the same time, for I fear we have been much misunderstood and misrepresented in the West.' I told him that I feared this was the case and admitted that personally I was puzzled to explain to myself why men of piety and philosophy should whirl like tops and should be grateful to him if he would take pity on my ignorance and explain the efficacy of the *Samaa* – Whirling Dance.

'That question', said he, 'you must answer for yourself, it should not be difficult to do so.' I said, 'Perhaps there is something in the Koran or the Hadijat of Mohammed which you construe into an order to spin.' 'As for that', said he, 'know that we are not limited by the Koran or the Prophet. God speaking to our souls is above all books and prophets. A Christian father said, Christ existed before Christianity and Christianity before Christ, and so Islam was in the world before Mohammed. There is but one religion as there is but one God, and all pure philosophy is true religion and all poetry and appreciation of beauty is recognition of God who is perfect beauty. It is not enough to be a Moslem or a Christian: one must realise one's descent from God and the necessity of reascending to him. The human soul is but an emanation from the "World Soul" always re-attracted to it, as the planets thrown off by the redundant life of the sun are still drawn towards the sun. "Return" the Greek "$\epsilon\pi\iota\sigma\tau\rho\circ\phi\acute{\eta}$"[2] is the whole duty of man: and the poets like our great founder, Jalal-el-Din, whose tomb we have just left, and Hafiz and Firdousi and all our spiritual fathers and the prophet Suleiman (on him be peace) have realised that the soul must be raised even by what seems doubtful or illicit means and hence they have sung of wine and women and flowers and beauty and love. Anything is better than apathy, which is spiritual apathy, except sordidness which is the soul's worst disease, and the work of the mystic – the business of the Maulavi – is to find means to free the soul from earthly clogs.'

'But', said I, 'if any so-called means of raising the soul is to be admitted

---

[1] A book in praise of the Prophet Mohammed.
[2] From the *Enneads* of Plotinus: 'return to the source of Being'.

and approved there is endless scope for sophistry and dangerous casuistry and the establishment of cults where the grossest material practices take the place of spiritual as in the Eleusinian Mysteries, the Bacchanalia, and the Phallic rites.'

'True,' he said, 'many are they who have gone astray, many even the saints who have been lost – it is important to choose amongst the least perilous means of exalting the soul.'

'Now,' said I, 'I think I can answer my own question, you adopt the *Samaa* as a safe and effective means of centrifugalising the soul', and he replied 'The *Samaa* alone, without fasting, renunciation of will, abstinence and the Divine Love would be in vain – with these, the Murid passes through the *Ahwal* (stages of ecstasy) into the *Alem-i-Misal* (the world of visions) where human pain and sense are lost, where power is acquired over deadly beasts and reptiles, immunity from fire and from poison, and knowledge of numbers and of mysteries, whose inward ears awake to unheard harmonies and inward eyes to things invisible: and then he may be snatched up by the Ineffable *Gezbed*, the Attraction of God, the foretaste of the ultimate merging of his soul in the great Soul of the Universe to which we aspire and strive. Listen, O my son, this is the golden parable of the human soul, of its origin and end, its separation and its Nirvana, its Paradise lost and regained; pure and white like the snow it became mingled with the earth and defiled and bound by it, but if the rays of the Sun of Righteousness shine not in vain, both snow and soul rise pure as at first to God.'

The old Murid (Initiate) seemed to be drifting into the *Ahwal* or the *Alem-i-Misal* and to be only subconscious of my presence, his Arabic became mixed with Turkish and Farsi, and in the torrent of his eloquence I could barely follow the drift of the stream.

Now he began to expound the Arcana of his Order and its insignia, the *tag* (conical cap) the *Paleuk* and the *tazbend*, the stone of consolation, the seven names of God, the ninety-nine beautiful names and the six *Erkian* or Pillars of the *Tesavvuf* (Spiritual life) and I in my bewilderment felt like the Ancient Mariner in the presence of the Old Mysterious Man.

At last an interruption came, in the shape of a young novitiate *Kara Kolak* (jackal) bearing light refreshments, he not having completed his thousand and one days of menial work, and some other Dervishes joined us, and seemed willing enough to answer most of my questions: and eager to question me. They asked me what was my idea of Nirvana, and I replied by the similitude of the Solar system – that once the Sun was undivided but that it threw off the planets and the earth and the moon, and if it again absorbs them that will be their Nirvana. I asked if their ideas of the Ultimate Union preclude the continuance of Individuality and they professed to attach no importance to individuality.

One said, 'We strive to lose ourselves, we have no names but that of our *pir*, spiritual father, the poems of Shamsi Tabriz were not written by him

at all but by his disciple and worshipper, his spiritual son, Jalal-el-Din
who renounced name and nature'. 'If', said he, 'you asked the beautiful
moon if he praises his personality, he will say, I am already cold and void
of energy and unless I merge in the sun I shall be dark and dead and lost –
ask of *Zuhal* (Saturn) if he prizes the beauty of his rings, and of *Zuhara*
(Venus) if she values her fair tresses in comparison with the infinite glory
and beauty of the sun to which they hope to return. . .'

On leaving they gave me some manuscript poems, one of which by
Jalal el-Din of Iconium on the Murid (the Initiate Dervish) I have
translated as follows:

The Murid[1]

Drunk without wine, full without earthly meat,
The Murid needs nor drink nor food nor sleep.
Mad with a madness passing wisdom, he:
A Sky pearl-scattering and a boundless sea,
Neither of earth nor water, air nor fire,
Monarch of regions past a king's desire.
Bookless: the pages of Truth with inward eyes
He reads, illumined by hundred skies,
A hundred suns and moons, a radiant throng
Of torch-bearers. To him all Right and Wrong,
Religion, Infidelity, are one.
In glorious company, rising through the spheres,
All-Being, Ineffable and One, he nears
The Murid-Treasure in a ruin, seen
By God-illumined eyes, by Shams el-Din.[2]

From Konia he proceeded by train and boat to Istanbul, where he was
able to find a room only in the expensive Hotel de Londres in Pera, the
Europeanised section of the city. Exploring 'the labyrinth of bazaars' he
saw in a passing carriage Mokhtar Bikheet, the son of his old friend the
Grand Qadi (Supreme Judge) of Egypt, together with a Turkish Sheikh.

STAMBOUL

In a second I was hauled into the carriage and in a few minutes was
taking sherbet with the Sheikh and Mokhtar and friends in an old house
by the aqueduct. The Qadi was not there having been honoured by the
Sultan with a special audience and being detained in Dolmabagshe to
lunch with the 'Emir of the Faithful'. He had luckily left with young
Mokhtar an imperial order admitting the Qadi's party to almost all the

[1] The Initiate Dervish or Man of God.
[2] The teacher of Jalal el-Din.

In holiday mood in the Mediterranean

places normally closed to visitors and on a member of the Turkish
'Ulema' (leading Sheikhs) calling in to do what he could in the
conducting line, I gladly accepted Mokhtar's invitation to make one of
the party. I was wearing a new Tarboosh of 'Stambouli' cut and colour,
so a little touching up and rehearsing enabled me to pass easily as a
kinsman of the Qadi's.

After a glimpse of the interiors of a couple of mosques and the tomb of
the great Sultan Mahmud, I found myself not without awe, in the mighty
enceinte of the Seraglio. It is hard, even after seeing it, to realise that such a
place exists in the actual world and in the twentieth century. Gardens
piled on gardens, palace after palace, throne rooms and museums,
treasuries containing untold millions in gems and masterpieces of art and
workmanship, ivory tables with ivory concealed by gold and the gold by
diamonds and rubies, golden goblets heavy with sapphires, swords
sheathed with gems; relics of the Prophet Mohammed and of the first
Caliphs whom the present Sultans represent by a kind of Apostolic
Succession, as Khalifa of the Moslems of all the world. Then the remains
of St Irene and other Christian churches, Sarcophagi of Constantine the
Great and many emperors, relics of St Chrysostom and other martyrs.
Council chambers, with rooms of execution of great Viziers, which
remind one of the Palace of the Doges: galleries of glorious sculpture
(and some painting) suggestive of the Vatican: keys of conquered cities

and implements of torture which recall the prisons of the Hague and the cage in which young royalties were brought up so that they might not aim at the sovereignty, suggesting nothing to me but Grimm's Fairy Tales.

Finally at Top Kapu we explored some of Abdul Hamid's hoard: it is whispered that millions of his treasure went astray in their journey from Yildiz, though treasures to the value of millions remain. Mokhtar nearly wept to think 'that the dear good old Sultan had been so robbed and that his sacred body had been so wickedly banished'. We went out by a different way, passing the colossal Tree of the Janissaries with its execution block, saw a gate where the heads of the Pashas were commonly exposed and where the pegs for their support still remain, passed the Gate of Felicity (Bab el-Saidieh) through which for four centuries no Christian (except a few kings and their direct representatives) passed – at least to return alive, for the 'Carnificers' and the horrible 'Mutes' were constantly busy in the marble and porphyry halls within with their scimitars and bowstrings. Here too, near the penetralia of the Grand Seigneur, mutinies were hatched and carried through, the Sultan Ibrahim was strangled, the Imperial Harem was violated and blood and gold flowed equally freely, in a scene where luxury and violence, vice and innocence, loveliness and hideousness exceeded the imaginative powers of the wildest dreamer.

Because of the Qadi's friendship, McPherson was entertained sumptuously in the palace of a Turkish Pasha ('dinner was served in a room whose marble slabs were joined by gold – or gilt – mortar'). On his own, he explored and ate in the district of Galata ('its dirty streets filled with bad music and odours'). The Qadi arranged to call on him one afternoon at his hotel – the Hotel de Londres – for tea.

However, I tea'd alone, to the relief of the hotel staff, who have a horror of turbans or anything truly native, and at 6 strolled out in the direction of the Funicular railway, when suddenly a carriage containing the Qadi, his son Mokhtar and Sheikh el-Khashaab drove up to me and stopped. The Qadi apologised for being too late for tea and added, 'but we shall be glad to have a little dinner with you instead'. Now the Qadi is the most hospitable and generous of men and I knew was invited to dinner at Ali Pasha's and had made the terrific effort of visiting Pera out of pure politeness and friendliness, but how about the 8 o'clock evening dress *table d'hôte* in the most modern of hotels? However, better to upset the hotel staff and guests than to offend the Qadi and I was just explaining to him that I should be delighted to have them but begged them to have a drive or stroll round Pera as dinner would not be served until 8. This feature of hotel life seemed incomprehensible to the Sheikhs but they acquiesced and we were driving off to the Taksim gardens when

I noticed another carriage pulled up behind that of the Qadi's and in it Sheikh Seif el-Din and two hangers-on. The Qadi's robes were magnificent and those of Sheikh el-Khashaab and of course Mokhtar was in perfect attire, but Sheikh Seif el-Din looked like John the Baptist at his wildest, and the others ready for the whirling dance of the Samaa. I wished myself back on Taurus, the situation seemed more hopeless, and I fancied the Qadi was beginning to see that his visit had not caused me unmixed joy. Just then he caught sight of the brilliant arc lights among the trees of '*Les Petits Champs*' and heard the band and said 'could we not go to that beautiful café of light and music and sit till dinner time, as driving is very exhausting'.

Now *Les Petits Champs* is a gilded hell, where western vice has triumphed over the East at its worst, but the whole party clamoured innocently to be taken there, and there we went. I gave a glance at the steps of the Hotel de Londres which is nearly opposite as we entered and spotted Cadman of Cairo and other people I know well, but they did not see us. I steered them through the strange company, too amazed at such an apparition to be aggressive and planted them at a table near the band and called for biscuits, gazoza and ice creams.

'What a host of beautiful women!' said the Qadi, 'unveiled too and many of them without their husbands and what lovely dresses, but oh, ye Sheikhs, it is time for the prayer of sunset'. Then they all arose and choosing a spot rather shaded from the blaze of light by many trees, they spread the praying cloths and publicly testified to the Greatness of God and went through all the prostrations. Occasionally a couple seeking quietude made for the spot and turned back bewildered.

That corner of *Les Petits Champs* has seen some strange sights, no doubt, but never one so incongruous. It was too much for Mokhtar and he returned to the band and I was busily occupied keeping the ladies of the Hemikosmos away from him. Then the Qadi and his disciples left their Gethsemane and returned to ice cream and meringues. Seeing their enjoyment of these delicacies, a ray of hope came to me and I plied them with more ice creams and stodgy custards and lemonade and before they could recover from their satiety I said, 'Now we must go to the hotel to get good places at the dinner table'. 'The dinner table now!' said the Qadi, 'impossible, we have already overeaten!' Mokhtar said, 'But we want to see Mr McPherson's hotel and we need not eat every course, it is quite rude to him to refuse to go'. The Qadi turned to me and asked me if I should be offended, and I assured him, 'No', but at the same time I pressed him as far as I thought was safe – 'No', he said, 'dinner is impossible, let us go with God's peace' and he rose and swept out with his followers at his heels, through the gaping groups of painted-cheeked peris, and I fancied the band stopped for a minute in the general stupefaction. We drove to Galata Bridge, but there appeared to be no boat, so the Qadi decided to remain the night at his Stamboul quarters, but there I knew there would be no dinner preparation and I was sure some of the party, if not the good man himself, must be beginning to feel that marrons glacés and meringues are not permanently supporting, so I insisted on them all coming to my Turkish place at Galata, and we were soon discussing macaroni and grilled quail and so on, and every one was selecting what he liked to experiment on. The time for the prayer of *Asha* was far advanced so we called at the great mosque Sultan Valide and then went, a merry party, to the quarters in Sharia Mahmud, Stamboul. When I left, Sheikh Seif el-Din accompanied me part of the way and wanted me to come back to *Les Petits Champs*. 'But no,' I told him, 'it is late and here is a saddle horse which will take me to Pera, so goodnight and the blessing of Allah'.

Later in his stay McPherson was conducted on a most privileged tour of the city by the Turkish Sheikh in the Qadi's party, the Aalim Fakr el-Din.

Even the most guarded tombs and carefully concealed treasures were opened and disclosed at the will of Fakr el-Din – a member of the Ecclesiastical and Imperial Court of the Ulema. No one suspected him of introducing a Giaour into the holy places. He was a simple and pious man but skillful in pious little frauds. At first he dismayed me once or twice by appealing to me on some Koranic problem before the very doctors of the Temple or by asking me to read him some of the inscriptions when his eyes suddenly and unaccountably failed him, but I soon realised that such questions before others were invariably on points which we had thoroughly thrashed out in our long conversations and which he had himself instructed me on or read to me shortly before.

My time and your patience would fail before I could narrate a tenth of the strange things he showed me: tombs of Sulieman I the Magnificent and the Sultana Roxelana: the Heroon of the Christian Emperors including Justinian under the Mosque of Mohammed II; Sinan's lovely masterpiece, the mosque of Shah-Zadeh; the Laleli Jami's Tulip Mosque commanding Marmora and the Seven Towers, the fossilised footprints of the Prophet at Eyub, his praying carpet at St Sofia, the glittering old parchments of Sultan Ahmed and its six minarets which so excited the envy of the Imam of Mecca that the Sultan had to raise a seventh *'madna'* at the Kaaba.

Sunday, after a round of the churches, ancient and modern, Catholic, Greek and Armenian – alone – I kept my appointment with the shade of Darius and the Lares of Jason and had my siesta at the Fanum in view of the Euxine and the Bosphorus and the mountains of Bythinia and Thrace and returned at sunset partly in a steamer, partly in a single-oared caique to dine in one of the abused restaurants of Stamboul and to wander from mosque to mosque and listen to the *Fikhies* and Imams.

Seated near the *Mihrab* of Bayezid I was so completely lost in thought over some problem of this strange city that I did not notice the Imams calling to the last prayer – the prayer of *Asha* – nor the thousands of people who had thronged in behind me, until I was seized by the arm and turning saw a black-bearded priest of Islam glaring at me. He gave me the greeting, *Salaam Alekum* (Peace be to you) to which I replied mechanically, but in order, *Alekum Salaam wa rahmet Alla wa Barakatuh* (and on you be Peace and the Mercy of God and His Blessing). This in Arabic, but he added in Turkish, 'Are you sitting alone, here by the *Qibla* (pulpit)? We, who have to lead this great Ramadan prayer!' and so saying he pulled me into line. Then I glanced round and saw row after row behind me of thousands of the faithful standing with their hands to their ears awaiting the '*Allah Akbar*' and on each side of me in perfect line a seemingly endless row of sheikhs and doctors and Ulema in the same attitude. There was no friendly column to hide me, not a moment to think out a way of escape (which an hour would not have discovered), in another second all these thousands of eyes would be on me, under the glare of myriads of lamps and candles if I made or omitted a movement to betray myself. There is nothing I object to, or that I think anyone could object to, in the prescribed prayer, which consists of certain Divine Praises, the opening chapter (*Fattah*) of the Koran, which greatly resembles the Paternoster, and in a general salutation to all present, the *Salaam Alekum*, and no reference whatsoever to the Prophet. Between the *Rikaas*, for each repetition of the above with the accompanying pious gymnastics is called a *Rikaa* (bending), the Imams chant prayers of Moslem scripture, which no one practically listens to, as everyone is at liberty to recite what he thinks suits his own case. I got through the five appointed *Rikaas* without incident but found to my horror that no one stopped. There were twenty additional *Rikaas* for the last prayer of a Ramazan day.

From a bodily point of view it beat forty minutes Sandowing[1] and as a spiritual exercise it was unique. I thought it was only honest to recite what I knew of the Koran between the *Rikaas*, but my supply ran short and had to be supplemented with Pater Nosters, Ave Marias, Credos, Antiphons and Compline Psalms and the Litany of Loretto. Even these failed at last to come to my mind quickly enough to keep my lips in the necessary perpetual motion and I was grateful to my memory for the Christ Church grace, a Collect for Turks and heretics, the Ancient Mariner and Abdul the Bulbul Ameer and scraps of Arabic poetry. Once I turned with the *Salaam Alekum* to the left when everyone else in the mosque veered to the right and nearly rubbed noses with my black-bearded Aalim in doing so, but that as far as I know was my only *faux pas*. It did not escape him, though he appeared not to notice it at the time, for

---

[1] The exercises of the famous German 'strongman' Eugene Sandow (1867–1925) who opened an Institute of Health in London.

when at last the final *Rikaa* was ended and I tried to slip away unostentatiously, I felt his hand on my sleeve again and he said, 'Do you then in your country salute first from the left?' 'Sometimes', said I, 'when they are so wrapt in prayer that these little points become beneath their notice, and in my land the most careless worshipper is too much occupied with his prayer to observe such a trifle in another.' 'I ask pardon of Almighty God – *astaghfer Allel el Azeem*' he said, 'and what land is honoured by your residence?' 'Ah,' said I, 'I live in Africa in the farthest protectorates of the Padisha (Sultan)'. 'Ah,' he said, 'that is why you talk Turkish so badly; why don't you master the language of the Padisha?' I retorted, 'I read the writing of the "Revelation" and talk the speech of the Prophet, is it not enough?' 'By Allah,' said he, 'it is enough, *astaghfer Alleha el Azeem.*' Then I thought I would carry the war into the enemy's camp, so I said, 'But of course your honour both speaks and reads the language of the Prophet.' 'Alas, alas,' he rejoined, 'I have indeed learnt the Koran by heart but can neither read it nor speak the language, *astaghfer Allaha el Azeem.*' 'But,' I asked, 'the *Fikhy* who is now reciting the Koran so accurately has read and understands what he is saying?' 'No,' he assured me, 'he has learnt it verse by verse, line by line, like a parrot and he has never read a word or understood it, and the rest are like him, and not one of a thousand of those who pray here but is more ignorant than he and myself, *astaghfer Allaha el Azeem.*'

The following day Fakhr el-Din amply corroborated this testimony and I tested it for myself on one or two of the *Fikhies*, finding them absolutely ignorant of any Arabic except the Koran which they had simply learnt by sound.

This was the last full day in Stamboul, Tuesday morning finding me on board the *Saidieh* bound for the Dardanelles, Mitylene, Athens and Alexandria. There was no chance of our leaving up to time so I made my final purchases in the bazaars and wandered for the last time in the Stamboul streets, now very dirty from the thunderstorms which had illuminated the city on Sunday night with a special glory.

Never have I found a place so remote from what I had imagined and had been informed. Stamboul, the stronghold of the 'Unspeakable Turk', the focus of Eastern vice, full of crime and violence!! that is what I had imagined and heard: instead of which I wandered with every feeling of security among gentle, steady, sober people, reserved but obliging, who seemed to like fasting and never tired of praying and never indulged in anything more dreadful than coffee and a pipe and an occasional Punch and Judy show: and left the Europeans and Christians of Pera the monopoly of vice and depravity. In fact Stamboul seemed more like a vast cloister than anything else, *seemed*, for it is impossible that my impression could have been wholly correct, but one can only describe places (like people) as one finds them. In any case I believe if the Turkish people were well governed, there would be little talk of the 'Sick Man' and disintegration of the Ottoman Empire: when badly ruled their utter ignorance and implicit belief in Moslem leaders makes them a menace to civilisation. Their endurance and fortitude is marvellous. I examined some transport waggons at Izmit, each one was to accommodate forty soldiers and its cubic capacity was 37 cu. metres, and a window area (total) of $\frac{1}{2}$ sq. metre – gross measurements from which must be taken space occupied by kit, etc., not by seats for they stand apparently during the long, long journey to Yemen or elsewhere, where they fight under the afflictions of hunger, thirst, cold and heat and are lucky if they get a fraction of their pay, and reckon themselves more lucky if they die for Islam and the Padisha.

The good old Aalim saw me off, and I vainly pressed on him a cigarette holder of coloured amber which I had seen him admire and had subsequently bought for him. He had given up whole days to me, and a cup of coffee on a solitary occasion was the only thing I ever prevailed on him to accept.

6

Sporting Life

For Allah created the English mad – the maddest of
all mankind!

RUDYARD KIPLING: *Kitchener's School*

Egypt provided Joseph McPherson with every sporting and open-air
diversion that his sometimes manic energy demanded: football, fishing,
swimming, sailing, shooting duck, hunting wolves, riding (but never polo,
which was for the 'insular British set'). Sometimes he extended his range,
which usually provided a set-piece for a family letter. One described his
creation of a golf links, and his exploits thereon, in a mixed area of desert
and waste ground near his chalet at Heliopolis. It was formally opened on
7 January 1909, the Greek Christmas Day.

To Mervyn   *Greek Christmas Day. 7 January 1909*

THE CLUNY LINKS[1]

I have practically abandoned the greens as they take too much making
and keeping up and camel drivers and others are not educated up to golf
and do not respect them. Permanent flags also are not used as native
women find they make pretty handkerchiefs, but you would be surprised
what a good game can be got, using a large hole, often natural or a circle
of a metre or so in diameter instead of the orthodox green and hole. The
drive off on Xmas morning was from the middle of my garden
(subsequently transferred to outside) and the photo shows Assad as
caddie, accompanied by the lad Hindy with two flasks of Chianti and
other refreshments for Xmas toasts at the sixth hole.

A row of trees and a ditch have to be cleared, and a cactus fence
avoided in approaching Green No. 1 (220 yds.). To reach No. 2 (170
yds.) a camel track and two ruined mud walls have to be crossed, and
with No. 3 (130 yds.) a short hole, either a lofty mud fence must be
cleared or the ball driven straight through an opening. A player would
use an iron, I suppose, I always try the brassie and have never over-
driven except Xmas morning, when the ball soared in an unprecedented
and I expect never to be repeated manner, clearing the road, missing

[1] Cluny: Scots for the chief of the Clan McPherson, and the nickname of a young nephew.

The Opening of the Cluny Links, Xmas Day, 1909: 'The Drive off in My Garden at Heliopolis, Hindy with Chianti to baptize the greens, Assad the caddy'

Cadman's house and landing in the next garden, to the alarm of a Syrian family. No. 4 (600 yds.) over a perfectly level and straight lawn of firm sand gives good practice with the brassie and is free from bunkers if one keeps reasonably straight: Cadman however, my opponent, getting wildly to the right, lofted his ball into a plantation of prickly figs and going after it startled a beautiful golden crested chameleon. Assad declares that he nearly trod on a snake in finding the ball in which statement Cadman's caddie supports him. I missed all this as going as much to the left as Cadman to the right my ball entered the only house in the neighbourhood and the Levantine owner was only willing to yield it up after I had taken coffee and mastic with him. No. 5 is over half cultivated land and *berseem* fields on the right and irrigation canals on the left must be avoided and over-hitting in the approach lands one in old tombs or a pond, though a straight steady player might easily negotiate the hole in three. No. 6 (210 yds.) from a very lofty sandhill is truly inspiring, it is like the pulpit hole at Saltford or No. 10 from Walton Castle at Clevedon, only more so. The hole itself is at the bottom of a kind of crater but a deep pond and a gully must be avoided and a number of tombs and holes and a ten-foot trench have to be passed over. I have twice done this in two, but on Xmas I took sixteen and Cadman fourteen and I had to help him out of one tomb from which he emerged with his ball and some human bones. I pulled my ball into the pond and Assad had to strip and go for it. It was here that a riding party joined us and we drank to home and beauty and baptized the Cluny links. I thought I had the secret of this hole having twice done it in two but I fear the party was hardly impressed by our performance on this occasion.

No. 7 (220 yds.) Little Pisgah, is from a lofty mound above the crater over all sorts of holes and bunkers on to a level plane, where one of the caddies as at the other holes runs on and plants the flag in the centre of the circle.

No. 8 (310 yds.) has no pitfalls but a rubbish heap and some Bedouin tents; but No. 9 (150 yds.) has walls and cactus trees and a tethered buffalo bull was there on Xmas and of course my ball went wide and touched him up and he got so excited at the approach of the caddies in their red vests that he pulled his peg out. We thought he was going for Assad who had the red flag and so thought Assad and fled. But no! he bolted towards the Bedouin tents where he got mixed up in the ropes and was finally secured. Green No. 9 is at my gate and ends the course at present. I seldom get round without some incident or some delay. If the ball gets amongst the Bedouins it is difficult to get away without having coffee and a chat in the door or one of the tents. One of my longest drives tickled up an old fellah who as soon as he had recovered from his surprise, pocketed the ball and only gave it up on being assured that it was highly explosive.

But I should think anyone who reads this long account is thankful that there are only nine holes and not eighteen.

The following year he embarked on an even more ambitious project:

A PILLAR OF FIRE BY NIGHT (IN THE TRACK OF THE ISRAELITES)

December 1910

The Feast of Sacrifice fell this year in the middle of December and meant for us a full week's holiday. I was rather out of sorts and was bent on a complete change and my inclination turned to a bike ride across the desert to Suez, an act of folly I have often contemplated. However I found that one of two gentlemen referred to as the 'Blither Brothers' in previous letters was contemplating the same thing, and although he, the

'Big Blither Brother', or BBB, is very harmless, I should have laughed at anyone who suggested our combining for even an afternoon's excursion. However he has been several times and is one of the few who has, always in the company of the same old Bedouin Mousa – or Moses – and a friend of mine, Cross, was going with him and urged me to come.

Several other schemes including a camel ride to the Fayoum and a horse journey to the Monastery of Wadi Natroun fell through and on the eve of the departure of the BBB and Cross their third man Kemp fell out and I met Cross at a Greek Theatre in the Esbekieh where they were playing *Oedipus Tyrannos* in the original Greek of Sophocles, and fixed up with him to take Kemp's place. I added more beer and water to the stores and sundry other articles that seemed advisable such as apples and oranges, kippers and haddocks, magnesium wire and a compass, and early on Friday morning, 9 December, we started on our bicycles sending Moses on before with a well-loaded camel. I was barely out of Cairo when my old bike snapped clean in two at the forks, so returning to the town I hired one and after lunch at Cross's we got fairly on the way. The route led through Abassieh and Heliopolis on the left – from which Moses and the Children of Israel started on the same route. Leaving the Land of Goshen out of sight, we passed a petrified forest and 'Moses' Well' where he is supposed to have practised his water-producing performance on a small scale; a little brackish, muddy water remaining as a proof. He did not repeat the experiment on the Egyptian side of the Red Sea, or anyway we did not reap the benefit of it. About 3 p.m. we reached Station No. 2 of the old post road which was abandoned half a century ago when the railway via Ismalieh was opened, but in places this ancient track which probably existed long before the post and long before Moses, was easily recognisable, in fact it was so well done up about a century ago for the Mails that it can be used now for motors twenty miles or so beyond Cairo.

We made a second lunch off cold pigeon and Chianti in the ruins of No. 2 Station, had a rest by the old well which was dug out by using a spiral track, up and down which the workmen went; and climbing one of the few surviving towers which were used last century for semaphore signalling (before the telegraph) we saw our camel on the horizon. This we overtook at sunset near Station No. 4 where we had decided to pass the night. To our great surprise we found part of this station still roofed in and some massive tables still remaining, on one of which we dined and slept without resorting to the tent.

Saturday morning we gave Moses (Mousa) a good start, arranging to meet him at sundown at the eighth and middle station and with a day's rations on our backs and bikes proceeded, sometimes finding the old road good, or firm tracks of sand, at others having to wheel or almost carry our machines through sand drifts or over boulders of some prehistoric water course. The sun was unclouded and the air like wine and the waste of sand and rock was broken by little shrubs bearing a dark purple kind of inflorescence smelling like apples. One tree we passed had a great shrike in it, the only living thing to be seen. He had been busy impaling beetles on the thorns of the tree, but where he found them we could not make out. The stations are from six to eight miles apart and at noon we were in the roofless ruin of No. 6, ravenously despatching our rations. I was enjoying an after lunch siesta, but the BBB was ruthless and bent on 'pushing on'. I pointed out that in that case we should arrive at No. 8 some hours before Moses and should have a cold wait at sundown and that it was better to rest here in the heat of the day. I could not convince him so I let him go on, and Cross, not knowing the BBB as well as I, went with him.

I started less than an hour after and expected to see them on the horizon and just caught a glimpse of them as they disappeared in the glittering waters of a great river which dried up to let me pass or heaped itself up in another direction. I caught them however (and passed the camel) between Stations 7 and 8 and just as the horizon was cutting the great sun, we halted at No. 8. How I blessed Cross for carrying a thermos full of tea and he me for the loan of my little brandy flask: and how we cursed the BBB for causing us to be so far ahead of the camel which bore our rugs at this, the chilliest bit of the day. I found it too cold to sit still and climbed on the ruin to search the horizon for our Bedouin, but no Mousa was to be seen in the wilderness and as we were in the centre of a widely extending basin I knew he could not come up for a couple of hours or so. I thought of Coupland and Young who in 1902 waited at this spot for their camel which never came. They pushed on thinking they had passed it until they were exhausted and slept supperless in the sand and pushed on the next day with no food and nothing to drink but a little whiskey, and no protection from the sun. Long before they reached Suez, Coupland, poor beast, was barking mad and Young had to beat him to prevent him lying down to die in the desert. He is in an asylum in England now I believe. Young has been wandering since in the Euphrates valley and is now in the Sudan. They were colleagues of mine at the Khedivieh School. The cold, and the blithering of the BBB and the taste I had had of the luxury of having the mirage and the desert to myself in the afternoon, made me long to wander across the sand to an old palace some miles to the North: so sharing my magnesium wire with Cross I set out.

The after-effects of the sunset were most marvellous. Two great columns of the most vivid crimson, black at the centre, rose in the West and a river of blood seemed to flow along the horizon. All this changed to green and long before I reached the palace of Abbas I, there was no light but that of the glorious moon in the zenith: and that lit up vast ruined halls, fathomless vaults, marble-columned barbican towers, ruined battlements, and quite a village of stables and the dwellings of the

followers of the princely owner. A tower with a winding stair like a
Christian belfry attracted me and climbing the stair I sat in a window
space and enjoyed the beauty and tranquillity of my surroundings. Not a
sign of life was there, not even of the smallest insect, except the evidence
of the stones of the castle and the palace that once life had asserted itself
here in the heart of the desert. On their chance of spotting it at the camp I
lit some magnesium wire and instantly the ruined tower and vaults about
me were full of wheezings and unearthly noises. I was too dazzled by the
light at first to see the beings I had evoked but soon found I was
surrounded by hovering brutes, huge like harpies and so near that I
struck out with my dagger to prevent an actual attack. Whether they
were vultures, eagles or harpies I do not know, for I vacated my perch as
soon as I could without breaking my neck and made through a kind of
amphitheatre across a spur of the barren hill to an ancient signal tower
and then made my way to the South. Had I gone by the compass only I
should have been all right but I struck an ancient road and as I had noted
a track from the palace to Station No. 8 I had no doubt that that was it. At
last the road blended with the desert and I found that in blindly
following it I had gone SSE. I tried then to compensate my error by going
slightly West of South, but after walking over an hour I came to the
conclusion that I had missed the Castle road and even crossed the Cairo-
Suez track and was in fact lost in the desert. I realised that the situation
could only be serious in the case of my walking so far afield that the
Station was out of sight when morning dawned, so walking back to a
comfortable sand drift and eating my last bit of chocolate and draining
my last drop of cognac I settled down to sleep after a smoke and after
burning most of the magnesium wire without response.

The moon and stars were most glorious and constantly great lamp-like
shooting stars wandered across the sky, suddenly I saw after a while a
white twinkling star shine out, more beautiful than them all, more
welcome than the Star of Bethlehem. It had faded in a moment, but I
replied with some of my wire and presently in place of the star a warm
glow appeared and sparks in a whirl of smoke and soon I was tramping
over the desert again guided by a Pillar of Fire until I saw a tabernacle
and three weird figures, in the glow, Cross, Moses and the BBB.

Night was very far advanced but the cutlets were still uncooked partly
because they were too alarmed about me and partly because they did not
understand the travelling Primus which I had brought. I soon had that in
full swing and whilst the cutlets and Cambridge sausages were sizzling, I
was trying to quench my unquenchable thirst. Although every drop of
drink, water included, was very precious, they voted me unlimited drink
in consideration of my happy escape from my perils which I painted in
the darkest colours, moving even the callous old heart of the BBB – and I
accepted – only muttering between the bottles of beer: 'Father have pity
on them, for they know not what they offer'. The BBB was still busy

cleaning up the dinner things, an operation on which he prided himself
and in which we encouraged him and in fact the one thing in which he
was some good, when I became drowned in a sea of sleep as the Arabs put
it. We were not far from the Hendali Valley, noted for its hyenas and
other prowling beasts and occasionally depredatory Arabs, and I had
had some misgivings that the column of fire by night might serve as a
guide to some of them as well as to myself, and I suppose the idea was with
me in my sleep, or else I was dreaming of the night in the Lebanon when I
met a brown bear face to face. Anyway I half woke with a strong
impression that something or somebody was prowling near the tent. By
the light of the remains of the fire of dried shrubs with the apply smelling
flowers, I could see the camel sleeping head erect and Mousa curled up
asleep in its lee and some distance behind them I saw the crouching figure
of a beast, but in spite of all efforts the waves of the sea of sleep
overwhelmed me again.

Suddenly I awoke again: this time there was no mistake: a huge
shaggy beast on all fours had already thrust his muzzle under the flap of
the tent and was crawling in. My weapon which had been carefully
placed under my rolled-up coat which served as pillow had sunk in the
sand and in my haste I could not find it. There was not a second to be lost
so one bound brought me on top of the intruder and I got a double grip
on its throat. So thick was the fur that I could make little impression and
was trying to improve my grip when the beast succeeded in gurgling out:
'it is I, Cross, you're throttling'. When we had sorted ourselves out a bit he
admitted that his enormous fur coat and the rough shawl wound round
his head, as well as his all-fours method of entering the tent had made a
very successful bear of him: and on subsequent occasions when he
wanted to take nocturnal strolls he woke me up to let me know.

Mousa prayed and sang and made all sorts of noises to wake us at dawn
about 6 o'clock and at last succeeded and after breakfast and seeing him
on his way, Cross biked to the Dar el-Raideh and saw my tracks amongst
the ruins and some enormous and remarkable ravens: he also found some
curious Greek inscriptions in a sort of dungeon under our rest house and
which as a Greek Honours man of Cambridge he made out.

We then pushed on and just as the noontide sun was making us thirsty,
he spied some luscious yellow fruit, round like big oranges with a
delicious apple like smell. He cut one open and inside it was like a
pomegranate. But Oh! the taste!, infinitely bitter: Cross declares
everything he used his knife on for the rest of the journey tasted like
strychnine. Some of the fruit too, fresh and orange-coloured outside, were
like ashes within. It was of course the '*Homdil*' – Dead Sea Fruit, the
apples of Sodom. A water mirage was shimmering to the South, trying to
lure us out of the track and we could well imagine a thirsty traveller who
had been deceived by the mirage finding the pippins of Gomorrha the
last straw. Luckily we had real pippins and oranges in our wallets and

'My inclination turned to a bike ride'

other refreshers too. We led our bikes through sand drifts and rocky hollows until we came to the tomb of Sheikh Takrousi near Station No. 9. He was murdered here on his way back from Mecca and then venerated as a Saint. His little shrine was open and on entering we found the catafalque decorated with innumerable votive offerings, hair, teeth, little flags, shells, beads, a sardine tin, tobacco pipes, and trinkets of all sorts – evidently no Yanks pass this way. We added some small coin, some coloured Turkish postcards and the silver paper from some chocolate and hope to have thereby earned the Sheikh's blessing and acquired merit and the approval of posterity for beautifying his tomb.

At No. 10 we rested and I had my siesta in peace but nearly got sunstroke as the sun found out my shady corner whilst I slept. Cross was busy tying rags round his bike tyres which were almost worn through and it was after three when we pushed on. A splendid run, only dismounting once between 10 and 11 brought us suddenly to the end of all traces of the old track: nothing but unvarying desert around us and no sign of anyone ever having passed that way: except in the distant ruin of No. 12. We reached it by moonlight and the night was so glorious that we pushed on to the valley beyond and camped in a pleasant hollow and dined sumptuously and slept peacefully. The next and last day's ride was through fine rocky, almost mountainous scenery; some of the hills glittering like snow in the sun, others rich dark shades of violet and purple, and though there was no trace of the old road, we never dismounted between 13 and 14. No. 14 was marked, not by the remains of the walls of the station but by the ruins of Fort Agroud, a couple of miles away and which Cross and I explored. This was once a Turkish stronghold and thousands of people are said to have been done to death here. Certainly skeletons were abundant enough in the vaults under the tomb of Sheikh Agroud. Near the fort are traces of an old railway station and track and a colossal water tank which might hold thousands of gallons, and also a ruined *Saqqieh* wheel and a well so deep that we could by no means see the bottom. It was apparently dry as stones fell with a hard sound taking between 4 and 5 seconds to make the descent, which indicates the incredible depth of over 200 metres.

Pushing on after lunch: a blue wall seemed to bar the distant view and ships were crawling up it and quaint porticos and minarets were at its margin. I thought we had struck a very erratic mirage but gradually was convinced that this was the Red Sea: Red forsooth! it is the deepest and most radiant blue imaginable, bluer than the Ionian Sea or the Italian Lakes or the sacred waters of Karnak.

This was the first day of the actual feast when Moslems slaughter rams wholesale in memory of Father Ibrahim's callous treatment of his son, and then make very merry for three days and nights, so we found the ancient town of Suez very much *en fête*. After tea and beer at the hotel, the Bel Air, I went off on my own: saw a native fair and many funny things and followed the reputed track of the Israelites, came to a ferry and on the other side a picturesque spot with a kind of well, known as Moses' spring. The natives asseverate very strongly that this is the true route of the Exodus: if so the wily old Moses chose about the narrowest spot for crossing and one hardly needs to fall back on a miracle or a mirage to explain the crossing of the Red Sea, and the dry old mummy of Pharaoh Menephtah does not seem so out of place in the Cairo Museum, after all.

We dined late at the Bel Air and had a long, long search for our Moses and the tent, finding him at last and passing our last night in the sand. Tuesday after a merry and interesting day amongst the holiday makers, we left Moses to recross the desert alone with only the camel for company: for the week was far spent and the train unfortunately was a necessity. We were all very sunburnt and much the better for the desert air and the exercise and the simple life and the long drink we enjoyed on arrival in Suez, and most of all for being absolutely out of the reach of official circulars, class bells and all appearance of red tape: and have the satisfaction of knowing that our names are added to the half dozen or so fools who have crossed the hundred miles or so of desert between Cairo and Suez on bicycles.

About this time, too, he took part in a 'primitive horse race', traditionally part of the opening ceremonies of a Moulid, or religious festival in honour of a Moslem Saint, held near his tomb.

I arrived at about 10 a.m. and being mounted on a very swift arab I was rash enough to take part. Competitors were allowed to use a stick to beat

On 'Buraq' with his colleague Cadman

their opponents' horses, or to baulk the riders, exactly as in the Palio raced at Siena on the Feast of the Assumption. After a little preliminary play to get used to these peculiar conditions, we raced and I won amidst vociferous and generous applause, partly because 'El-Buraq'[1] was better fed than the other horses, and had had good practice at the Gezira Sporting Club, but more I think through the mild use they made of their sticks where I was concerned. My triumph was short-lived, for I was entirely outclassed in the management of my mount at the finish, they pulled up almost in a length and I committing some havoc in the crowd before I could stop. Riders and onlookers took this with the same chivalrous good temper. Even the people whom I fear I hurt, refused any compensation; but a picturesque vendor of *Qara Sus* or *Erq Sus*, a drink made mainly of sarsaparilla, I fancy, was on the spot and I bought up his stock for the liquid delectation of *quicumque vult*. As I rode away I heard his cry, *Sibil Allah ya Atshaneen!* (Fountain of the Lord, Oh ye thirsty ones),' and saw him thoroughly well mobbed.

Many years later writing his book *The Moulids of Egypt* (much of which was a record of vanished customs), he recalled this occasion, not only for the horse racing, but also for his anthropological observations during the *zeffa* – the ceremonial procession.

---

[1] Also the name of the white mare given by the Archangel Gabriel to Mohammed for his miraculous flight from Mecca to Jerusalem and back in a night.

There was a great crowd about the tomb, with acrobats, conjurors, dancing girls and the rest; and the streets were so thronged that my progress was most difficult, and I had to take a short cut through a harlots' quarter, almost deserted at that early hour, and out of the route of the *zeffa*. At the beginning of the *Suq*, the main street of the little town, further advance was impossible, and I was immobilised for quite an hour watching the pageant pass, and there I spotted W., another Englishman in the same condition. After the usual '*Turuq*' with their banners, music, sashes, and insignia, came endless carts bearing groups dressed up to represent some guild or some fancy, and others drawn by one horse or donkey and bearing thirty or more children and women in gala attire, then I noticed approaching a large cart with a raised platform at the front. At the centre of this was a throne, and before it was standing a very handsome lad of fourteen or fifteen, perfectly naked except for a little crown, and an open bolero of crimson stuff embroidered in gold and bearing little epaulettes, through which almost invisible cords passed. Brightly coloured circles had been painted round his navel and nipples. A 'Wazir' in gorgeous robes adapted from syces' costumes stood on each side of the monarch, one holding a gilt chamber pot and the other a basin, which with low obeisance they presented to him at intervals. Musicians beat *tarrs*, *tablas*, and *darabukas* on a somewhat lower platform behind. But the amazing thing was that the little king's virile organ was dancing to the music in seeming excitement, turning to the right and left, dipping down, and then flying up and down as though actuated by a spring. The royal car paused for a minute or more a few yards from where I was and I could detect a fine cord attached to the anterior portion of this marionette of flesh and blood, passing under one of the epaulettes and descending from behind to the lower part of the cart, where obviously a string-puller was concealed.

It is worth noting that the Moulid of Sheikh el-Herera, does not, (now at any rate), follow the Moslem Calendar observed by nearly all the others, but is held on Sham el-Nesim, the Easter Monday of the Coptic and Greek Churches: and I suspect the *Zeffa*, with its phallic elements, dates back to pre-Islamic, and pre-Christian festivals in honour of Spring.

7
1913

Surely there never was a time in the life of the world when it was so good, in the way of obvious material comfort, to be alive and fairly well to do as it was before the war.

C. E. MONTAGUE: *Disenchantment*

In spite of Joseph McPherson's blithe ability to shrug off intrusive worries and distractions, he was showing certain signs of restiveness in the year or two immediately before the Great War. Perhaps his enviable life – and he was well aware that it was enviable – began to seem a little static. And the international scene was full of alarums.

In 1913 he again visited Istanbul, the centre of an Empire in convulsive decline. In the war with Italy in 1911–1912, the Turks had lost Tripoli and the Dodecanese Islands; and the First Balkan War, just concluded, had deprived her of almost the last vestiges of her territories in Europe. Attacked in 1912 by an alliance of Bulgaria, Serbia, Greece and Montenegro, Turkey had been forced back to a line based on Chatalja only twenty miles from Istanbul. However, the victorious allies had quarrelled amongst themselves, and on the very day that McPherson arrived, Bulgaria had attacked Serbia and Greece. Turkish forces were soon to issue from the Chatalja line and re-occupy Adrianople (Edirne).

Moreover, two weeks before his arrival, the head of the government, Sevket Pasha, had been assassinated, and the city was still in a turmoil.

Fascinated by the excitements in Istanbul, he lingered there for a week, and then took a ship up the Black Sea to Odessa, from where he went by train across Russia and the Continent, en route to England. On board ship, he set down his impressions of Istanbul from the moment of his arrival for his nephew Campbell.

To Campbell   *S.S. Odessa,*
            Cie. Russe de Navigation à Vapeur et de Commerce July 1913
I was awakened at dawn by the ship stopping in answer to a challenge at the mouth of the Dardanelles and Tenedos was in sight. We steamed slowly through and stopped at the little town of Dardanelles for an hour. The shore bristles with forts but they don't look very deadly: the passengers were much more interested in possible invisible mines. Slowly as we passed the Hellespont, it was all too quick to disentangle the maze of myth and history which it recalls. Troy and Simois, the Mount of Ida

Lord Kitchener, British Consul General from 1911, at the opening of a new quay in Cairo. He was recalled to Britain in August, 1914 and appointed Secretary of State for War. *Inset:* McPherson sometimes attended official receptions at the British residency, but having little interest in 'big bugs', rarely mentioned them

and the homes of Heroes, Gods and Goddesses. Soon we were amongst the lovely Isles of Marmora and looking out for the most superb city in the world. The sun was at its brightest, sea and sky dazzling – only one lowering cloud where Byzantium ought to stand and gradually we realised that the cloud was a smoke wrack enshrouding a burning city. Troy in imagination was burning behind us and in reality flames were bursting through the smoke in the midst of Constantinople. It was a most distressing sight! It was like watching the suicide of Dido and so great was the conflagration that though we were nearly two hours distant from the city and the minarets of Sultan Ahmed barely visible, there was no mistaking the flames.

Night was coming on when we entered the Golden Horn and I lost no time in transporting my luggage in a caique to the Scala near the Seraglio, leaving it in the Hotel Anadol in the heart of Stamboul and making for the scene of the fire. There was no approaching it however: the city was full of soldiers, mounted or infantry and a cordon was drawn for miles round the burning area. The city is of course under military law and the state of siege was interpreted by the soldiers at its strictest. The palace of the Minister of the Interior, Talaat Pasha, was utterly consumed and this had been threatened for this very day and carried out in spite of all precautions that cunning and force could take. The Sublime Porte and other Powers had also been threatened and were in danger and so the military authorities were thoroughly exasperated. Armies of firemen were accompanied by troops, and trains of ambulance wagons and the artillery were in the Hippodrome ready to crush any revolutionary attempts. There seemed to be no light in Stamboul but the light of the conflagration and of innumerable torches. These and the general uproar frightened the horses and many took fright, crushing people and adding to the confusion and panic.

One spectacle very characteristic of a Stamboul fire was to be seen from time to time: a party of youths running and bearing a small hand fire engine, surmounted by a sun object in brass exactly resembling a pyx. When new to Stamboul I used to salute this, thinking it contained the Viaticum, a mistake which the bareheaded white-robed and girdled bearers made fairly excusable: the priest, I thought, had gone on to the sick house with the holy oils.

The idea occurred to me to watch the fire from the tower of Eski Serai but this again was forbidden, but luckily by the mosque of Bayezid I found an unguarded lane and got as near the blazing quarter as the heat would allow. There, near Talaat's palace, now gutted, was a lovely mosque partly in flames and smoke and fire curling up the minaret. Before long I was spotted by a Turkish officer and roughly ejected.

Hassan Bey, one of my table companions on the *Ismaliah* [the ship from Egypt] though he had not been to his home at Scutari for seven years,

A Turkish fire brigade in action

was so keen on seeing the fire that he had remained at Stamboul till the last boat was gone and I met him near my hotel and offered to put him up as I had a double-bedded room. We went to Galata first and found excellent beer and plenty of it and then turned in. The bedding, sheets and all looked spotless and the room beautifully clean but I was awakened after an hour with swollen hands and eyes, and before I lit a match the intermittent light from the burning area revealed troops of 'takhta bitti' (bugs) scaling the bedroom wall. An examination indicated that they were entering the bed by means of my shirt which, hanging on the foot of the bed, touched the wall. After raising this drawbridge, putting all intruders to death and making a cordon of Keatings round the bed legs, I slept in peace, as the bed itself, it turned out, was free. A glance at Hassan Bey revealed a similar state of things in his quarter, but the bed touched the wall on two sides and I thought it would neither be kind to him nor to the takhta bitti to awake him. I woke once or twice and saw scouts grouped on the arm of the sofa nearest me and at various points on the wall eagerly seeking a vulnerable point on my frontier: these were slain as spies and I may as well say at once that my tactics were so successful that I spent a comfortable and happy week in this room. It had a marble-topped writing table, mirror, cupboards and so on and served as sitting room as well as bugwalk, but to wash or bathe one had to use a tap and receptacle outside of the room and common to all on my floor. My bill for the week was 65 piastres (about 10/4). Breakfast I took at a laiterie opposite where café au lait, yeost (curds) and eggs came to about 2 piastres. Lunch and dinner I generally took à la Turque at a Stamboul restaurant where the bill of fare was in Turkish only (or possibly Armenian or Greek) and these I found cheap and clean and the Turkish cooking good. Sometimes I had a meal de luxe at Pera at the 'Tokat Lian' or in the 'Petits Champs' and sometimes when I was riding or boating late or came down the Bosphorus by the last boat at 9 p.m. I did not dine at all, but went to a beer house where 'maza' is given free. At one place in Galata where I called for a glass of beer, $1\frac{1}{2}$ piastres, the waiter always brought ten little plates with all sorts of little luxuries, and every additional beer entailed two or three new dishes. The table being small, these formed a kind of pyramid in time when one was thirsty. I append a rough sketch of my table one evening at my third beer [see opposite].

Tuesday morning Hassan Bey left me and I wandered about mosques and markets, quays and ruins and took a boat for an hour or two at sunset on the Golden Horn. I greatly missed the dogs – such a feature of Stamboul – which the wretches marooned on an island of Marmora and still more I missed the horses which were good and cheap and could be hired almost anywhere in the streets. Nearly all the horses have been commandeered for the war and it is hard to get a cab, the trams – which were horse trams – no longer run, and the few remaining saddle horses are crocks.

He looked up an old acquaintance, the Chief of Police in Istanbul, Othman Effendi, whom he had known as the Christian Dr Nolan in Cairo, a leading medico-legal expert.

We met later in the day and he showed me bits of Stamboul which would be known and open to few but the heads of secret police, and then we dined tête-a-tête in the *Petits Champs* overlooking the Golden Horn and the Heights of Ayab. He seemed to know everyone dining at the other tables or promenading in the garden and after dinner we joined or were joined by various individuals and groups: diplomats from the Embassies, naval and military officers, war correspondents, nondescript people whom I took to be spies of the government or his own, women of rank or beauty or both; and the personalities and conversation I found intensely interesting as nationality after nationality was presented and language after language was employed.

The groups rearranged and I found myself with some Austrian naval officers who were denouncing the French fleet as being rotten to the core in points of ships, guns, ammunition and personnel, particularly as regards the drug-besotted officers. The conversation was nearly always war and politics (politics of a sort much more vivid and interesting to me than the usual paper article). A Japanese admiral was denouncing Churchill, 'There', said he 'you have the deadliest danger to the Empire, I have no doubt he is in the pay of the German Government and if he could engineer a civil war at home or disaffection in the Colonies he would be well thanked and rewarded by his august master the Kaiser.'

'But', said a young Oxford war correspondent, 'he is always refusing to reduce the British fleet except so far as the German naval programme is curtailed.'

'And that attitude pays his Imperial master well, for it saves his country expense whilst it lowers the sea power of Great Britain and

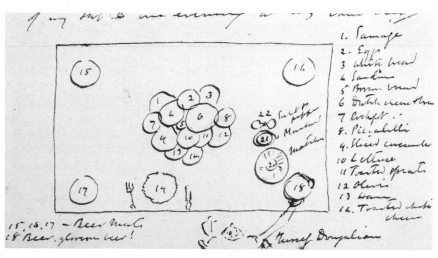

meanwhile the attention of the British public is not drawn to the fact that
the Italian naval preparations are going on by leaps and bounds, nor do
they reflect that it is from Italy the blow will fall as far as sea power is
concerned.'

'Yes,' laughed an Italian attaché, 'under cover of the German bogey
and with the help of British Naval economists we hope to fly our flag
along the whole north coast of Africa east of Tripoli.'

'Including Egypt?' I asked.

'Especially Egypt', he replied and called for mixed vermouth and
olives. We thought the evening was over and my companion was off to
his unknown abode, telling me he would have a house to entertain me in
on my next visit, and I was taking a horse to my hotel, when an incident
happened that was within an ace of entirely changing the rest of my life.
Just as we were shaking hands, up came the Oxford chap with Raouf
Bey, Director of Foreign News.

'Here's a pretty go,' he said, 'troops ordered to Tchataldha next
Tuesday and not a war correspondent about prepared to go with them,
must raise some specials.'

'Here's one for you,' said Nolan pointing at me. The Bey who seemed a
busy man of business instantly opened a little catechism, of which I
append the gist of my replies.

'But can you write stuff for the papers?'

'I can write rubbish and plenty of it.'

'Excellent, the very thing, but you need a little Turkish.'

'I know a fair amount of bad Turkish.'

'Capital: the worse the better with the soldiers.'

'Any Greek?'

'Yes.'

'Better and better. Do you mind being shot at?'

'I rather like it.'

'First rate, but are you afraid of cholera?'

'Been through it in Upper Egypt and found it very interesting.'

'Magnificent! Do you sketch?'

'No, but take photos when I've a camera.'

'That could be supplied, but can you start Tuesday, the day after
tomorrow?'

'Yes, if I go.'

'Do you tire quickly in the saddle?'

'That's where I rest from choice.'

'Good! I think I can easily fix you up, any preference for papers?'

'Preferably not the *Daily Mail* or similar halfpenny gutter rags.'

'They're all gutter rags nearly, would that prevent your going?'

'No.'

'When can you give me your decision?'

'Tomorrow before 10 a.m.'

'Magnificent! Any questions to ask me?'

'Would it involve my giving up my post in Egypt?'

'Probably.'

'Should I be free to return when I liked?'

'Probably not.'

'Should I return at all?'

'*In sha Allah* – if God wills.'

'Should I see anything of the fighting?'

'If the General wills.'

'Will he will?'

'Probably not.'

'Will my accounts be censored and changed?'

'Certainly.'

'Can I communicate with my friends in England whilst at the front?'

'Possibly – are they a sporting lot to understand and appreciate your sudden change of plan?'

'Yes.'

'Then tomorrow at ten.'

It was 2 a.m. but I dragged the clubs trying to find Percival Graves,[1] *The Times*' correspondent, an old acquaintance of mine, whose advice I thought would be useful, but I could not find him, so after a couple of hours in bed thinking out pros and cons and almost resolved to go, I got up and packed and was at Graves' house in Pera long before he thought of turning out of bed. He received me in pyjamas and dressing gown but threw the coldest water on the enterprise.

'Don't you know', he said, 'that practically all the war accounts were fiction, the correspondents being kept out of sight and knowledge of all fighting and manoeuvres and even their impressions censored out of recognition?'

'But you', I said, 'and your contributions to *The Times*?'

'All concocted in this easy chair and written in this room in touch with our Legation and the Embassies, with books of reference at hand and atlases, and take my word for it all the best correspondents did the same.'

'But now', I queried, 'you are off with the troops, are you not?'

'Do you take me for a fool,' he said, 'to be stowed away in a plague-stricken, bug-ridden camp, leagues from and hidden from the front, to be treated like a camp follower only with more suspicion? . . . no, my easy chair is good enough for me, and good enough for the damned, besotted, selfish, shortsighted British public who don't want news that affects the destiny of nations (or the doom of the Empire – Turkish – or British if it came to that) – they want pettifogging little economies, paper football, any twaddle, God knows what they want.'

---

[1] Philip Perceval Graves (1876–1953), son of Alfred Perceval Graves, half-brother of Robert Graves; *The Times*' correspondent at Istanbul, 1908–14.

With Saleh outside the Esbekieh Gardens, Cairo

Graves always was an egotist and a pessimist but would certainly know something about the troubles of war correspondents, so considerably shaken in my wish to go to Tchatalda, I bade him farewell, hoping he would look me up in Cairo soon. 'Soon,' he rejoined, pessimistic to the last, 'it will have to be fairly soon, if I come before the Italian flag flies over the Citadel.'

I had not much time to decide. A special Russian boat was getting up steam in the mouth of the Golden Horn and I was still undecided when I reached Raouf's office. What he told me decided me – whether for the better or worse I shall never know. 'The departure of the troops was postponed for ten days or so; he feared there would be the usual procrastination.'

That settled it. I might fritter away the rest of my holiday waiting for the start, and the rest of my life waiting for my pay and for my chance – anyway I would not procrastinate – drive, you devil, to the Hotel Anadol – chuck the luggage into the cab – hang on to the change, hotel waiter – buzz the chattels into a caique – swing them on board – and damn the Turkish officer who wants to see my passports and papers 'for a moment', and rather out-of-breath and with no ticket, but my goods and passport intact, I was steaming up the Bosphorus within a few minutes of thanking and bidding farewell to Raouf Bey.

Family group at Bristol, Somerset: Dougal, Irene, Constance, Gladys, Ja, Jack

McPherson proceeded via Russia and Europe to England where he spent a long leave. His thank-you letter from Egypt to the wife of his eldest brother Ja evokes an idyllic England in its last year of serenity before the First World War (as well as explaining why he was long remembered in the family as an extravagant practical joker . . .)

Dear Pollie   *February, 1914*

After the most delightful of a series of delightful holidays in England, I should like to thank you as chieftainess of our branch of the clan, and through you all the others, for your continued and if possible increasing kindness and hospitality every time I come home. I cannot thank you all, especially my hostesses adequately, and I am sure you realise what I cannot put into writing.

I doubt if there are many families where the brothers hold together so clannishly as we, and when the scape-grace of the family can be certain of such a warm reception from all his elders; but it is certainly remarkable that all their wives should show such invariable kindness and make their homes mine during my long and frequent visits.

Certainly it is not on account of any merits of my own. Did I not through playing ghosts, cause you to twist your ankle, which I fear has given you trouble ever since? Did I not upset poor dear Flo terribly by

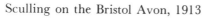

Sculling on the Bristol Avon, 1913   'Pleasant days on the river'

'Ariel Rowing Club McPhersons': *Left to right:* Dougal, Ja, Duncan, Joseph, Campbell, Jack

surreptitiously introducing a frog into the salad, and put her permanently off sausages by dubbing them mysteries? Did I not frighten Alice's life out by fishing for my boating cap, (though I don't think myself there was any real danger?) and did I not very nearly roast Nellie and her tender offspring alive at the Tower, by letting down fireworks from the turret? And as for the brothers did I not drain their finances to complete my Oxford course, and to get out of the clutches of the infernal tradesmen? All this, and much more, alas, have I been guilty of! *Mea culpa, mea maxima culpa!* And yet the fatted calf, and hot buttered toast and beer are always waiting me.

The visit has left me full of pleasant reminiscences: the jolly times and merry meetings of the clan at your house, culminating in my birthday party; the rambles with Dougal and 'Rene on the moors in the home of the wild red deer, and my daily gallops with Charlie on good sound Devon and Somerset hunters, and the little meetings and picnics he and Gertie arranged, and the fun on the beach with the kiddies; then the pleasant days at the bonny Bungalow; and the boating and rambling, and raspberry and currant pies at the Exmouth Boathouse.

Then the pleasant days on the river. How nice it was to sit amongst the cushions and watch the skilful lady oarsmen make the little boat fly in spite of the weight of sin they had on board in the shape of uncles and dads, – even as they and we all made the bread and butter fly at the Wingrove, and the bread and cheese, piccalilly and beer at Hanham! And what a unique crew in the four-oar, five brother Macs with another of the clan in the sculler, and the leading lady of the younger generation acting as photographer.

The crowning memory of all my holiday, the end of the pilgrimage, so to speak, was the visit with the brothers to the little burial ground at the Rookery, the lovely, holy, long home of her whose life was love and holiness, – *lux perpetua luceat in ea,* – the only spot remaining to us of the few acres, with orchard and garden and the old home which was our little kingdom, complete in itself. The old Rookery reminds one of the 'Fall of the House of Usher' – it has barely survived the family. The giant elms are gone, leaving only the poor old 'Bear-Tree' truncated and moribund; and the beautiful walnut trees are no more, even the mulberry and pear tree in the orchard and the ribstone pippin have fallen, and the old house which cracked across the front is 'improved' to death, *et sic omnia . . . .*

But if I start reminiscing about the Rookery, or attempting to recall a tenth of the pleasant times and the kindnesses I enjoyed this holiday, time and light will fail entirely. It only remains to be said that the holiday ended as it began, without a cloud.

Here, too, in Egypt – if it were possible to forget the pleasures of home, which it is not – there is all to make one oblivious and to render life pleasant, and to bridge over delightfully the two years or so which separate me from you all.

Looking forward to that happy time, with lots of love and thanks to you all,

Your loving brother,
JOE.

It was McPherson's last serene letter for ten years.

PART TWO

THE HAPPY WARRIOR
1915-1917

EDITORIAL NOTE

The War Letters differ somewhat in format and intention from the earlier ones. On his Gallipoli experiences, McPherson wrote three long letters to his brother Dougal, scribbled on pages torn from a pocket notebook while he was in hospital or on board ship. They form one continuous report.

During the Desert Campaign, he often wrote letters to England which were not addressed to a particular family member, but merely numbered, as despatches from the battlefield. After the war, he collated all letters into a personal war history.

In part Two, 'The Happy Warrior', we have followed his narrative intent.

8
Gallipoli

The greatness of the prize in view, the narrowness by which it was missed, the extremes of valiant skill and incompetence, of effort and inertia, the malevolent fortune that played about the field, are features not easily to be matched in our history.

WINSTON S. CHURCHILL: *The World Crisis*

'I got a mild dose of shrapnel.'
J. W. McP.

Turkey entered the Great War on the side of Germany on 6 November 1914. In Egypt, which was still, technically, a province of the Ottoman Empire, the British acted to regularise their anomalous position. A formal Protectorate was proclaimed, replacing the 'veiled protectorate' which began in the 1880s. The Khedive, Abbas, who was absent in Turkey, was declared deposed, and his uncle Prince Hussein Kamal was installed as ruler of Egypt with the title of Sultan. The British Consul-General was upgraded to High Commissioner.

The main military threat to the British in Egypt came from Turkish forces in Palestine and Syria, which could be expected to advance across the Sinai Desert to the Suez Canal, and prompt action was taken to strengthen the canal's defences.

Joseph McPherson had first joined a volunteer reserve unit formed by members of the Gezira Sporting Club, and known derisively as 'Pharaoh's Foot'. Though he was nearing fifty, this was not at all to his satisfaction, and in July 1915, he managed to get himself enrolled as a Red Cross Officer, with an immediate assignment on the hospital ship *Neuralia*, bound for the fateful beaches of Gallipoli, where a massive new Allied offensive was about to be launched.

The original Allied landing on Gallipoli had occurred over three months before on 25 April. The objective had been to overwhelm the Turkish defenders on the Peninsula, and so enable British and French battleships to force the Straits of the Dardanelles, as a prelude to knocking Turkey out of the war. The plan had almost totally failed. After suffering heavy casualties, the allied troops were pinned down in two cramped beach-heads: the Australians and New Zealanders at Anzac Cove, the British and French at Cape Helles; the naval assault on the Dardanelles had been, at least temporarily, abandoned. Now a new effort was planned,

With a Volunteer Unit formed from members of the Cairo Sporting Club
known as 'Pharoah's Foot'

with massive reinforcements to the Allied strength. Its aims were to break
out of the Anzac beach-head, to mount a diversionary assault from Cape
Helles, and to make a new landing at a third point, Suvla Bay. Then,
according to the plan, the advancing fronts would link up, sweep the
Turks off the commanding heights and dominate the Straits.

Thus was set in train one of the most grievous of British military
disasters. The new landing on 6 August and a (limited) Anzac break-out
were achieved, at great cost, but the decisive advance never took place.
Indeed, though fighting went on for much longer, the battle – according to
the British Official War History – was lost three days after it began,
largely because of the astonishing inertia during the first twenty-four
hours of the landing of the general commanding at Suvla Bay. In those
three days, out of 50,000 troops engaged at Suvla and Anzac, casualties
were at least 18,000; and the Turkish forces were still firmly established on
every vantage point.

The hospital ship *Neuralia*, on which McPherson was Red Cross Officer
was one of twenty hospital ships assembled to ferry the expected casualties
from Gallipoli to the island of Imbros. McPherson sailed from Alexandria
on 6 August, the day of the landing at Suvla Bay, and arrived off the
beaches of Gallipoli on 10 August.

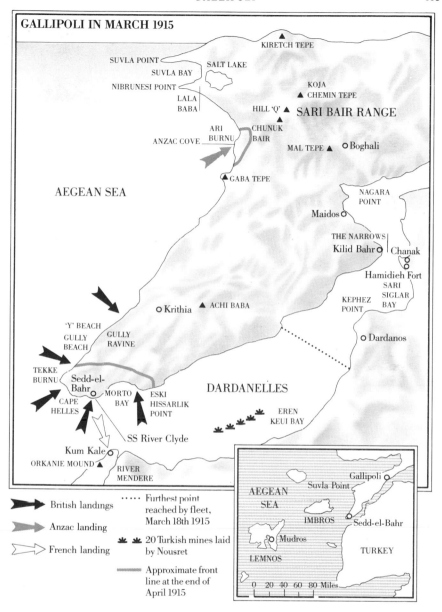

GALLIPOLI IN MARCH 1915

KIRETCH TEPE ▲

SUVLA POINT
SUVLA BAY
SALT LAKE
NIBRUNESI POINT
LALA
BABA
KOJA
▲ CHEMIN TEPE
HILL 'Q' ▲
SARI BAIR RANGE
ARI
BURNU
ANZAC COVE
CHUNUK
BAIR
MAL TEPE ▲ ○Boghali

AEGEAN SEA

▲ GABA TEPE

NAGARA
POINT

Maidos ○

THE NARROWS
Kilid Bahr ○ │ Chanak

Hamidieh Fort
SARI
SIGLAR
BAY
KEPHEZ
POINT

○ Krithia ▲ ACHI BABA

'Y' BEACH
GULLY
BEACH
GULLY
RAVINE

○ Dardanos

TEKKE
BURNU
Sedd-el-
Bahr
CAPE
HELLES
MORTO
BAY
ESKI
HISSARLIK
POINT

DARDANELLES

EREN
KEUI BAY

SS River Clyde

Kum Kale ○
ORKANIE MOUND ▲
RIVER
MENDERE

British landings

Anzac landing

French landing

····· Furthest point
reached by fleet,
March 18th 1915

20 Turkish mines laid
by Nousret

Approximate front
line at the end of
April 1915

AEGEAN
SEA

Suvla Point

Gallipoli ○

IMBROS
Sedd-el-Bahr ○

○ Mudros

TURKEY

LEMNOS

0 20 40 60 80 Miles

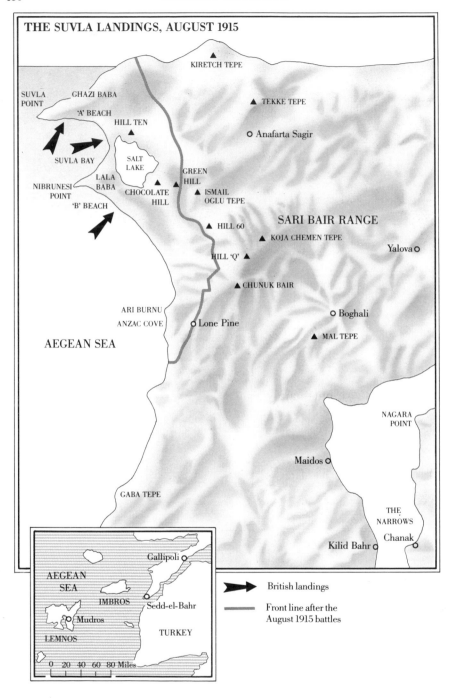

THE SUVLA LANDINGS, AUGUST 1915

KIRETCH TEPE

SUVLA POINT

GHAZI BABA

'A' BEACH

HILL TEN

SUVLA BAY

SALT LAKE

TEKKE TEPE

Anafarta Sagir

NIBRUNESI POINT

LALA BABA

'B' BEACH

CHOCOLATE HILL

GREEN HILL

ISMAIL OGLU TEPE

SARI BAIR RANGE

HILL 60

KOJA CHEMEN TEPE

Yalova

HILL 'Q'

CHUNUK BAIR

Boghali

ARI BURNU

ANZAC COVE

Lone Pine

MAL TEPE

AEGEAN SEA

NAGARA POINT

Maidos

GABA TEPE

THE NARROWS

Chanak

Kilid Bahr

AEGEAN SEA

Gallipoli

IMBROS

Sedd-el-Bahr

Mudros

TURKEY

LEMNOS

0 20 40 60 80 Miles

British landings

Front line after the
August 1915 battles

Anzac Beach 'The Bathing Season'

At dawn we anchored under the shore near Gabe Tepe. The battle was in full swing, and I should think it is seldom a non-combatant or even a combatant has had such a magnificent view at close quarters. The Turkish guns in the 'Olive Grove' were enfilading the beaches on which we had to descend to bring out the wounded. There was a continuous roar of musketry and machine guns, and a constant booming of cannon, partly on shore but mainly from the battleships behind us.

The hills reminded me of Etna as once I saw it, with its lateral craters in action. With glasses we watched our men attacking on a ridge above

Howitzers in Action at Gallipoli

Anzac, which I take to be '971', but they were beaten back by hordes of Turkish reinforcements; then we felt rather sick to see Turkish batteries, trains of mules, and all sorts of engines of war brought on to this vantage point, especially as shells were crashing into our beach camps and stores under our eyes. But suddenly over our heads sounded a roar like the rush of an express train, and a lyddite shell struck the ridge where the Turks were thickest. It was from a 14-inch gun of a monitor exactly behind us, and she continued to land colossal shells with marvellous precision on the ridge; the discharge of each shell being followed by a detonation so terrific, that it can be heard, as I have found since, at Lemnos, sixty miles away. With the naked eye we could see mules and carriages blown into the air, and gaps made in the enemy's ranks. To the North, Anafarta was being bombarded from the sea, and its guns, which had long enfiladed our beaches with deadly effect, were being silenced.

But we were not able to give our undivided attention to the spectacle long, for a small first batch of wounded came alongside, and a few of us went ashore with the boat to help in bringing more. We were soon in the thick of it. The beach and the gully behind it were full of wounded, dying and dead, and as furious fighting was going on in the gully, an incessant hail of bullets came down, wounding or killing the already wounded, and their stretcher bearers and helpers. The Red Cross is no protection, some say that the Red Cross to a Turk is as a red rag to a bull, my opinion is that they simply ignore or mistrust it, or in most cases do not even recognise it; on subsequent landings I took the badge off because the white part makes a mark for the sniper at a distance at which the cross does not show.

Red Cross Tents at Anzac Cove

It was difficult to select the most urgent cases. Men had lost arms and legs, brains oozed out of shattered skulls, and lungs protruded from riven chests; many had lost their faces and were, I should think, unrecognisable to their friends. So busy was I for one, that I was only vaguely conscious of the ceaseless rattle of rifles and machine guns, of the whistle of their bullets, and the intermittent bursting of shells. I was helping one poor chap, already wounded and roughly bandaged, to the boats, when suddenly I was deluged by a spout of blood, and found he had been shot through the forearm, severing an artery, I suppose the radial. I was surprised how easy it was to stop the deadly haemorrhage by digital compression of the brachial artery, and as there was neither time nor opportunity to apply a tourniquet, I dragged him along by his brachial, got him in a boat, and finally up the gangway and into the operating theatre, though now and again I had to change hands or relax the pressure, when of course the blood spouted afresh. He was soon put right, and saline solution injected in quantity into his chest, and I felt consoled for not being in a position to wipe out a few Germans, and by being able to do the next best thing and save one of our own men's lives.

The more serious surgical cases came in for operation, and Col. (Doctor) Warren set me on to chloroforming, until he or one of the other doctors spotted that I did not shape like a fully qualified medical man. They retained me in the operating room, however, my main duty being to hold legs and arms in position whilst they were being amputated. Sometimes there was not much left to hang on to.

Then I dashed about the wards, bringing up bad cases or going back with them after the operation, with special instructions as to their treatment to their nurse or orderly.

The bravery of the wounded was marvellous, and their fortitude incredible. One youngster who had a shattered hand and other injuries, and whose clothes were completely saturated with blood, came out of the chloroform smiling, and remarked that he had had a first class sleep, the best for a month, and he only wanted a good feed to be in heaven.

Many were keener on food and drink, or on a cigarette than on having their wounds dressed. One poor chap, Captain Shote, I think, had lost his nose and most of his face, and we were obliged to take off an arm, the other hand, and extract two shrapnel bullets like shark's teeth from his thigh, besides minor operations. It was really a precious hour or more wasted, for I saw him next morning, being carried to the mortuary.

From the operation room windows we could furtively watch the volcanic coast, and see the shells bursting, whilst those from the 14-inch guns of the Monitor shook us from stem to stern as they rushed over our heads; and we got to know where to expect them to burst; they never, or extremely rarely missed their mark.

After a time I went on shore again for a change: things were quieter; but on the way back to the ship, several casualties from the rifle bullets occurred in the boat, many poor wounded chaps were seasick, and two died on the way.

So the day passed; everyone at the highest pressure, and no time for meals. A thousand wounded passed through our hands, of which about three hundred light cases were bandaged and sent back to try their luck again, and seven hundred were after full treatment, supplied with beds below or mattresses on deck.

Night brought little slackening of hostilities, or of our work, but we stole a bit of time at about nine o'clock for a good dinner, our first meal, and a little more to watch the fireworks. The naval guns lit up the Peninsula with star shells, and red and white rockets went up on shore from the Turkish lines, while muskets and machine guns kept up a continuous rattle, which increased enormously every time a star shell or rocket lit up an objective.

Anafarta, near the salt lake, was blazing furiously, and occasionally a munition store went up, with a flame and a roar.

It was about three o'clock when four of the doctors, myself and Father Cavendish, the Catholic Chaplain (who had been unremitting in bandaging wounds and administering extreme unction all day), met in the saloon for tea, and then turned in.

All who had spare bunks in their cabins, except perhaps the 'sisters' gave them up to wounded officers; I handed over my spare one to Captain Hopkinson, who had been shot through the pelvis. He fought his battles over again, urging on imaginary troops to the attack. I assumed superior command, and ordered him to dig himself in, and preserve absolute silence. I hardly noticed whether he obeyed orders, for I had been on my hind legs for a solid twenty-four hours, and little short of a bayonet attack would have roused me. The Lascar cabin attendant, however, succeeded in doing so, at about six o'clock by dint of mild persistence, and the usual cup of tea, biscuit and apple. Luckily for him I did not know enough Hindustani to curse him satisfactorily. I opened my eyes on the Bay of Imbros, and a military biplane hovering near, and on going on deck, found that we were already transferring all except the bad cases to the hospital there. One stretcher bearer, whom I had noticed mortally tired overnight, and to whom I had repeatedly lent a hand in spite of his protests, failed to turn out to resume his work; we found him in his bunk stone dead.

No time was lost at Imbros; for getting the work of transferring the wounded over quickly, we were back again for more before eight o'clock, anchored close to the coast near Anzac, among cruisers and destroyers.

It was Wednesday, 11 August, one of the hottest days of the whole campaign. Furious attacking and counter attacking was proceeding, whilst the Artillery and Naval guns never slackened. Stray bullets came on board, and as on the night before, shot several on deck. Once a bullet smashed into the operating theatre, and at one time a machine gun apparently was turned on our upper deck: but so far the land batteries kept their fire for the land and particularly for the beaches, and seldom replied to the fire of the warships.

I had no possible chance so far of landing my medical stores and other things, and today the difficulties were likely to be very great. I at last got permission to go down with some pickets and letters in the launch which towed out the wounded. It was absolutely necessary to leave the main stores until dusk, as they were sure to draw fire. When I found myself on shore with these documents, the difficulties in the way of finding the destinees were prodigious, in some cases insurmountable. Dr Bean, for whom I had a private letter and things, had been shot in the wrist and had gone to hospital, probably to have his hand removed; but I found his brother the Australian journalist[1] at Headquarters with General Birdwood,[2] and he was very delighted to receive them, and as he had been sniped through the leg and was very lame in consequence, he was glad of my help up to his dugout, high up on Anzac.

(Anzac, by the way, I had looked for in vain in the atlases, believing it to be a true Turkish geographical name, but Bean explained that it was an invention for which he took some credit, compounded of the initials of Australian New Zealand Allied Corps[3]. It now appears on the war maps.)

I also had a little packet for Lieutenant Macauley, erstwhile my next door neighbour at Ibrahimieh, at that time a civilian. They told me he was up in the trenches somewhere, but the quest was wholly in vain, as far as finding Macauley was concerned; though by no means regretted as it gave me an opportunity of seeing something of trench life near the fighting line.

Everywhere I was well received, and besieged with questions about the outer world, and the progress of the war on the other fronts; as also with invitations to partake of trench fare, and I enjoyed my walk immensely among the whistling bullets: and on my way down was entertained by a Captain Shuler in his dug-out to whisky and soda: a rare luxury on the Peninsula, and a costly one.

I returned on board in time to get away with the remaining things at dusk. As a matter of fact I had very little to deliver at Anzac, but an Australian who went down with me had about twenty tons of Australian Red Cross stuff: so of course our launch and the loaded lighters drew fire.

The splashing of bullets in the water round us I took at first to be fish rising, until one or two struck the launch.

It became necessary to extinguish our candle, and as no shore lights were showing, there was little to guide us, and so it became a difficult and

---

[1] C. E. W. Bean, later Australian Official War Historian.

[2] GOC Australian and New Zealand Army Corps.

[3] Correctly, Australian and New Zealand Army Corps. There is, in fact, a very similar Turkish word *ancak*, meaning 'hardly' or 'barely'.

lengthy business, getting alongside one of the ramshackle piers.

The launch boy had instructions to take me back to the ship when I had completed my business; so arranging with him to be at the same pier at an appointed hour, I made for the Red Cross Clearing Station, and soon after was amongst the trenches and dug-outs again.

Macauley I utterly failed to trace, so I left his parcel with an officer friend of his at headquarters.

But what headquarters! No one could accuse General Birdwood of living in ease and safety out of range of shot and shell! His dug-out differed little from the rest, except that it seemed particularly exposed; and as he sat outside of it with a large lamp on a rough table, conferring with members of his staff, he appeared to me to be a particularly easy mark for a sniper. A few days before his aide-de-camp was shot dead at the door of the dug-out, and a shell entered the dug-out exactly opposite in the night, blowing the occupants to bits.

When at the appointed time, I went out on the pier between the bales of hay, put up to protect from snipers, neither launch nor launch boy could be found, and I wandered searching for him, on lighters piled with stores, until I was accosted by a naval officer in charge, who shouted out, 'I suppose you know, Sir, that's gelignite you're throwing your cigar end on; – it's no good looking for anyone to put you out to your ship, I can't do it, I've got too damned much to see to; – you'll have to look out for yourself'.

He is the only surly person I have met so far in the war zone; and I was about to answer angrily, but reflected that his job was calculated to make any man irritable; officers in charge of the piers and stores are the special mark of the most expert snipers, and from the nature of their work they are constantly exposed, and go on for a few days having chips knocked off them, until sooner or later they succumb to a well-aimed bullet or shell.

So I thanked him as politely as I could, and went to the casualty clearing station, hoping that there might be wounded going off to our ship. There I was informed that nothing could be done from Anzac that night, but that they believed our hospital ship had been signalled to proceed to a hospital beach near Suvla, to remove wounded from there, and that if I cared to risk it, I could probably get there along the coast and through the saps.

I should much have liked a little more time at Anzac, but my Mudros and Helles stores being still on board, not to mention my own kit, I was in a quandary; for the Captain had warned me that he should sail as soon as he was full up with wounded, and that he expected this would be the case before morning.

I decided to walk to the beach indicated, and at first the way was easy enough, along the beach and through a deep sap, but I soon lost my way among the ramifications of the latter, and got down to the mortuary, and then somewhere up near the firing line. An NCO – a Ceylon planter – very kindly took me a lot of the way, but he too got mixed up in the dark. In some places the sap was roofed over for protection, and formed a deep tunnel, in others it fizzled out, or had been shelled to nothing, and I had to skirt the beach, or cross gullies without protection.

Now and again I came upon bands of Ghurkas with mules; once I had to pass a Maori sentinel, who challenged me, and to whom I gave the countersign. Sometimes I stumbled over dead or dying, or met stretcher parties worn out with fatigue and wounds. Sometimes I hurried past ghastly objects which emitted a horrible smell.

From time to time the darkness was broken by rockets or a star shell, or by the searchlights of our fleet, and though the transient light showed me the way, it always caused the Turkish musketry, which never ceased, to become trebly fast and furious, and bullets sang loud and more near.

At last I reached the casualty clearing station near the south end of Suvla Bay, and saw what I took to be the *Neuralia* lying out, with its crosses of red electric lamps, and the long string of green lights.

But, Oh, what a piteous sight was the beach! Thousands of wounded lying in the open, or on stretchers, patiently waiting their turn to be taken off, or dying quietly as they lay; exposed to the sun all day, and to bullets and shrapnel by day and night.

The '75' guns in the 'Olive Grove' were shelling the beach intermittently, even at this late hour, and the Medical Officer, when I reproached him for not making use of our ships and getting the wounded off to it, replied: 'I should be only too thankful to do so, and indeed we have orders from headquarters to that effect, but we have applied to headquarters for boats and help and can get neither. Three thousand casualties have been brought in to us in the last forty-eight hours, and we have dressed and tended the lot, as well as an originally short handed and now decimated staff can possibly do it, without operating room or appliances. They have been shrapnelling us off and on all day and even tonight, and the front part of the hospital camp has been carried away, as you see, and lots of the wounded and our own staff killed. Stretcher bearers and medical helpers are sniped wholesale, the mortality amongst such, and among the Army Service Corps having been lately out of all proportion.'

As he spoke, his remarks were more than once punctuated by a shrapnel burst, and realising that it was useless my staying there I promised to report the desperate condition of this beach at headquarters, and set out to find my way back to Anzac, hoping that, if I could not rejoin the *Neuralia*, I might get a passage on a trawler or something to Mudros, and join her there: for our port of destination is always kept strictly secret, Mudros is generally called at for orders, going and coming.

As I strolled back to Anzac in the dark, made darker by occasional

search lights, star shells, rockets, or glimpses of burning villages I nearly
fell over a stretcher in that salubrious spot known to Tommies as
Shrapnel Gulley, or Sniper's Delight, and recognised the party as one
which I had met near this place on its way to Anzac: but in the interval
one of the bearers, a young New Zealander, had been shot by a stray
bullet, inside the right thigh. Having one remaining dressing on me, I
fixed him up, put him on the stretcher with the wounded man, and lent a
hand in carrying the load: but was jolly thankful for the arrival on the
scene of a party of New Zealanders, who took charge of the lot; and so I
left them and hurried on.

Now and again the whirr of a shell overhead, going apparently to the
ill-fated beach, relieved the monotony of the sing-song of the bullets, and
the rattle of musketry amongst the hills and rocks.

Suddenly a short pitched shell passed near my head, and burst in the
sand a short distance behind me, and I fear in the immediate vicinity of
the stretcher party I had just left, and near a train of battery mules.

I put my arm up to shield my head, and received a shower, apparently
of sand and pebbles, which bruised and lacerated my arm and side. One
bit, harder and sharper than the rest, a piece of the shrapnel itself, got me
just above the elbow. It did not pain a lot, but a feeling of tiredness and
drowsiness, which had been creeping on for some time, became almost
overwhelming, and I was glad to sit down by the nearest rock, and wait
for the New Zealanders to come up; for I had neither water nor dressings
to render first aid to myself.

But the New Zealand party never came, and whilst the intense gloom
was broken for a minute, a bullet splashed on the rock, suggesting to me
that this was no abiding place. At the same time I discovered that I was
not alone – another form was sitting propped against the rock regardless
of the bullets. He was quite dead and cold, but his natural attitude had
evidently deceived the snipers, for they had wasted many bullets on his
dead body, quite a silvery halo of lead marks round his head.

Despairing of seeing the New Zealanders again in the body, I did my
best to find the sap end; but missing this I found myself in a rocky and
wooded gully, down which a land breeze wafted an unholy smell towards
the sea; and where the sharp crack of rifles sounded at close range. This
may have been some acoustic effect of the rocks, but there were other
indications that this glen was the valley, not of the shadow of death, but
of its very substance, and that if any rest were to be expected here, it was
likely to be of a sempiternal nature.

Finding the sap at last, and arriving at an outlying dug-out of Anzac, I
had no thought but for drink and sleep. An obliging sentry woke up the
sole occupant, a friend of his named Taylor, saying to me: 'Here you are
Sir, you're in luck, for a shell got in last night, when Taylor was out for a
minute, and smashed up his mate, and as the dug-out is built for two,
you'll have plenty of room, and Taylor will be glad of a new mate.'

Taylor was very friendly, and I took such a long pull at his water bottle, that there was no water left for other purposes, and in fact I was too sleepy to bother about anything else.

With my tunic under my head and a rug belonging to the dead man on the natural floor of the dug-out, I was conscious that he was telling me tales of blood and steel. The never-ceasing musketry of the Turks changed into the lullaby of innumerable frogs croaking at Giza, and the constant sing-sing of the bullets outside the sand-bag walls and biscuit tin roof was like the ping-ping of mosquitoes in Egypt, and I heard neither cannon nor bursting shell, but enjoyed as sound, peaceful, happy and dreamless sleep as I have ever had in my life.

An army of great sticky flies, and the pain of a stiff arm woke me about six o'clock, to peep out through the little opening in front of the dug-out, framing a lovely bit of blue sea, dotted however with battleships, busy at work even at this early hour.

Some very bonny-looking New Zealand lads, who had occupied a similar hole, near ours, had received an unwelcome visitor at dawn, in the form of a shell: this had found its way in through the biscuit and oil tins, had shattered their rifles, torn their sand-bags, and made a devil of a dust, from which debris they emerged – I am told – grinning and unhurt: one of those miraculous and unaccountable escapes, of which, happily there are lots of instances.

Though their arms and kit had been ruined, a telescope had escaped from the wreck, and with it we examined the shipping. There were two hospital ships lying off, but no *Neuralia*; so accepting the still half-sleeping Taylor's invitation to breakfast later on, in the case of my not being able to get away quickly, I made for the Anzac beach.

How I longed for the prohibited camera, to photo this picturesque place with the morning light upon it. From the sea it looks as if the hillside were honeycombed with hermits' caves – on the spot it might be some quaint Indian settlement, more or less perpendicularly planted. There are no straight lines, no hard angles; the narrow dusty tracks amongst the dug-outs wind about in bewildering curves, and away above stretches beautifully hilly country, with well-trod hollows and grassy slopes, and patches of scrub-covered woodland where doubtless, arbutus and dwarf rhododendron and bracken flourish, and sleepy tortoises are rudely wakened up. Even in its present aspect of smoke and fire, its never-ceasing thunder and all the forms of death, and of the engines which scatter it broadcast, concealed in every copse and under every shrub, it makes one long to stroll to the top and gaze down on the Aegean, and the Hellespont, and the plains of Troy; and away to where Athos towers dimly above the heads of the Samothracian mountains.

After reporting my visit to the unlucky hospital beach, and the state in which I had found it, and the urgent need of helpers if they could be obtained, I went to the casualty clearing station, and enquired about the

Neuralia. They could give me no information about her, but informed me
that the wounded would be sent out to any ship willing to take them.
There were lots of men bathing; swimming out to our sunken vessels,
whose stacks and masts formed convenient objectives and resting places.
Hundreds of bathers have been lost in spite of the barricade of empty
petrol canisters, behind which they usually dress, and in spite of the
fallacious idea that ducking is a protection against shrapnel; but this
morning, Beachy Bill, as the most attentive gun in the Olive Grove is
called, was silent; and I was about to go in and give my arm a salt bath,
preparatory to having it properly dressed, when I saw a launch about to
go. I instantly joined the party of wounded, and we were soon hailed by a
nondescript-looking vessel like a huge armoured trawler, and were told
that any walking cases might come aboard.

I was about to accept when I spotted a Red Cross ship remarkably like
the *Neuralia* steaming in, and persuaded them to take me on to that. It
turned out indeed to be the *Neuralia.* She had been out to bury her dead
and had come back to take on her full complement of wounded, and my
satisfaction at meeting her again was considerable.

We had got out as far as the nondescript vessel without attack, but
either that or a destroyer lying close to the *Neuralia* tempted some of the
shore batteries, for a hot shrapnelling commenced, and lasted an hour or
two, and we were splashed in our lighter again and again, before I
could board, and then on deck we watched a great display of bad
marksmanship: for the Turks, who have the range of beaches exactly,
seem little good at floating objects.

Shrapnel burst over our heads, sometimes almost in the rigging,
sometimes at a great height, struck the water a few yards from our stern,
and under our bows, and generally played with, and gave us a fine
display, without hurting us.

We came nearer to being hit than the other more deserving craft, and
it looked as if we were the main object of the fire, but I can hardly think
that that was really the case, but had we been hit, I doubt if the Turks
would have deserved the obloquy inevitably heaped upon them, for these
Red Cross ships take any risks and go anywhere, with regard for nothing
but the best and speediest way of getting sick and wounded aboard, and
we are generally in the invidious and dangerous company of belligerent
vessels, munitions stores, and such like; and I fancy many of the smaller
craft which have no claim to immunity cultivate our vicinity for a sort of
moral protection. In any case we are constantly between the Turkish
land forts and our war vessels which are bombarding them, and
naturally, with the best intentions on both sides, we are liable to have a
warm time.

Divided between the interest of watching bursts of shrapnel, and the
usual volcanic phenomena on shore, on the one hand; and the pain and
discomfort of my arm on the other, the latter at last prevailed, and

whipping off my bloody and filthy clothes, most of which went overboard, I soaked in a delicious bath, ate an enormous breakfast, and then revisited the operating theatre in my new passive capacity.

After a minor operation on my arm, and its thorough dressing, I remained on for some time in my old capacity, hanging on to limbs whilst they were being removed. Many of these, unlike the fresh cases of the first day, were maggoty and gangrenous, from long waiting on shore, or too often from a first aid tourniquet having been left too long and continuously. But the doctors soon packed me off for an arm bath, hot fomentations and bed.

That night septic poisoning and fever set up, and gave me the devil's own time. In no position could I rest, so I roamed about the ship, feeling that I should like to howl. I think I should have done so on shore, but here I was ashamed of myself with my little puncture, and seven hundred poor chaps lying patiently and almost silently yet suffering from every ghastly wound that bullets and shells, and worst of all, hand grenades could inflict. I could only admire their heroic fortitude the more. Hardly a groan throughout the ship, and very little restlessness; and so quietly did they die that they sometimes eluded the last offices. The Tommies as I roamed around greeted me with a smile and seemed to have no wants but a cigarette and a drink.

The well-filled Officers' ward was silent as a charnel house, and smelt rather like one in spite of good ventilation and all sanitary arrangements.

Shot through the lungs was Brigadier-General Cooper, always in a sitting position, silent and sad: a remarkably high-bred, noble-looking man, so little self-assertive that he was put into the big ward in the hold with hundreds of the rank and file, when first he came on board, and when his orderly came to enquire about him, it took him and us an hour to find him. Only once on board was he known to assert himself or his authority, and that was when a wounded officer spoke impatiently to the hospital orderly, and the Brigadier roused himself to remind him sternly that the orderlies and sisters were already worn out with overwork and must not be expected to do impossibilities.

No wonder that the Brigadier was sad, victim of a tragedy happily rare enough in our warfare!!

On Sunday the eighth, some of our troops (East Lancs., I believe) occupied the most coveted Hill 971, which dominated the Peninsula, the Narrows and to some extent Achi Baba; but unhappily one of our battleships, taking them for Turks, shelled them. Of course they had to retire, but the Royal Irish Rifles, Carson's Darlings,[1] meeting them, and perhaps for other causes which I do not know, got panic stricken, threw

---

[1] The Official War History tells a different story of a hand-to-hand struggle with the Turks: 'Accurate details of this grim struggle have never come to light . . . The 6/Royal Irish Rifles lost half its rank and file and nearly all its officers . . . Br.-General Cooper was severely wounded and every officer of 29th Brigade headquarters was either wounded or killed.'

away their rifles and equipment and bolted down the gully, forsaking their commander, Cooper, and leaving him and their officers to their fate. The very few survivors of these were on our hospital ship; and not a few of the craven riflemen were there too, in spite of their flight. There were other troops involved, under Cooper's general command, the Hants., I have been told by some. Another Irish regiment, the Connaught Rangers, marching up at the time, met the fugitives, who shouted that the whole Turkish Army were on their track, driving them into the sea. An officer of the Connaughts, who, wounded, occupied the bed next to mine in the hospital at Mudros, told me it was the most demoralising incident he has ever known: his men wavered, but bucked up and proceeded up the hill, finding nothing to justify the panic in the least. They seemed in a way to have saved the situation, but neither they nor any other of our troops have been able permanently to occupy this point of vantage. . . .

Friday, 13 August – able to do nothing because of my arm, and too restless to do that properly; the OC found me a job to my mind. It was to interview six wounded Turkish prisoners on board, and get their names, numbers, regiments and other particulars required for the official entries: and incidentally, but at the particular wish of the CO, and of Col. Warren and others to find out their true attitude towards their German officers, their views regarding our men and their fighting, the issue of the war etc.

Some time ago, in my interviews with Turkish prisoners at Qasr-el-Nil, and at Meadi, I had the greatest difficulty in getting anything out of them, that was definite or direct. When I asked them if they loved their German officers, they replied, 'We love God and our Prophet'. 'But surely', I said, 'there are some amongst the sons of Adam, whom you respect'. 'Oh, yes,' they replied, 'we love the good English officers, who are so kind to us here, and we love dearly the gentleman who is with you now', pointing to Capt. Ross-Bain, a young, jolly, good-tempered, and very good-looking chap, who was taking me round, and who had bet me that I would not elicit an opinion from them. Then after much expenditure of cigarettes, and of talk about Stamboul, their homes in Turkey and Syria, and Asia Minor, I cornered a Smyrniote with the leading question; 'Don't be afraid,' I said to him in Greek which he understood, 'I am not a spy, nor here officially – but tell me,' I added in Turkish, 'do you love your German officers or not?' He replied, 'We are forbidden to talk about these matters, particularly about the German officers, but' – making a grimace, he turned round and spat copiously, and the Turks understood, grinned and did the same. Ross-Bain, who comprehended neither Greek nor Turkish, understood the action, and acknowledged that I had won the bet.

Mindful, therefore, of the previous difficulties, I did not put this crucial question to the prisoners on board the *Neuralia* until my third visit. They had comfortable quarters in the padded chambers of the mentality ward, whose doors were freely left open, and I was able to sit or lie down on some cushions, and talk to them at my leisure.

The first visit was taken up in obtaining answers to the official queries: Regiment, – Number – Rank – Name – Nature of wound, – and in seeing that they were supplied with clean togs, cigarettes, lemonade, and other little luxuries, rendered more allowable by this being the first day of the great Moslem feast of Bairam, which follows Ramazan: and the second in getting further into their confidence, by more cigarettes, and such like, and extensively yarning about Ramazan, the Salamlek, the Padishaw, and their native land, and copious reference to, and quotations from the Koran.

On my third visit the conversation turned naturally on to the fighting, and they chatted with such complete freedom, far as they were from German, or even their own officers, that I think I might have saved myself half the preliminaries. They said the British officers fought like lions, and their men like devils, that every Turk admired them, and longed for the time when English and Turks should fight side by side as in the past. They professed absolute lack of faith in the new, so-called friendship of Germany, and the professed sympathy with Islam and they declared that they utterly hated and loathed the German leaders, and would far rather have the killing of them than the slaying of the British. 'The German officer', they added, 'is harsh, brutal and tyrannical, demands impossibilities, and shoots us without ceremony for not doing them: listens to no request or complaint, however well-justified, and treats the man who makes it as a criminal.' 'God curse them', one of them ejaculated, and made a grimace and spat on the floor. Some of the others followed his example, and all were in full agreement except one wooden-faced fanatical-looking creature, who gave vent to some platitudes about the will of the Prophet.

Though they held that God must give the ultimate victory to the sons of the Prophet, their views on the Gallipoli farce were precisely the same as my own, and of nearly everybody I have met on the spot: namely that all the fighting and killing and expenditure of stores and ammunition was absolutely fatuous. 'We cannot turn you off,' they said, 'but we can prevent you moving on, and the campaign on present lines may go on indefinitely, without result either way.' They could tell me, and probably knew, little as regards their resources in munitions etc., and they had a far higher opinion of our fighting men's abilities than of their equipment, and seemed particularly amazed at our lack of machine guns, or the little use we made of them. They admitted a wholesome dread of our naval guns, and the slaughter by them of enormous numbers of their men; and cited cases of our searchlights spotting them in the open attempting night movements, and wiping out whole battalions with a few accurately placed shells.

Our conversation was interrupted by the chief spokesman, a powerful, thickset, merry-looking ruffian, being hauled off for an operation. He had a compound fracture of both arms, and lots of other injuries, but he went off smiling, (though the first time we had put him on the operating table he was convinced that his last hour had come, and commended himself to Allah). He got me to ask the doctor how long it would be before he could get about again, and on being told, – about six months, he remarked that that was nothing.

Friday evening, August the thirteenth, we moved to Imbros; sooner perhaps than we should have done, but for a little incident which happened. – We were watching a cruiser a little further than ourselves from the shore, as it let up a captive balloon, when without the slightest warning or previous shelling, a high explosive shell fell bang in the middle of her deck, smashing everything, and killing everybody round about, but not sinking the cruiser. The report came after, from right across the Peninsula, probably it was a long range shot from Asiatic Annie.[1] It was either a magnificent bit of marksmanship at an unseen object, or an egregious fluke; probably the latter, for the rapid series of shells which followed, apparently from the same source, came nearer hitting us than the cruiser.

Anyway we decamped right speedily, and the cruiser was not long in taking up a new position. We shortly after got wireless intelligence of the torpedoing of the *Royal Edward* Troopship, and this made our little destroyers, if possible, additionally active: for our bombarding vessels made excellent targets.

The next day McPherson landed at Lemnos, and was promptly hospitalised. He wrote: 'I was faced with a grimmer foe than Beachy Bill or Asiatic Annie – none other than old Father Tetanus himself, from whom the Lord preserve you – but thanks to big and repeated injections of tenanus anti-toxin, and on one occasion, artificial respiration and Dr Stanley's skill and attention, he was put to flight.' After a week, he managed to get himself discharged, and, pleading that he had important letters to deliver at Gallipoli, contrived passage on a minesweeper to Cape Helles.

Mine-sweeping is a fascinating form of sport; and except when conducted under the enemy's guns, or on a cold and boisterous sea, it presents little danger. You wear a cork jacket, and if you wish, overalls, also a pneumatic collar round your neck. A looped steel cable runs from the Sweeper to the Consort Trawler, and this carries two weighted skeleton triangular prisms, about ten feet long and four feet base, and when you nobble a mine, it is hauled up and exploded automatically, making a lovely bang and a very effective fountain. . . .

[1] Turkish long-range gun on the Asiatic side of the Dardanelles.

Turkish Battery on the Asiatic shore of the Dardanelles

We got well up the Dardanelles, and I never saw the waters of the Hellespont looking so blue and lovely; but in the middle of the fairway, like the back of a whale, protruded the unfortunate *Majestic*. On the shore the cliffs were honeycombed with dug-outs, and I noticed a few tents and marquees, the only ones I have seen on the Peninsula, except three at Anzac; although, by the way, the *Graphic* and some other illustrated papers introduces them freely into pictures, as well as horses, animals as unknown here as Ichthyosauri.

Sedd-el-Bahr and a few other ruined fortresses were changed, but looked as picturesque as when I last saw them in their Mediaeval glory, but no guns were visible, and only the somewhat distant roar of cannon, and the feeble rattle of machine-guns and rifles disturbed a beautiful scene.

We had seen in the morning a periscope near Imbros, probably that of the submarine which about this date torpedoed the *Southland*, but to us it was an object of interest merely, for our old tub was hardly worth an eight hundred pound torpedo.

Here in the straights again we saw one, this time the periscope of one of our own submarines, bobbing up to the surface on its return from a raid in Marmara. The conning tower quickly followed the periscope, and an energetic little destroyer came puffing up to escort her out.

Taken altogether we were too much for the patience of the Turkish gunners, and without warning there sounded the whirr of shells, the detonation of their bursting, and terrific splinters in the water unpleasantly near us; and an aeroplane marked below with the Iron

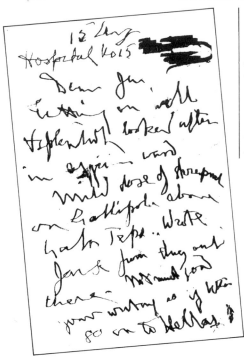

PERSONAL.

Mr. J. W. McPherson, of the Ministry of Agriculture, has been severely wounded at the Dardanelles.

Mr. J. W. McPherson, of the Ministry of Agriculture, who was wounded at the Dardanelles, is reported to be in hospital at Mudros and to be going on well.

15 Aug. Hospital No. 15
Dear Ja,
  Getting on well & splendidly looked after in officers' ward. Mild dose of shrapnel on Gallipoli above Gaba Tepe. Wrote Jack from dug-out there. Not much good your writing as if better go on to Helles, and won't go to base hospital. Had a great time. Would not have missed it for anything. Love, Joe.

Left: The first postcard home after being wounded in the arm. *Right:* Reports in the *Egyptian Mail*, Cairo on 18 August, and 7 September

Cross, came and hovered over like a monster hawk. There was a general order to 'Get', so we got and stood not on the order of our going, and reaching Helles about an hour before noon we put into the pier behind the breakwater of sunken vessels.

  In obedience to orders to present myself immediately on landing to the Commandant, Major Watson, I went up the 'High Street' so called, and found that gentleman in a very modest dug-out, high up on the cliff. He was very friendly and chatty, but gave me bad news of the death of his cousin and my friend Basil Etherington-Smith, of Oxford University Boat Club, and 'Varsity Boatrace fame. At our last parade at the Sporting Club before I left Cairo, he and I commanded adjacent platoons. He was keen on coming to the Peninsula, but his recent marriage and other things prevented his doing so, and he remained 'in safety' in Egypt, and died of diphtheria.

  Watson, as I said, was kind: he was indeed too kind, for he went out of his way to find me a passage back to Mudros on the *Clifford*, to sail at sunset.

  I had therefore to make the most of my limited time, so after a visit to the Red Cross tent, a drink and then lunch with a Major McDonald in his dug-out, I got a day's rations, with a 'Maconochie chicken' thrown in, from the Quartermaster, had that and my kit taken to the *Clifford*, made friends with the Captain, Lieutenant Randall, got a promise from him not to go before 7 p.m. and set off with my precious letters along the new beach road.

Tommies were bathing everywhere, and all was peaceful, and I reached 'Gully Beach', and Beach 'X' without incident. I have so rarely found the original destinee alive (or not wounded and sent away) that it was a pleasant change and surprise to find Col. Parker alive and uninjured in his roomy dug-out of sand-bag walls and roof. He informed me that Lieut. Mackay who had long ago given me the letter of introduction, and whom I believed to be in Malta, was a few miles off in the advance trenches; and showed a telegram from Mackay's mother asking if he were still alive or had gone down when his transport was torpedoed, or had come to any other untoward end. He added, 'I am sending that and other papers to Mackay by an orderly and though it is not strictly speaking permissible, you may accompany the orderly if you wish and are willing to take the risk'.

I suspected the good Colonel of wishing to resume his interrupted siesta instead of entertaining an entire stranger, and fully sympathised with him, so blessing his drowsy soul I set off with the orderly.

The road passed for a while groups of naked Tommies, enjoying the calm warm sea, but rounding a bluff, it changed abruptly to a lonely desolate track, gruesome in spite of the bright sun, as the Valley of the Shadow of Death. The beach north of the bluff, 'Shrapnel Point', is entirely exposed to an enfilading fire from the guns of Gaba Tepe as well as those of the Asiatic batteries, and there being only a few yards of shingle and a rough path between the sea and the perpendicular cliffs, there is no escape except in an occasional cleft in the rock. Even in the case of a badly-aimed shell, the shrapnel bullets are kept along the track and concentrated, so to speak, by the cliffs. It was here, I believe, as the Commandant had told me in the morning, one shell had wiped out 113 mules.

The jetsam here was of a ghastly and suggestive (sometimes offensively smelling) type; torn tunics, shattered boots and rifles, scattered ammunition, riddled helmets, bones and ration tins. In one place a cave had been partly hewn out of the rock as a shelter but it had never been finished, and pick heads and shattered tools lay about with khaki garments and other things to indicate that the work had been rudely interrupted. I longed to collect some of the shells which lay about, to replace those I had abandoned on Anzac, but the young orderly hurried me ruthlessly on, till we came to a little ravine full of moss and shrubs and containing a few dug-outs. Here through a sap he led me to the advance trenches, and I found poor Mackay anything but in his element. I was about to thoughtlessly look over the parapet, when someone dragged me back and told me to use a periscope. I took it and was amazed to find that the Turkish trenches were just in front, almost within a stone's throw. Though so near, some of the men assured me that they had never seen a Turk, as there had not been an attack since they had come to the trenches. Some of the older inhabitants had seen too much of them, and one new hand told me an amusing yarn of how he had rubbed noses with brother Turk. He had crawled out at night over the rough ground with a hand grenade – a form of sport and nightmare for both parties – had crouched behind a mound preparatory to making his last rush, and on suddenly raising his head, came in contact with a Turk who was on exactly the same game of carrying a hand bomb to the British trenches. They were both startled, but Lorrie (my informant, and known in the trenches as lousy Lorrie) recovered himself a second or so before the other, which made all the difference and accounted for him being alive and back in his own trench.

Mackay and Major Somebody, a friend of his, came back with me through the sap to the ravine, and we were enjoying a lime-juice on the mossy slope, when whirr bang – a shell rushed over our heads, bursting on the rocky face. We were well within the killing zone (from spreading and rebounding shrapnel), so we retired as speedily as we could without spilling our drinks, to a dug-out, like rabbits to their hole. Only one other came, aimed badly like the first, at a masked battery at the head of the ravine.

The rush past of a shell is an impressive sound: it fascinates and attracts one, and is awe-inspiring like the wings of the Angel of Death passing by; and even if at some distance it has the effect of being extremely near, of rushing at you in fact.

As no more shells came, I started back alone along the Valley of the Shadow, picking out on the way two of the most perfect shrapnel shells I could find for use later as beer mugs. There were scores to choose from, as well as shells of other calibres too heavy to carry.

I got back to 'X' Beach at four o'clock, very hot and dying for a cup of tea. The beach was almost deserted, but in the Officers' Mess dug-out, I found Col. Parker and a couple of his staff with a pot of tea before them. They supplied me with lots of this delicious beverage, and sardines and bread and jam, and a delicious cake with almond paste, a present from home.

Col. Parker told me to take my time, but to excuse him as his regiment was just about to go into action. He explained that information had been obtained indicating that the enemy had been 'sapping up' lately, were likely to attack, and as we were hardly strong enough to resist the attack in force or to push through a successful counter-attack, it had been decided to take the initiative and bombard their trenches with our combined batteries supported by some of the naval guns.

I told him that I had an important letter to deliver to Major Gibbon of the Howitzers, somewhere near the beach. 'But he will be in action', said the Colonel, 'above here, and the bombardment begins at five o'clock sharp and it is now four-thirty'.

Of course I exaggerated the importance of the letter and the necessity of delivering it at once in person, and Parker replied at last: 'Well, it is not usual to have anyone near the guns, but you seem to be a pretty free lance, and Maj. Pilkington here is going up to observe the action, and if you would like to take all the risk and responsibility, you may go up with him'. Risk and responsibility be damned, I thought. Here was the chance of a lifetime to see a real engagement at close quarters on the actual battlefield, a sight I have longed to see all my life, and was told was very difficult of realisation.

The Major, provided with powerful field glasses and a fund of military knowledge, conducted me without delay up the track, half cliff path, half sap, leading to the batteries.

I could not see Major Gibbon, but delivered the letter to a gunner of his battery, whom the Major made directly responsible to the CO for its safe delivery; and choosing a little knoll behind the guns, near the cliff, my companion explained to me how the land lay.

Our trenches starting from the cliff, ran inland for some miles, at right angles to it: the Turkish trenches being nearly parallel to ours and ridiculously near. They diverged a little inland, where was a hillock and a vineyard coveted by both parties, and towards which the sapping had been mainly going on.

Sharp at 5 p.m. our land batteries opened fire on the Turkish trenches, avoiding with care our own advance line. The Turks did not reply at first, but when they opened fire they shelled not only our trenches but rained high explosive on our guns and battery positions, putting out of action I am sorry to say (temporarily at least) four out of five newly placed howitzers. Soon however they concentrated their fire on our trenches (fearing, the Major said, an attack under cover of our fire); in spite of the disabled howitzers, our remaining guns kept up a lively and very accurate fire, mostly with lyddite, and the plain was soon smoking and flashing and hidden in places by columns of dust. Aeroplanes came up and hovered like great birds of prey, and the red and white flag and the black ball went up at the Signal Station to notify the advent of German aircraft. I expected to see some fighting in mid-air, but in that I was disappointed; all the aircraft were too busy with reconnaissance and I suppose with signalling to be quarrelsome, and the next move in the drama I took to be more or less under their guidance.

Suddenly the Major passed me the glasses, pointing to the hillock. Turkish soldiers were swarming towards it, not apparently from their main trenches, but out of saps running forward nearly at right angles. It did not appear to us an ideal moment for occupation of the hillock and vineyard, but perhaps their saps were becoming untenable. The Major was too intent, and the roar of the guns too deafening to ask him many questions. I passed him back the glasses, but without them I could see our troops also in the open near the hillock. Their bayonets gleamed in the evening sun, and something else on their back like little mirrors or tin plates glittered continuously.[1]

The tussle at the hillock and vineyards was almost hidden by dust and smoke; and about this time, two new voices from the sea made themselves heard above the general uproar. They came from a Monitor and another battleship bombarding the Turkish guns, invisible as they were from the sea.

In the distance behind us, all Helles that was free to do so had clambered up to get a glimpse of the battle, and there was also a few observers, very few, like ourselves, near the guns. One chap, possibly a privileged War Correspondent, not far from us, appeared to be sketching or writing notes.

The hand to hand tussle seemed to have ended (like all our fighting in Gallipoli so far, and as far as one can predict, in the future until the campaign is abandoned) in smoke and carnage. The artillery duel however continued, and with our naval guns thrown in, it seemed likely it would throw the casting vote in our favour. I was enjoying the general effect and watching the aircraft, when suddenly I felt a sharp pain in the head and a sort of crash as though everything was breaking up, and the very ground seemed to vibrate – not the dull pulsation caused by the guns, but a definite quiver, akin to an earthquake.

Deaf and dazed, I had the more difficulty in summing up the situation as the geography of our immediate vicinity was fundamentally changed. In place of the mound on which our late neighbour, the sketching man, had been perched, was a yawning crater, for both mound and man had ceased to exist. I doubt if their debris could have been disentangled. From the crater there arose an immense white column shaped just like a lily,

This sketch of the shell-burst, done virtually on the spot, was later drawn more elaborately, and in colour, in the typed copy of the letter

[1] An innovation to assist the artillery was that every man in the assault was to carry a large triangular piece of biscuit tin tied to his back. It was intended that these shining triangles should subsequently be placed on the parados of captured trenches, in order to show the furthest points attained (*Official History of the War*).

with its petals relaxed, high up in the air, and round its base was a calyx
of a darker colour, made up of shell splinters and other things. The high
explosive shell which had thus deprived us of our neighbour, suspended
our faculties and given us a magnificent spectacle, had not come from the
usual direction, but as I realised when my companion pointed back over
his shoulder at a distant flash, another voice was making itself heard from
the Asiatic shore. Before the report corresponding to the flash was heard,
another shell was upon us, not so uncomfortably near as the first, but
unpleasantly near the guns and I felt much less a spectator than during
the first phase of the fight.

Our attention being thus drawn to the Asiatic side it was rivetted there
for a time, not only by the fascination of the gun flashes, but by the lurid
magnificence of the sun, setting over the Plains of Troy, an appropriate
blood red, in a wrack of smokey cloud; and the Major suggestively
looked at his watch.

I did the same and realised that if I were to catch my boat, sprinting
would be necessary. But that was out of the question: my kit, such as it
was, might go to the devil or the government: I might never see such a
sight again, and I could not tear myself away, so I put the *Clifford* out of
my mind and sat on till the end. That came, however, before nightfall.
The batteries on shore seldom fire after dark, for that, so the Major says,
gives away their positions much more than day fire.

The German doves and albatrosses[1] had already soared away to their
nests at Chanac, and our aeroplanes were flying home to their eyries on
Tenedos; ambulances were going out and wounded brought across the
plain which was still smoking everywhere and in places blazing where
the dry scrub had taken fire.

Except for a little rifle fire, all became very still; so the Major climbed
down and I took my way along the top towards Helles, sometimes gazing
back like Lot's wife, on the plain which had suffered a rain of fire;
sometimes enjoying the peaceful and lovely view in front; the blue
Hellespont and Aegean, and lofty Samothrace behind and between the
Isles of Lemnos and Imbros; Rabbit Island and Tenedos lurking under
the Trojan shore, and Mother Ida watching over the tombs of Ajax and
the dead heroes of Ilium; and faint sinuous lines, which may be the
Simois and Scamander winding seawards.

It was McPherson's last glimpse of the doomed enterprise; he embarked
that night and was back in Alexandria in a few days.

Four months later, in January 1916, the allied troops were evacuated
from Gallipoli and the campaign abandoned. Of the 500,000 men who
had landed on the Peninsula, over half had become casualties. On the

---

[1] The *Albatross D.I.* was one of the first German fighter planes to be effectively armed with two
forward-facing machine-guns; the *Taube* ('dove') was a scout plane. But some of these planes may
have been *Fokkers* (see note p. 168).

Turkish side, the grim statistics were much the same. Half a million men had defended those terrible heights; half of them had been killed or wounded.

Of the Allied soldiers who had survived Gallipoli, some were sent to the Western Front, some to Mesopotamia, and others fought their way across the desert from the Suez Canal to Jerusalem and Damascus.

9

The Battle for Sinai

'Anyway I have refused military promotion and civil rank and an unique chance of a soft, safe and honourable job in Cairo, like a fool doubtless, in the glamour of the name and the impulse which sent our ancestors to the Wars of the Cross and Crescent in the days of King John.'

J. W. McP.

At over fifty years of age, and already wounded, Joseph McPherson could doubtless have found some Base job. However, when he was declared fit after four months with his arm in a sling, he chose to be commissioned in the newly formed Camel Transport Corps, a vital unit in the battle plans of the British command in Egypt. The idea of a defensive line on the Suez Canal had been abandoned. Instead, an 'offensive defence' was envisaged, in which the Turks would be confronted in the Sinai Desert, and ejected from the positions they held in strategic oases and along the coast. The task of the Camel Transport Corps would be to supply the fighting troops in the desert with stores, particularly water, and to carry back the wounded. It was, physically, one of the most demanding military roles. In the training camp at Ain-el-Shams, near his old home at Heliopolis, McPherson had a harsh introduction to it.

Life at times at Ain-el-Shams was rendered exciting and even perilous by the savage disposition of many of the camels. Nearly every day one or more men went to Hospital with camel bite, and frequently when a camel got loose at night and excited the others, the Camp was kept awake practically all night.

The Australian Officers undertook to lassoo them, but I never knew them to succeed, except on one occasion, when the lassoo went well over the animal's neck, the camel bolting with about a dozen natives hanging on to the rope, and the Australian as well. A large wooden erection for a useful purpose was in the way and the rope coming across this, the camel's progress was stayed for a moment, as the friction of the rope gave the men a purchase. After a few seconds the wooden house moved on and finally capsized, and harrowing shouts from an unfortunate officer inside were heard above the general hubbub. One singularly vicious beast who got loose, crushed tents down, and putting his head into one, hauled a native out of bed in his teeth and hurt him very badly.

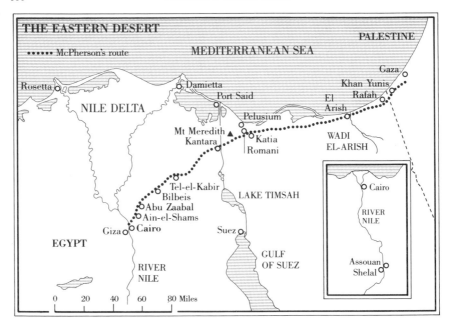

I have yet to meet the hero who will stand up to the really mad 'man-eating' camel. Our OC, Captain P——, a little god in the eyes of the natives and a pillar of dignity and valour, gave us 'useful hints' on how to act. We were to calmly await the onslaught, step aside and smite the brute on the nose with the butt end of a whip – that would stop and daze it – then a blow over the knees would bring it down, so that its legs might easily be tied. One moonlight evening he was with us in the lines when a great brute ran at us. I was on top of the *Tibn* dump (hay pile) in about two seconds and the other officers except the gallant Captain. He stood his ground hoping the brute would pass by on the other side. It did so, but whether it heard his laugh at us, or what caused it to turn I do not know, but turn it did and Captain P—— did the best eighty yards in his life, finally tripping up in the guy ropes of a tent full of natives, into the midst of which he pitched head first.

I had never been the definite object of a direct attack, until one day when superintending watering, I noticed a brute giving sidelong glances from bloodshot eyes and warned the Adjutant not to come too near him. I had hardly spoken when he left the water and came for me open-mouthed. As I turned the horse, his jaws met so near my bare knee that he covered it with foam. I was splendidly mounted, but the horse could not get sufficient pace on at once, and the camel missed me again, fixed his teeth in the pony's flank and hung on, literally the incarnation of grim death. My poor beast reared, tried to bolt and finally foundered in a pool of blood, quite done for; then the camel turned his attention to a native, picking him up by the head and shook him till his neck broke. I came off scot-free, but a few days later was not so lucky. I was knocked down by a brute and got a nasty wound in the legs, which necessitated a small operation and made me a cripple for some time.

While still crippled, he was sent deep into Upper Egypt to recruit cameleers from the local people.

I hunted for recruits but all in vain – the natives muttered something about war and the sea and they all shook their heads. So I commandeered an engine and went to Assouan to the Mudir, the Lord Lieutenant, over whom as well as all officials and civilians I had temporary authority.

He was willing to obtain press gangs and supply a native armed guard to keep them to their work, and (as a *pis aller*) I told him I might accept this, but before doing so I decided to try pacific means. I got him to send back with me a *Sarraf* (Money Payer) with £70 (to the CTC A/c) in silver, and then in the bazaar of Assouan and on the shores of the Cataract and amongst the tents of the Bisharin, I announced that I would take on anyone who liked to work temporarily at Piastres 7 (1/6) a day and leave him free to quit when he liked. Anyone wishing to be properly enrolled, liable for service anywhere, would receive Pt. 50 (half a sovereign) on being sworn in, Pt. 7 a day and rations.

At Ain-el-Shams Base Depot of the Camel Transport Corps

'My staff in Upper Egypt while recruiting'

No one swallowed the latter bait, but sufficient men and boys came in on daily terms to take down, line out and look after the new camels. The next day, 8 February, a few old men and boys offered for regular service and received a handful of silver, loaves, dates and onions. The people are horribly poor in these parts: a low Nile, . . . and the repercussion of the War generally had united to reduce their slender means to a minimum and their mouths watered at the sight of this wealth and feasting. Moreover I kept my military authority as a trump card in reserve, visited the villages, dosed their sick and tipped their kids and talked all sort of rubbish to their Sheikhs; employed them to push my trolley, sail me in a felucca over drowning Philae, get me geological specimens from the mountains and go with me wolf-hunting.

Pickets were chosen from them at night, and head men appointed, and little treks were made into the desert to exercise the camels, and a little manoeuvring and drilling done. They began to enjoy the whole thing as a great game and to get keen on seeing more of the world, so that on 11 February when it became imperative to send away nearly 300 camels and to find 60 men to go with these and I once more brought the *Sarraf* and piled up notes and silver on the table, I had no difficulty in swearing in over a hundred men, all of whom took the King's half-sovereign, affixed a seal or thumb mark and were sealed round the wrist.

> The Camel Transport Corps eventually numbered 30,000 camels and 25,000 drivers. An Egyptian Labour Corps to assist the fighting troops was also formed; by the end of the war a million and a half Egyptians were serving in it. This constraining of the Egyptians to assist the British against the Turks was one of the prime causes of the nationalist upheaval after the war, not only because of what was done, but also because of the methods employed. Later in the war, McPherson had sharp criticisms of 'the scandalous evil – the shameful and corrupt way' in which the recruits were enlisted.

The men and youths I brought from Upper Egypt and Nubia – recognised as the flower of the natives in the service, were genuine volunteers, but my methods of enlisting them were not acceptable to the usual recruiting officer, with more general military knowledge than special acquaintance with the native and with more limited time than was at my disposal, and with more rigid instructions.

The method usually adopted was to ask the Mudirs (Governors of Provinces) to obtain a certain number of troops in a given time. The Mudirs ordered the Mamurs of the different Divisions each to provide a certain proportion, and these farmed out the procuration until as a rule it was in the hands of the Omdas or Headmen, of the village, and these in a horribly large number of cases, delivered over their personal enemies, people who were likely to supplant them, husbands of pretty wives whom they lusted after, and generally those unable or unwilling to pay the exemption fee extorted.

Many feeble old Sheikhs, fathers of families, only sons, physical weaklings, and other unsuitables, have I discharged somewhat irregularly; and much friction has there been between me (since I came into power at Base), and certain English Recruiting Officers, who suggested that the native magistrates into whose hands the recruiting had been placed, knew their own people better than we could, and should be trusted, and that they could not see why I should interfere with the system.

McPherson's apprehension of the resentment among the Egyptian peasantry at the British demands on them, particularly as enforced by the local authorities, was soundly based. Throughout the country, a verse was being chanted:

> Woe on us England
> Who has carried off the corn
> Carried off the cattle
> Carried off the camels
> Carried off the children
> Leaving us only our bare lives
> For the love of Allah, now leave us alone!

In his letters from Sinai, McPherson gave the name 'the Crusaders' to the army of which he was a member. It was a colourful mixture, for alongside the English, Scottish and Welsh County and Yeomanry Regiments marched the Australian Light Horse, the New Zealand Mounted Rifles, the Hyderabad Lancers, the Rajputana Lancers, The Bikanir Camel Corps, and the Hong Kong and Singapore Camel Battery. This army was opposed by strong Turkish forces well used to the desert (the British commander reckoned that the Turkish infantry marched through the sands almost as fast as his cavalry could ride) aided by German planes, and German and Austrian artillery and machine gun units. To defeat the Turks, the British had also to subjugate the desert, and a vital part of their plan was the laying of a railway and water pipeline to parallel their advance.

By June 1916, they had advanced thirty miles into Sinai from the Suez Canal, and occupied Romani, an important sector of the Katia (Qatiya) Oasis area. The railway had been laid to Romani, but the water pipeline was lagging behind (as it was to do throughout the whole campaign), which meant that the front line troops had to be supplied with water by convoys of camels from the pipe head and from wells.

In July, the Turks massed for an assault on Romani; their aim was to eject the British from this strong point, and use it as a base from which their artillery could shell the Suez Canal thirty miles to the west. McPherson's unit was ordered to the front.

The night was passed in equipping and preparation, and the following day, 21 July, we marched out with 2000 camels, 20 riding dromedaries,

"Inundatio camelorum"

The camel lines at Ain-el-Shams. 'Inundatio camelorum'

12,000 natives, OC., Adjutant, 5 Sectional OCs including myself, a
number of NCOs and the usual attendant details – saddlers, ambulance,
vets, batmen, orderlies etc.

The gallant colonel of the CTC led us out, and I fear I lost a good deal
of what respect I had for him, for he made a most pathetic muddle of it.
As is the custom of these big bugs, the more they go wrong themselves, the
more they curse their inferiors in military rank, who pull the chestnuts
out of the fire for them. He had always been polite to me before, but after
getting my section hopelessly muddled up, he handed over the command
of them to me and was very violent because they were not instantly in
perfect order. He said, 'Good God, did you ever see such a damned
muddle?' I remarked, 'NEVER, SIR, although I have led them myself
scores of times'. More I dared not say lest he should abuse his temporary
and arbitrary power by putting me under arrest at Headquarters and
doing me out of the trek.

We got sorted out finally, and made a short march and bivouacked,
and the next morning marched from 4 to 9 a.m. through Abu Zaabal,

where an immensely powerful wireless installation is at work, past the Basalt Quarries, halting from 9 to 3 p.m. near a little village in a palm grove with a canal (like an English river) flowing through it. There we watered man and beast, had a swim and a rest in improvised wigwams of the usual type which takes very few minutes to erect and consists of a blanket stretched across camel saddles. In weather such as we were having it was necessary to make sure that through movement of the sun, no part of the body should become exposed.

A miscalculation as regards the head would probably mean death, and as regards a limb, very severe burn.

We were able to buy fowls and eggs in the hamlet, and when after marching from 3 to 6, we bivouacked for the night, my cook Mahmud Abu Silah, now looking after my horse, made a delicious dinner and we slept until 3 a.m. under a star and moonlight sky. On the morning of the 23rd, after marching from 4 to 6.30, a halt was called a few miles from Bilbeis, an ancient city of some repute and the See of the present Catholic Bishopric. It was Sunday, and I should have liked to have gone into town, but the OC put it out of bounds, and in violation of the rule that no camels be marched between 9 and 4 except in the cases of exceptional urgency, he decided to push on at about 11, and forced on the march till 6 p.m. with hourly halts of about eight minutes.

He might have been warned by the terrible march to Kharga[1] in the Western Oases a couple of months ago, when nearly every Englishman and scores of natives got sunstroke and many died, both men and camels. But he is one of those cocksure idiots without judgement or common sense. The heat was most intense and the sand burnt and cracked the natives' feet. Half of them were unprovided with water bottles in spite of the reports and urgent requests for them from the Section Officers for months past. It was a pitiful sight, the poor devils fainting with thirst, heat and weariness, falling out or plodding on blindly. I and my NCOs soon exhausted our water bottles on the worst cases and though we were well mounted on horses with dromedaries to fall back on, we felt it a great deal, and I think I never suffered so much from thirst. There was no time allowed to open one of the *fantasses*[2] I had luckily brought with me. When I saw a man actually falling out, I let him mount one of the camels and ride at least a short stage, but this caused the greatest annoyance to the OC who ordered many to be taken down and flogged. Lieut. Hill, one of our officers, went mad and tried to kill himself.

At last we halted for the night some miles from Tel-el-Kebir, and I was able to give each of my 120 men three-quarters of a pint of warm water: many had to have it poured down their throats as they lay half dead on

[1] The Kharga Oasis, 90 miles West of the Nile Valley, had been held by the hostile Grand Sheikh of the Senussi earlier in the war, and reoccupied by a British force in April 1916. Most of the troops had been conveyed by train, but the Camel Corps marched.

[2] A small metal tank. A camel carried two.

the ground. One old Sheikh, quite a big man in his own Sudanese village, and a head man with us, was in a very bad way and we had to carry his water to him. To my surprise he only sipped it, though he was dying of thirst, and taking the rest of it in a pannikin of his own, he proceeded to wash his beard. As the dark dye came out he said, 'It is helpful for a *rais* (headman) to appear young before his men, but I dare not go before my God with a lie on my beard'.

Thanks to my *fantass* of water (about fifteen gallons), I lost only two of my men, but in some sections the natives made for Tel-el-Kebir to obtain water and many of them never returned. Whether they deserted or died on the way is not known, and this fool's march was quite unnecessary.

The next day we marched in a fairly reasonable manner to Kassassine, had a swim in the canal and bought lots of fruit. I was Orderly Officer, so I had a restless day and a sleepless night, and was much annoyed when we marched out at 3 the next morning to find myself delayed for twenty-three minutes by the OC's baggage which was not ready when everything else marched out to the minute. The Adjutant remained with me, and two hours later when with difficulty we found the column (for it was dark when we started out) I found the OC having some sick men of mine flogged for riding their camels without my express sanction. I pointed out that it was difficult for them to obtain it when I was looking for his ------ baggage and protested very strongly against his action.

I was glad at 6 o'clock when the ranks of the Section next in front opened and allowed mine, the rear and Orderly Section, to push through, thus terminating my twenty-four hours as Orderly Officer.

Our progress towards the Suez Canal was barred towards sunset by a fresh water canal, but bridges were arranged in the night, and by 4.30 a.m. we were across. We had to proceed in single file, a procession seven or eight miles long, except one Section, which tried a short cut and got terribly bogged. It was twelve hours' march before we were across the big canal, and camped at Kantara. The once picturesque village of Kantara, with its mosque frequented by pilgrims on the route to Mecca, no longer exists, but an enormous camp stretches for miles on both sides of the Canal. There is much congestion at the water troughs and the pontoon bridge, artillery, camels, cavalry bustling each other. In one of these scrambles my horse took fright, tried to jump limbers and generally behaved absurdly, until he and I came head over heels. A gun wheel just missed going over my neck, and I was half-stunned for several hours, but all right by the evening.

Half and more of our company moved on to Romani, but my section and half of another were kept at Kantara from 26 July to 3 August. All sorts of rumours came through to us. Three Divisions of Turks were massed in the Katia region and they were penetrating towards the Canal. Their battle planes were bombing us at times, and Romani vigorously. Some ten thousand CTC camels were massed at Romani and innumerable troops and an attack was imminent. Officers who came through suggested that the plan of attack was to sacrifice Romani and then cut off the Turks in it and that was the reason why provisions and water were kept short there.

At 4 p.m. on 3 August, a sudden order came to march to Gilban at once and we were on the way before five. Night had hardly fallen when we missed the Company OC who was supposed to be leading the column. I had to take command, made a long halt, sent out scouts, and finally marched to a suitable spot and bivouacked for the night (Hill 40). No tidings of him at dawn so I led the column on. Movements of troops delayed us an hour at Hill 70, and always to the sound of cannon we marched to Gilban. Trains crowded with troops were hurrying to the front. After hurried interviews with Brigadiers and Colonels, and conflicting orders, I handed over five hundred camels to their drivers and NCOs and to the 1/27th Brigade, and attached myself and the remainder provisionally to the Worcesters 1/125th Brigade in the same (1/42nd) Division.

My special duty was to take water to the Worcesters who had none but a few drops in their water bottles, and also provisions. I had filled thirty-six *fantasses* when the supply stopped, the Turks having penetrated the ground I had marched over in the morning and cut the pipes. I left hundreds of empty *fantasses* at the tanks belonging to people who were in urgent need and marched out.

A Lieut.-Colonel and about 150 troops, besides officers and NCOs escorted the camels and their precious burden, but the Colonel insisted on my taking command. We followed the new railway from Kilometre 17 to 25 and then went S.E. The bulk of my escort were soon engaged in fighting a way for us, and I handed over the general command, retaining that of the camels and troops immediately attached and from time to time we joined hands with strong patrols.

We learned from one of these that the Turks had attacked Romani, and that its fall was rumoured, and that the whole region we were traversing was at present a battlefield. Shells and bullets whistling over us, the rattle of machine guns and rifle fire, and the roar of artillery made that obvious to me, but few of my Egyptians had been under actual fire and I was a bit anxious as to their behaviour when the fact was brought home to them. We were still in a hollow, but extended before reaching the ridge. It was well we did so, for on reaching the exposed summit, we were greeted with a few shells; one 'coalbox' falling between our lines getting a camel and slightly hurting its rider. There was a bit of stampede, but I managed to persuade them it was a great joke – fireworks at the expense of the Turks and Germans, better than those let off at Abbassia on the Prophet's birthday. I also pointed out that I should be obliged to use my revolver on the first who deserted or disobeyed and that the rest would use their rifles if necessary. They swore that they would stick with me and obey, whatever happened, and I may as well say at once that they behaved splendidly through stirring and sometimes trying times.

The way to Hod Nagur Ali where the Worcesters were supposed to be, lay over many similar ridges, but a higher ridge to the North provokingly spoilt the view of the main battlefield. When however we reached Hod, the regiment had left and were in the thick of the fight, leaving a party to wait for us and bring us on. 'Can the camels manage a beeline across the hills?', asked their leader, 'as they are absolutely without water and every minute is precious.'

The acclivities were such that no camels would be put at them under normal circumstances, but luckily I had trained my animals to beeline marching, and circumstances were anything but normal, and it was really wonderful how they took the slopes.

Some fool described this country in *The Times* (I think) as unpicturesque desert; it is anything but that – flat plains with salt lakes and bogs are broken with lofty hills of sand, steep on one side and often precipitous on the other, and nearly all of these shelter a tiny oasis of the most brilliant emerald, chiefly palm trees. These oases, seldom more than a few acres in extent, are exceedingly beautiful, backed by bold lines and graceful curves of the sand hills.

We had struggled up a steep hill, Mount Meredith, I think, and found ourselves stopped by a precipitous drop. Far down below appeared the tops of palms but no sign of life, and my men longed to climb down to the well that was hidden doubtless in the green. We had nothing to obstruct the view now, and the battle scene below us I shall never forget. A mass of the enemy were intercepted and our cavalry were charging them until they surrendered.

A Taube[1] was being shrapnelled and the shells burst apparently close to it, a snake-like vaporous spiral descending from each towards the earth. Suddenly hell opened beneath our feet, out of the peaceful palm grove came shot and shell – not in our direction, and our troops responded with terrible effect. A hail of shrapnel crashed into the trees and a fusillade opened upon it. Men rushed out and attempted to climb and remained dead, framed in the sand. Horses and camels burst out and fell spouting blood. The same happened at a very tiny oasis a few hundred yards away, and I realised the scheme of things and for once admired our strategy. Our apparent retirement towards the line and canal had tempted the Turco-Germans to occupy all the wells and besiege Romani, and our forces had filled the ridges of the hills east of these. They had no natural water supply, but that is where our camels come in, and the CTC, little appreciated, justifies its existence in carrying water, ammunition, forage etc. It was now 5 p.m. of 4 August, and the

---

[1] German reconnaissance plane. But the British tended to use the name for other German planes, and McPherson's 'Taubes' (or 'Doves') were almost certainly Fokkers.

In camp in the Sinai Desert with his horse, Tammuz

battle had resolved itself into an attempt of the Turks to extricate themselves.

Our escort at once took shelter in a sand hollow, but I was so fascinated by the sight, and it was so theatrical and dramatic that I felt rather like the occupant of a stage box at the fifth Act of a tragedy.

Heliographs were flashing and signals being passed from point to point, and I found a party of our horse, who had ridden on to reconnoitre and get tidings of the Worcesters, were signalling to me desperately. My signalling is about on a par with my typewriting, pace kills me, and so was only just deciphering something to the effect that we were a mark for shells when one buried itself in the sand on our ridge. Others followed, but we were soon in shelter; and then a Taube swooped into the hollow and opened on us at close range with a machine gun. I was busy doling out biscuits, dates and onions to the natives at the time. The next moment I was trying to arrest a stampede of camels, and the Regulars were simply trying to save their horses. Several of these were hit, but there were no other casualties and after a quarter of an hour or so, we collected our forces (with a few exceptions) on the flank of the hill. I don't know how we should have got down without this little stimulus. After adjusting our loads we cut slap across to the little oasis at the foot of 'Royston Hill'[1] and barracked the camels and tethered the horses outside the trees: within was full of dead men and dying men and animals. The Red Cross was at

[1] The 'hills' and 'mountains' were high dunes, named after British Commanders.

work and as regiment after regiment came down after sunset, all my energy was taken up in protecting the water. I was luckily able to conceal about half; it was sad to see how the men drunk with blood and mad with thirst wasted the precious stuff in their eagerness to drink, and their officers seemed powerless to keep discipline at this stage.

At 9 we all, a considerable army, moved on to Pelusium, guided by the Pole Star, and at midnight after a twenty-one hour day and fifteen and a half hours in the saddle without food except a few biscuits nibbled on the march, I settled down to bully beef and tea and made an attempt at sleeping. It was a futile one for it took me all my time to keep my guard, who were dead tired, sufficiently awake to protect my stuff and horses from rapacious Australians and others. Then the rest of my column or the bulk of it came in from Gilban by a devious route, and I had to see a couple of hundred camels out loaded with ammunition, with a pursuit column, at dawn.

The Turkish attack on Romani had completely failed in its objective. Out of a force of 18,000, over 4,000 had been taken prisoner, and perhaps 2,000 killed and wounded. British casualties were around 1,000, with a low proportion killed. However, the Turks escaped to the east with their main force still in being and their artillery intact. McPherson and his cameleers joined in the pursuit and the series of skirmishes over the next few days, supplying the infantry and cavalry with water, rations, and ammunition, and picking up 'innumerable Tommies' in danger of death from exhaustion, thirst, and heat-stroke. He made his base camp in an agreeable oasis, and at night would ride out on his horse Tammy, reconnoitring and observing 'the weirdest sights' for instance, a Turkish 'camp of the dead', littered with the bodies of men, camels and horses.

Death must have come on man and beast with marvellous suddenness, for some of men were lying in their shelters and others sitting up against the trees, and horses had their nosebags on, and camels their boxes of ammunition. The effect of the intense moonlight through the palms was extraordinary. As I lay on the sand in the windward side the company seemed to come to life. I could have sworn that the resting figures moved their lips and even limbs, whilst all nature to the most delicate palm frond seemed petrified to eternal rest and solitude. I must have dozed, though I seemed to myself to be always gazing on the scene, for I seemed to be in the country of the living; living Turks stood motionless to their guns, riflemen covered the hilltops with their *sheshkhamas*, sentries were at their posts and knights of the Red Crescent bent over the wounded.

Suddenly I was jerked violently from my position. Tammy, my faithful steed, who had stood by me like a statue, the snaffle rein under my knee, had shied at something or at nothing and seemed in mortal terror, and it took me all my time to pacify and mount him, and as I did so I thought I saw figures, really living and moving through the palms on the far side, so I took a devious way home.

The next day, 8 August, passed in perfect isolation and without tidings or orders, but withal very pleasantly until the afternoon when one of my scouts reported that he had found a large party astray in the desert exhausted, and at the end of their water and rations. I told him to let them all come, and over fifty mounted troopers rode in with two officers, about as many infantry, over fifty natives and a hundred camels. They had lost their way trying to find the ammunition dump on Mount Meredith. It has seldom been my privilege to dispense hospitality on such a scale, but thanks to our Turkish loot [rations, equipment and weapons gathered up the previous day], every man and beast had as much as he could eat and drink and when they left near sunset, I fixed them up with forage and rations and water for a day, and sent a guide with them to the ammunition dump. They brought good news with them: Katia the Turkish stronghold had fallen to our British Arms and they were sent for ammunition for the pursuit further east. On the other hand they were the cause of our losing our protectors, for the battalion of RE who should have gone, decided to move on at once to Katia. I should have marched out with them but my scouts, despatch riders and others were out and could not be collected in time.

The Engineers marched out with my guests and I rode with them a mile or so, and had hardly returned to the palm grove when I heard a few rifle shots followed by a sharp fusillade. It was rather disconcerting with our minimised defences, and we were glad of the explanation when our guide returned with one of the scouts. The latter reported that seeing a party of mounted cavaliers to the S.E. and thinking them to be our men, rode to meet them, and found his mistake in time to bolt to the guests and Engineers. Their front guard followed up by a strong body, turned the tables on the pursuers, who were hostile Bedouins making for the wells in our little oasis. So our guests had done us a good turn, and though there was little hope of their horsemen capturing the Bedouins (except by lucky shooting), for a horse is no match for a camel on soft sand for more than a quarter of an hour, there was little probability of a Turk or Bedouin approaching our wells for a bit, much as they must covet this well-known watering place. Precautions were however necessary, so I held a pow-wow with the chiefs in front of my wigwam, commanded silence, and forbade all light, strengthened the line of scouts and put a strong guard, armed as well as possible round the grove and on top of the overhanging hill, then all the rest laid down, sword or bayonet (Turkish) in hand.

In case of the picket sighting the enemy, I was to be awakened silently and my orders awaited in absolute silence. If in my opinion the hostile party was overwhelmingly strong and too well armed with rifles or guns for us to have a dog's chance, I was to give one gentle blow on my whistle

and invite our hostile visitors to water, coffee, and kill them one of their own fatted camels if necessary, only reserving to ourselves the right of lying about the movements of our troops and watching our opportunity.

On the other hand, if there appeared any chance of success, I was to give two shrill blasts, and every man was to attack and make a hell of a row so as to lead them to suppose that the wood was full of men. As they wanted a war cry I gave them: '*Seif el-Din wa Clan Chattan*' – 'The Sword of the Lord and of Clan Chattan'.[1]

In silence, and by the light of the moon they prepared for either emergency, and I was amused to find that to make a still more terrifying hubbub they had at hand metal vessels and *ballases*, earthen pots. After posting the guards, I also '*ad utrumque paratus*' turned in and slept soundly until about midnight, when I was roused by a trembling hand, and a trembling voice told me that the enemy occupied the east end of the oasis and were still coming on. On the heels of this guard came another, who in deadly alarm, assured me that the dead Turks who had lain in the sand slope and whom we had lightly buried, had risen from the dead and were coming down on us. This last intelligence rather reassured me, as it suggested that both tales were the result of fear and imagination, but on going to a clearing in the palms I had to admit myself that the dead men had reappeared and were moving, or that I was the victim of some illusion. Passing through my lines I found the men silent and motionless but intensely alert and awake, then like two idiots from Fenimore Cooper, the first guard and I crawled from palm to palm towards the east end. Slight but distinct noises indicated that this part of the grove was occupied, and feeling sure that the objective of an enemy would be the water, I placed myself so that I would see the approach. I had not long to wait, several figures advanced stealthily to the wells, but in the moonlight I saw that instead of enemies they were harmless neutrals on four legs. In spite of my precautions they detected me, and a dismal howling and stampede followed and the disinterred dead rested once more. Whether our visitors were hyenas, jackals, wild dogs or what I could not determine, but I suppose the last named. They sang to us and the moon mournfully at a distance, but attempted no further corpse-lifting.

When daylight came, without waiting longer for missing details or orders, we set out eastwards in quest of Katia, all the better for the two or three pleasant, peaceful and profitable days passed in the beautiful but uncanny little oasis.

Towards noon we were brought to an abrupt halt by finding ourselves on the brink of one of those precipitous sandhills I have described, and looking over, the green tops of palms were visible, so as we were ready for rest, shade and refreshment, I ordered the men to find their way down

---

[1] The McPherson Clan. Cf. *Judges* 7 : 18, 'The Sword of the Lord and of Gideon'.

Bir Mameluke east of Katia. 'My NCOs at the Oasis'

and rest for two hours in the oasis. This fell in with the views of old and young, and the latter were soon up in the palm trees like monkeys, stuffing mouths and pockets with ripe dates.

A tree of delicious ripe green figs was reserved for me as '*spolia opima*', and in digging for water, as the supply I rationed out was limited, some of the men found buried provisions and medical comforts. One found forty-two tins of milk. The place was strewn with rifles (Turkish) with sights intact, but all bolts gone. The place must have seen bloody fighting, and a succession of occupation, for English, Turkish and German accoutrements and bloodstained tunics were mixed up everywhere. Soon after emerging we came across a number of dead camels and some human remains. The saddles were of the, to me, well known CTC type. Shells of all types, including the mighty missiles fired by our monitors, were lying about, and thousands of shrapnel bullets on the sand.

One of my flank outriders reported beer, and galloping over, I found the mortal remains of a German between the barrels, one beer, the other water, both nearly empty, and round him a circle of Apollinaris bottles and wine bottles labelled *Ungesteiner Rotwein*, mostly broken or emptied unfortunately, and empty tins which presumably contained sausages. I took his card, 'Lieut. Grippa', and wrote his epitaph on the beer barrel: HE DIED AT HIS POST. Incidentally I drank to his enemies in *Ungesteiner*.

Deir Bietar – Sinai. Bathing under machine-gun fire

The Battle for Sinai lasted another five and a half months. The Turks established their main force at the coastal town of El Arish, seventy miles from Romani, leaving strong garrisons at various advance posts. The British Command, chastened by the exhaustion of the troops after the Romani battle, concentrated on subduing the desert and making it habitable for British troops. The railway and water pipe line were pushed ahead, a network of roads laid (on pegged-down wire-netting) ; reservoirs, hutted camps, aerodromes and signal stations were established. McPherson and his cameleers shuttled backwards and forwards between the supply bases and the slowly advancing forward units. It was gruelling work, and in October he had a near-mutiny on his hands. McPherson had few disciplinary problems with his cameleers during the whole campaign. He does report ordering twenty-five lashes for 'a case of real insubordination' while on his recruiting mission. Generally, he commanded by appeal of personality rather than threat of punishment, and he once received a note from a jocular CO saying that it was known that 'your besetting sin was over-indulgence to the natives, that you cursed them a bit when they deserved flogging, and only flogged them when they deserved hanging'. But an acute problem of discipline arose at Romani when orders came to move out with an infantry division.

This sudden order to advance from Romani came unfortunately and tactlessly on the eve of the 'Great Bairam', the greatest Moslem feast, which ranks in Islam quite as high as Christmas with us. My two hundred natives were nearly all past the end of their contracts and entitled to discharge, and they believed that they had been brought back from Nighiliat for that purpose and for payment. It would have been hard enough to have been kept at Romani during the feast, even had they been allowed light duty and permitted to feast and keep up their traditional ceremonies, but to have to march out at dawn eastward to toil and perhaps death was more than their patient hearts could bear.

Trouble began in some companies under orders overnight, but my men took the order in silence, and I hoped a little coaxing and pressure in the morning and the lure of extra rations and new water bottles would be sufficient with them as they were a good lot and very much attached to me. However, I was awakened before five by angry mutterings outside my tent and when I went out I found about 150 fanatics surrounding it. I ordered them to fill their water bottles, draw their extra rations and saddle up, but their head man explained that whatever happened they would draw neither water nor rations nor load up nor march out on their feast day and they demanded their pay and discharge. I parleyed and ordered without effect for a bit and noticed that they were concealing weapons. Suddenly a great handsome black devil about 6ft 4ins. high (named Jesus) came threateningly forward and I covered him with my revolver: to my disgust I found it was choked with sand and would not revolve, so I whacked him twice over the head with the butt end. It was a heavy Service weapon and he fell senseless in a pool of blood. Then I ordered my own bodyguard to bind him hand and foot and they obeyed hesitatingly and trembling. Then I invited any other 'gentleman' who did not want to march out to come forward, but they all assured me they only wanted to fill their bottles and to work. I don't think there would have been any further trouble, but my NCO came on the scene and several bodies of British troops, and the two hundred natives were divided up amongst three Brigades (seven Batteries) of Artillery, two Field Companies of Engineers, the Glasgow Yeomanry, a Mobile Veterinary Section, a Machine Gun and a Wire Line Section, these being the units of the 1/52nd Division to which I was attached.

This advance was the prelude to successful attacks on the Turkish forward posts. As the Turks pulled back, the British followed hard on their heels. On 20 December the Turks, to avoid being enveloped, evacuated El Arish, and two days later, after a night march, the British forces moved in. El Arish, with its groves of palm trees and cultivated fields, signalled an escape from the desert for the British and – though the biggest battles lay ahead of them – a chance to celebrate a triumph. McPherson arrived soon after the main force.

It was our ambition to spend Xmas at El Arish, and we had a merry and jubilant time, especially as wine, whisky and beer came up just in time. The fall of El Arish meant to us a peaceful and uneventful Xmas: troops, Camel Batteries and all sorts converged to the vast camp. I collected up a lot of beasts and men no longer wanted for the present with the first line and marched them into the prepared camp on Xmas Eve. We should have got in for Xmas Eve, but a great salt lake intervened:

'My first dug-out at Ganadil'

these areas are very dangerous, we often got horses in up to the girths in the neighbourhood of the lakes and in places there are awful quicksands where horses entirely disappeared in a few minutes.

I therefore called a halt for the night, but when I rode round later on to see that the guards were properly placed, I went down to the lake and very carefully crossed not only the dried up bog, but the lake itself at a narrow part. It was quite firm and so exactly like a frozen lake in England very lightly coated with snow that I did not think anyone could distinguish between the two with the eye.

I had Reveille sounded at 4 (or 0.400 as we now have to write it) and consulted the native NCOs as to the feasibility of taking a short cut across the lake. They were unanimous in declaring that the whole convoy would be swallowed up. I told them that nevertheless that was the route I intended to take and not a protest was raised. Whether their compliance was due to an unbounded confidence in my lucky star or to sheer helplessness to combat my pigheadedness I cannot say, but they followed to a man.

We had reached an island in the middle of the frozen lake when Xmas dawn broke: all the stars had faded except one wonderful star in the east, which had been a thing of great use to me as well as beauty in the campaign and which all the natives call *THE* STAR. In places the ice cracked and water oozed up through, but for the most part all was firm as an arctic sea. A great awe seemed to have come over man and beast. I halted and looked down the line, it was quite uncanny for there was neither sound nor motion. Tammuz was a rigid statue. We might have been there for ages, frozen or bewitched. When I stalked on the ghostly procession followed soundlessly, then weirder than all in this place of infinite solitude, music came from some near but invisible source: '*Adeste Fideles*' and 'Hark! the Herald Angels', and about the same time there was a pulsation as of many wings overhead – a host of aeroplanes had turned out to see who was crossing the lake.

Then the sun broke gloriously and soon we were in camp where a warm Xmas welcome and breakfast awaited us.

The day spent almost entirely in the saddle in the bracing air gave me a great zest for Xmas dinner at 7.30 at which nearly all the officers in the neighbourhood – about twenty – were present. Bagpipes escorted the flaming pudding and natives masquerading as Father Xmas, Bloody Bill, Harlequin and Columbine etc played weird instruments at dessert as they processed round the board.

Being invited to another Xmas feast on St Stephen's night at another camp, I walked miles over the frozen lake and back the same way. Summer had reigned unbroken so far, but a change came that night: thunder roared from every crag and the silver surface of the lake flashed every second in the lightning.

It was a brief respite before the arduous advance resumed towards the 'Crusaders'' goal – Palestine.

10

Tammuz and Gad

Come saddle my horses, and call up my man;
Come open your gates, and let me gae free.
SIR WALTER SCOTT: *Rob Roy*

Joseph McPherson's horse Tammy figures often in the letters, at times
described as 'glistening like a flame in the sun' – his name was short for
Tammuz, the Phoenician sun-god. They were companions from the
beginning of the campaign.

I was the last officer to join up to B Company in the CTC to complete
establishment, and when a few days later a batch of delightful Arab
ponies was provided I had last choice. They were the best and most
sporting mounts I have ever seen for Army purposes, but *primus inter pares*,
in my untechnical opinion was a flame-red Arab pony of singular
beauty. To my amazement the OC, the Adjutant and the Section Officers
passed him by until there was only one other officer beside myself left to
choose him and another pony between us. He chose the flame-red, but
was not keen and finding that I was, kindly handed him over to me.

At mess that night I found that his reputation was well known to the
others, and that had damned him. He had kicked an NCO's brains out,
injured several others by bolting madly and was well known among the
troops by the atrocious epithet of the 'The B----y P--p'. It is rather
curious how this foul name was transmuted into that of the ruddy god of
beauty. It was first paraphrased by me into 'The Scarlet Pimpernel', (but
this flower being tinged with the blood of Adonis and sacred to that god),
I rechristened him by the name of the equivalent deity in the Phoenician
cult – TAMMUZ.

Tammuz certainly proved a handful, but being forewarned was to be
forearmed, and I never if I could help it let him have his head except with
the desert before, and when on occasions he got it in spite of me, and I
could not pull him up, I practised bringing him round in decreasing
circles, but except for his wild desire to fly, he never kicked or showed
any real vice with me, and came to know me and make friends with
me . . . .

We drifted apart when in March I was sent to the confines of Nubia to
collect more men and camels. I was sent for a short time also to the Sollum

McPherson convalescing at the Sirdar's
house after being thrown from his horse: 'A
Broken Head'

district but got no tidings of Tammuz, but one day in April, when back in
Ain-el-Shams a party of B Company returned, lo! Tammuz was in the
van with an Australian astride.

Within five minutes I was on his back and within seven I had just
escaped a smashed knee as he bolted with me past the corner of a wall.
How I wangled him from the Australian I don't know. I fancy he was fed
up, and how I over-rode all regulations, I don't know, but from that day
Tammuz was mine again.

I shall never forget my sunrise and sunset rides on him: or the days
when I manoeuvred the whole Company, 2000 camels in the desert, and
had to be in several places at once – which was easy, thanks to Tammuz –
but alas, one day in June, Tammuz, who had no nerves and was afraid of
nothing, pretended to take fright at some practice bombing and without
the smallest warning, bolted with me at top speed on ground full of pits,
barbed wire and other obstacles. I put him at an embankment impossible
to jump, but the fool tried it and we both described epicyclic curves in
space.

When I came round and pulled my scalp back off my face and mopped
enough blood out of my eyes to look round, Tammuz also bleeding in
several places was standing by me, a model of penitence, and when at last
I managed to crawl on to his back, and night and day alternated at the

rate of about three times a minute, he carried me gently and quietly to the Field Ambulance, and after I was sewn up, took me just as gently to the mess in time for dinner.

The Camp Commandant, Major Flower, sent me to hospital where I had a pleasant time, but Tammuz he utterly anathematised and sent to be cast to the Remount Depot declaring that he should kill no more of his officers or men.

I did not know that, and when after my time at Nassia Hospital, and a tranquil spell convalescing at Sir Reginald Wingate's house on the Gezira I returned to camp and asked for my Tammuz, Major Flower brutally told me that he had taken damned good care I should never see him again. Nevertheless, owing to a shortage of mounts, he was reissued to an Australian NCO by the Remounts, and the fates brought us together again at Kantara.

'It's strange we've met,' I thought, 'but stranger still if we part', and I wangled him again from the Aussie, and we never did separate again, until death did us part.

On that great decisive day, the Battle of Romani, 4 August 1916, he carried me on the battlefield and off it, fifteen solid hours, and after the twelfth hour on our way to Pelusium, when I gave him his head to gallop back in search of some of my men who were missing, he succeeded in bolting and nearly handed himself and me over to the Turks.

With practically no rest we were off again on 5 August in pursuit of the Turks, and through a long blazing morning, when Tommies dropped dead of thirst and heat stroke, Tammuz was fresh as a lark. Now and again when I called a halt I dismounted and instantly went sound asleep, resting against and in the shade of Tammuz, and he never moved a limb.

The next morning on Mount Meredith, when by a mistake of Colonel S——— I was abandoned in No Man's Land by the Brigade with a lot of crocked natives and sick camels, Tammuz gave me the most *mauvais quart d'heure* of the campaign.

He slipped his headstall and galloped off towards the enemy. It was the sixth of the month and I had not taken boots or clothes off, nor had any consecutive sleep since the second, at Kantara, and here I was, abandoned, with an unarmed band of natives, and little water. Somehow we must dodge the enemy or be killed, and find water or die, and I looked to Tammuz to see us through and he had bolted.

But for the men who depended on me for their lives and moral support, I should have wept bitterly, but whilst I was struggling – with what success I do not know – to persuade the men that all was well and to buck up myself, I saw Tammuz ambling towards me down the slope, and after feeding out of my hand, he let me bridle him and mount him, and then followed a few of the happiest days of my life.

When I was poisoned with the effluvia of dead Turks, he flew with me through the pure air and over the pure sand, until not a trace of the miasma remained in my lungs. He was with me on my moonlight visit to the Camp of the Dead in the doomed oasis and he carried me gaily to Katia and all about Sinai.

At Rabah he was slightly wounded and had a narrow escape of being knocked out. A bomb fell behind and another in front of him and very near and several horses and British officers and men were killed at his side . . . .

He suffered, poor beast, more than the coarser-grained horses, from lack of fresh, pure water, and lost something of the sunny glory of his coat, and his ribs became more apparent. Brackish water he loathed but soup he did not mind and he never lost an opportunity of going round the camp and stealing the water set out at the tent doors, or at the mouths of the dugouts in the little green canvas basins, whether it had been used or not. Many is the string of tall oaths I have heard from officers or NCO's at finding their water stolen. Had a mate done it they would have wanted his blood, but Tammy, as they called him, became a privileged person, almost a mascot to the camp.

He became strangely humanised as we proceeded across the desert, and his little trials such as the water question were blessed to him. He never lost his fiery nature, particularly when one was on his back, but it became blended more and more with a superequine gentleness and camaraderie.

When camped at the outposts I often found it inexpedient to be mounted, and on these occasions (sometimes at a moment's notice of danger) I dismounted, gave Tammuz a friendly slap and pointed towards the camp, when he kicked up his heels and galloped straight for the horse lines, even if we were quite newly posted. Sometimes I watched him through my glasses and invariably he pulled up a little before he reached the lines, went round the camp stealing every drop of water he could find, sometimes peeped in on one or two of his friends amongst the officers or NCO's and then stood in his own place in the lines, waiting for his native servant to attend to him.

He was a delicate eater, as he was a fastidious drinker, and his chief weakness was for dates. When on the march or when watering neither of us missed the groves of date palms, and whilst I sat in or stood on the saddle picking the fruit which grew at some height, Tammuz helped himself to the usually riper fruit lower down. He could not fill his pockets, but he expected me to do so, and invariably examined my pockets a few hours after one of these occasions. Once when on the march we both had a fill of ripe dates about sunset and shortly after I went to sleep on my camp bed under the stars with Tammuz some twenty yards off tethered to two heavy sandbags. I was awakened in the night by a great tugging at my bedclothes and soon found myself uncovered: then a cold nose poked me in the ribs and rubbed itself over my face. It was Tammuz who had dragged his sandbags with him and was bent on

Rabah, Sinai: 'Tammuz outside my Dugout and Palm garden'

something. I was puzzled for a minute and then thought of dates and produced my little hoard which Tammuz felt I was keeping for him. He plainly told me he was content and that I might sleep in peace, and he kept his word, for I soon fell asleep to the sound of crunching and munching dates, and only woke when a blaze of direct sunlight fell on my face the next morning.

His somewhat attenuated condition and a good deal of hard riding developed saddle galls, and the vet. wanted to send him to the Base, as he said he would not be fit to carry a saddle for months, but I easily got over that difficulty by regularly riding him barebacked, a luxury in riding I much enjoy with a smooth-going beast. Tammuz was that in excelsis. When at the height of the wildest gallop he was like a top at full spin, and one could have slept on his back: and on the cold amber mornings before the sun was up, instead of the chill of the saddle I enjoyed the warmth of his flanks to my bare knees.

Tammuz had a wonderful faculty of orientation – far greater than that of Du Maurier's *Martian* – and often in my long, solitary, delightful rides when I was utterly at sea, the bonny beast piloted me home by the shortest and best route.

His other great comrade-in-arms was his batman, Gad, who was to remain with him for another thirty years, though their first acquaintance was not promising.

Gad, or to give him his agnomen, cognomen and patronymic, GAD el-MOULA ABD el-RAHIM Abu el-ZAGHAZIR – which being int reted means – The Dignity of the Lord Worshipper of the all-merciful Father of Little Birds, first made his appearance with a batch of native recruits at el-Mazar in Sinai in December 1916. Just then it was difficult to keep pace with the demand, so that this batch was rather a scratch lot and not very highly drilled.

After making out the nominal role, I put them myself through some simple drill, and manual exercises, and found that at least they numbered smartly, until it came to Gad, who had either to be roused from a reverie, and failed utterly to think of a number, or gave an entirely wrong one with great celerity and confidence. There was a good deal of tittering in the ranks at about my fourth repeat, so I rode up to the offender, and gave him a cut or two with my rhinoceros whip. The next attempt he shouted out what he hoped might be an acceptable number, long before his turn. Finally he and a few other bad cases were handed over to a native NCO, and drilled till they were black and blue, until he was reported fit to re-enter the ranks.

Once more I took him, and this time he stammered out the right number with great doubt and diffidence, looking right and left to his comrades for confirmation and support. He even acquitted himself fairly well at forming fours, except when he was blank file which utterly floored him. Then on his squad being proved, he was so proud at accomplishing his right-about-turn, that he did not notice the command '*Aley*' – 'As you were', and on the order to march, he took the opposite direction from the rest, till he collided with a camel.

He really was a hopeless case, but his patience under chastisement and his cheery comical manner soon made him a source of amusement, rather than of irritation . . . .

Gad had his virtues: he could ride any beast, camel or horse, barebacked or any way; and he had so honest and open a countenance, that I set him to sleep in the orderly bivvy, in which certain thefts, and rummaging of documents had recently taken place, and he distinguished himself, about the third night, by catching a man *in flagrante delicto*, with evidence on him, enough to send him to Intelligence for examination with a view to trying him as a spy.

Gad had a natural gift for cooking, and several times on the march, when he had looted a chicken roost, or wangled a bird out of his natives, he sat on his camel, and left a little trail of blood, then a long one of feathers behind him, and at the halt instantly dismembered the victim into a dixie of water on an improvised fire; added onions, potatoes, salt and pepper, and any herbs available and a little rice, and in a marvellously short time, served up a mess of pottage, as succulent and savoury as that for which Esau sold his birthright.

As the campaign progressed, Gad showed himself to be completely devoted to McPherson, and also an 'unabashed coward'.

Gad el-Moula – the new recruit
'The Great Galumph'

His one comfort was his spade, and the celerity with which he dug himself in at even a short halt, was worthy of a burrowing beetle; and when during the ensuing weeks, we settled anywhere, even if for a few hours only, he and the others delved me a palace in the bowels of the earth, and Gad's little rabbit hole was never far off.

Again and again, I heard Gad's voice emerging from his hole in fervent prayer to his favourite saint, Saida Zenab, that she might divert a shell which seemed to be coming in our direction on the head of Captain Scraggs,[1] who had burnt his British clothes and blankets, and many a candle he vowed to light at her shrine, if she acceded to his pious wish. I often reminded him that he was running up a serious candle account with Saida Zenab, that he had already got into three figures, and had better go cannily.

A rabbit in a common constantly shot over, could not be more chary of emerging from his hole, than was Gad of coming out on to the shell and bomb-scarred plain. He grazed my horse, whilst sitting in his hole, by means of a long rope, at which he tugged vigorously whenever he scented danger, dragging the animal back into the Wadi.

However, Gad, the 'great Galumph', as McPherson called him, was to show his true mettle during the greatest ordeal of the desert war – the Battle of Gaza.

---

[1] Gad had unlawfully acquired some equipment, which was confiscated by the CO, Captain Scraggs.

11

The Battle of Gaza

Gaza: The Greek form of the Hebrew 'Azzah' (fortress).

The British advance into Palestine was barred by the strong Turkish garrison at Gaza, traditionally 'The Gate to Palestine'. It was a formidable obstacle, with the approaches to the city protected by high thick cactus hedges or by trench lines commanding open ground. As Gallipoli had shown, the Turkish soldier in strong fixed defences could be unyielding, and was never averse to sallying forth on a fierce counter-attack. The British assault began early on 26 March, first with an artillery barrage, and then with cavalry and infantry. Towards evening, there were hopes of a quick victory, since the defenders had withdrawn into the city, which was almost completely encircled. But relieving Turkish columns were marching from the north and east, and, fearing a flank attack, the British commander ordered his mounted troops to pull back. Next day, the Turks counter-attacked, and the battle continued for another forty-eight hours, made more desperate by a fiercely hot desert wind.

When the British broke off the action (known to military historians as the First Battle of Gaza) to prepare themselves for another battle two weeks later, they had suffered four thousand casualties, twice the Turkish losses.

During these three days of battle, McPherson was twenty-five miles away, getting confused reports of the fighting, and suffering from the same desert wind.

The beautiful spring weather gave way to a Khamsin with a shade temperature of 110 degrees and no humidity at all, and when I took my camel over five miles of sand nearly at the temperature of boiling water to the camel wells near the beach, they and the men almost fell into the troughs in their eagerness for water and then we all rushed into the cool sea before fighting our way back against a burning sandstorm. The next day the temperature rose even higher and not the faintest breeze stirred, camels dropped dead grazing and in the lines. Altogether I lost seven and was congratulated by the Assistant Divisional Veterinary Surgeon on having lost so few compared with other companies.

Under these conditions of climate a couple of Divisions of our troops made a disastrous attempt to rush Gaza and our dead and wounded reached many hundreds, I should think, probably thousands. We however saw a lot of German and Turkish prisoners, including a General, a fine Austrian battery complete and other trophies, but our mules stampeded with the Lewis guns into the Turkish lines. One of our CTC officers with a convoy of 180 camels and ninety-five men taking water to the trenches came under heavy shell fire and only seven camels and two men escaped.

Altogether the CTC losses were pretty heavy.

'But it's an ill wind etc.', it gave me my chance of getting back to first line work, for my four hundred depot camels were reduced in filling up casualties to 98 and every one of these was wounded, so on Colonel Whittingham turning up on March 30th, he considered that these could be left to the Adjutant and NCO's and asked me if I would like to go up to the firing line.

I told him 'Rather' and he said 'There's a convoy going up from the dump at five, go up by that'.

It was then well after four, so, by no means to my regret, I missed the convoy and set out very nearly a free lance with a British NCO, my native Orderly and syce, a *murasla* (messenger) mounted on a *Hajine* (riding camel) and the burden camels and two horses and rations for man and beast for three days.

We were soon over the Jordan, so to speak, and marched by moonlight to Khan Yunis, – the birthplace of Delilah – commandeered a garden of fig and orange trees surrounded by a fence of prickly pear, fed, mounted a guard and slept under the stars.

Up betimes we spent an hour exploring this ancient city of the Philistines, its old bazaars and graves and narrow, picturesque streets, photographed its extraordinary castle, watered horses and camels, filled our haversacks with magnificent oranges, and pushed on until we found some of the units to which I was attached in the autumn, drawn up in battle array a few miles from Gaza.

After a night with the Lowland Field Ambulance and a consultation with some superior officers, I offered to fill a gap with the 21st Field Company Royal Engineers (Lowland TF), who were well-sinking under the nose of the Turk at Gaza.

They received me with open arms, and I am still with them – though we have moved camp from a hill above the village of Deir Beulah to a lonely spot in the grove by the shores of a sweet water lake and close to the sea. The trees and tangles of most luxuriant creepers and bushes conceal also some field batteries and hundreds of tons of shells and high explosives. Behind us are our heavies and cavalry and very near in front our entrenched infantry with whom we are in touch. Absurdly near to these are the Turkish positions, trenches and redoubts.

As we crossed the plain and a little ridge of hills to my new position on Palm Sunday, Turkish HE shells were falling pretty freely, but in a seemingly rather aimless way and the same desultory fire kept up all Monday. Aircraft and anti-aircraft guns were busy nearly all the time keeping up a constant hubbub.

I had taken a big party of men, horses and camels to the sea and all were enjoying themselves when the erstwhile calm sea began to boil a little way out and little fountains rapidly approached us on the surface. Nearly everyone took the phenomenon for a shoal of fish coming in, but I remembered that type of fish at Gallipoli and ordered all hands (and legs) instantly to take shelter under the sandy cliff – there the machine guns could not reach us. All escaped except ten camels, one of which died, the others were only slightly wounded.

The next day, Tuesday 3 April, the Turks attacked and I was lucky enough to have a sort of front seat for the whole show, including the repulse of their infantry onslaught. Our position became quite untenable and we came down to our pleasant place by the lake.

Since that day neither side has attacked in force, but there has been a continual artillery duel, and great activity amongst the aircraft, even by night by the light of the full moon. As I write I should think there are at least three hundred smoke wreaths floating above us in the sky, some black, some white, the only clouds in the serene blue: A Taube and an English plane are manoeuvring and occasionally getting in a shot at one another: more English planes are coming up through a barrage of shell bursts and pieces of our own shells are falling in our own camp, almost a greater danger than Fritz's bombs.

On Good Friday we were eating in our subterranean mess when a succession of shrapnel shells burst in our camp and the bullets rattled on the double sheets of corrugated iron over the entrance. All hands pretty nearly went to earth. Amongst them Gad el-Moula, my native orderly, who unfortunately lay in a funk hole appropriated by a family of scorpions, one of which stung him on a very sensitive spot. Another shell burst just as he emerged into the open (we were also on top) and he had a most narrow escape, but he got off with some slight concussion. Poor chap, he had a bad time for a bit, but strong pot. perman. externally, and strong rum and coffee internally, worked wonders.

In the afternoon a couple of my messmates, RE officers, suggested my accompanying them on a reconnoitring expedition. We saw parties of Turks and mapped down new trenches they had made, got sniped at incidentally, and had to travel a good bit of the way on our bellies.

We visited eight Tanks[1] which have just come up, and I spent about an hour inside one of them called 'War Baby', a 105 HP youngster with four Hotchkisses and two auxiliary guns. I was much interested in War Baby, its guns, revolver, loop holes, periscopes, dynamoes, differentiator etc.

---

[1] These tanks were of an early pattern, and had been used for training in England. It was found that they operated best in the desert if the tracks were not greased; the sand then ran through cleanly.

The personnel consists of one Officer who sits by the driver, four gunners on bike seats and two greasers, eight in all (1 Officer, 3 NCO's and 5 men) . . . .

At night (Easter Eve) our planes, and to a less extent, the Germano-Turkish, took advantage of a full moon in a clear sky. Tons of bombs must have been dropped and thousands of shells wasted on the practically invisible aeroplanes.

My night was less disturbed by this cause than by some little beast, probably a jerboa, who scratched at the parapet of my dugout and brought sand and dirt into my face. I had snakes and scorpions on the brain rather, and switched on my electric torch several times to find out who was walking over my face or sharing my blankets. Beetles, caterpillars, scarabs, black ants nearly an inch long and mole crickets were amongst the offenders, and finding nothing worse, I at length went deep asleep and slept till the Easter sun peeped in at me and Gad el-Moula roused me. The big guns were roaring, and above all earth and air were vibrant with the crump of trench mortar shells.

What a salute for the risen Lord! I thought, and having promised myself an Easter holiday, went to sleep again until it was nearly time to go to 5 o'clock Field Mass.

A stranger Mass I have never assisted at. I found about two hundred soldiers round Father Lean (or some such name) and an improvised altar in the open, in the middle of a burnt-up corn field.

A Bedouin family was looking on curiously and as I handed my reins to one of these aborigines I remarked 'I am afraid we have made a mess of your barley fields'. 'Oh no,' he replied, 'Judge Samson did that long ago – he caught many foxes, soaked their tails in petrol, set them alight and drove them into the corn which was harvested in those days by the Philistines – that was before my father's and grandfather's time, but the corn always comes up rusty.'[1]

An orderly came up before I could obtain any more local information concerning Judge Samson, took my horse and drove off the Arabs, and I took my place in the congregation.

The good father was hearing confessions in record short times, whilst the rest of us sat round in the boiling sun with our helmets on.

The plain was a fine spectacle, tens of thousands of camels winding across it to the lake, or bringing up ammunition and rations, camps in all directions and Gaza and its fortified positions dominating all. Thousands of cavalry rode past us to protect our right flank, limbers, guns, GS wagons etc. clattered past smothering us in dust and lines of infantry reaching as far as the eye could see came slogging along. Two regimental bands were playing, one at a C of E service not far off, and a kilted crowd

[1] Judges 15:4–5

were skirling (is that the right word?) not far off either on the bagpipes.

Mass commenced, accompanied by no other music than the above except that some gun or other supplied nearly every stop of the organ – the deep base of our heavies, the shrill treble of the whistling bullets and all intermediate notes by Archibalds, Howitzers and other instruments more numerous than those in the band of Nabuchodnosor Rex. The crump, crump, crump of trench mortar shells and the rattle of machine guns supplied the drums and kettle drums.

The good father made a pretty little sermon and proceeded with Mass, but there was every sign that the battle (by far the biggest in this campaign) was starting in earnest. Suddenly he said, 'I'm sorry I couldn't hear all your confessions, but don't be shy, boys, I'll give you two minutes to dispose yer hearts and then you shall all (who wish) come up for the Blessed Sacrament – if I stopped to hear about half your sins, many of you would be dying in them.'

He was as good as his word and nearly everyone came up. Then we all sang out 'Faith of our Fathers' and dismissed.

Mass over, the guns with a few exceptions, lapsed into silence. It seemed almost as though they had been firing the Easter salute and I was forcibly reminded of an Easter Mass I once heard at a Russian Orthodox church. At the 'Christos voskres – ve istine voskres', guns were fired and rockets went up and at the 'Christe Aneste' at the Greek churches there is a veritable fusillado and firework display.

After an early, hearty lunch, to give camels, horses and men under my command a holiday, as well as myself, I brought them all to the beach for a swim, and then to a field of rich pasturage where all the beasts, lightly hobbled, are grazing to their hearts' content whilst the men sit in the gaps of the lofty hedge and do nothing.

I have been ensconced in a mossy flowery bank under the luxuriant hedge, writing this letter, to the wonderment of tortoises and lizards, green beetles and golden birds, with just enough bombing and shelling going on to remind me that my present role of gentle shepherd is not the main one. Gad el-Moula brought me tea and biscuits at 3.30 and the men's rations were sent out to them, but the sun has now set gloriously over the sea behind the trees and swarms of fireflies are coming out to make the most of their little electric torches before the big moon mounts itself, bright stars appear for a moment in the sky and give place to thick black smoke rings, whilst others, paler but more permanent, gleam gently without smoke, a battalion of flamingoes is manoeuvring overhead, wheeling and deploying, advancing in echelon and now, at the alarms of a Turkish shell, advancing at double march in extended order towards the lake, where armies of frogs and crickets sing in rivalry, and from the direction of the camp comes the sound of a bell, the Angelus perhaps, though I think it is more likely to be the Gas Alarm, and I have not my muzzle.

Man musst den Tag nicht vor den Abend loben[1] but so far Easter Sunday has been a Happy and Tranquil Holiday.

At this time, while the British were preparing their second assault on Gaza, McPherson's batman, Gad, had been offered his discharge from the Camel Transport Corps, and had appeared delighted. Nevertheless, when on 16 March, secret orders arrived that the attack would commence at dawn, and McPherson led his camels towards the front by night march, Gad was still there.

Gad after doubtless a great mental struggle, had resolved to reject his chance of being sent down and demobbed; and would not even wait at the dump. He seemed impelled to come on and I tried in vain to dissuade him. He asked 'Whom will you find to put on your puttees as evenly as I do? Some bigger "Galumph" than myself will surely put your spurs on upside down; and you will never notice it until you have been let in for drinks all round to the mess! Who will get your gun-fire tea in good time in the morning?'

So Gad on his camel, never far from my horse, took part in the weird, dark and silent march.

McPherson made his home and his headquarters in a deep nullah which he called after the Biblical river Kishon.

Enemy shells pass over us as harmlessly as our own, as the Kishon bed lies from twenty to forty feet below the general level. We lay down anywhere in the night, but Gad el-Moula, with some help from sappers and natives has turned a fissure in the bank into a wonderful retreat. I have tried to sketch it but failed. It is twelve feet high, twenty five feet deep and ten wide, with a deep trench at the bottom and funk holes at the sides, for use in case the enemy uses high burst shrapnel.

Its one drawback is the lack of view of the battle, but we have steps up to the top and can run up the slope and get a full view, and if unlucky, a taste of the conflict.

We saw 'War Baby' go up into action this morning with the infantry behind it. Another Tank stuck and before it could get out, was demolished by three direct hits from Turkish shells. Personally I think these Tanks are white elephants and more likely to do harm than good, anyway in this country. When six of them marched out from Deir Beulah on the 14th, two of them stuck in the sand before they had proceeded a mile and were only extricated by the help of the others and a powerful traction engine, and at the expense of several of our two and half inch ropes.

I commenced this in my palatial cavern, but now I am finishing it on

[1] Don't praise the day until the evening.

the ridge by the cistern domes, now safe from snipers, as we hold the
Mansura Ridge. Rich yellow cornfields, red with poppies and blue with
cornflowers stretch away to the Brook and far beyond, and I have had
foraging parties out all day with billhooks, reaping for our beasts, where
others sowed (where those others are I cannot tell, since leaving Deir
Beulah I have not seen a native).

As St John saith: 'Others have sowed and we have entered into their
labours'.

The sun's light is going and no other is allowed, so I must hasten back
to my twilight dinner in the cave.

Wednesday, 18/4/17 our attack on Gaza continued in a desultory way,
our great effort being reserved for Thursday, 19/4/17. 'Intense
bombardment' was ordered for two hours at sunrise, to be followed by a
combined attack, our Division to take the centre. A French cruiser and
four monitors which were to assist, and 100,000 gas shells were in reserve,
but it was understood that the General considered these inhuman and
probably unnecessary.

We, the 2/1st Lowland RE, were to follow up the Infantry of our
Brigade to consolidate the trenches as they were taken. The Australians
who went out on 16/4/17 to blow up the Beersheba line for five miles
were to cut off retreat in this direction. The only fear seemed to be that
the Turks might escape by the seacoast track to Jaffa, but a Division of
Cavalry was to hasten round to the N. of Gaza to prevent this if possible.
We were to enter Gaza in the evening.

My own view, of no military value, was that the Turks would not
seriously join issue so near the coast but would retire on Beersheba away
from Monitors and our source of sea supplies, *but* that if they were strong
enough to contest Gaza at all in face of our seven Divisions and the
British ships, we should find them strong indeed in point of position and
numbers.

This alternative view proved to be the correct one, for when at 5.30
yesterday morning, our 120 cannon gave voice, a host of Turkish
batteries at once replied. It was a magnificent effect, and it was war. It
was moreover music, and reminded me of the diabolically inspired music
of Wagner. On a count and estimate there were over a hundred major
detonations per minute, including the crash of bursting shells, some
vibrations common to these formed a sustained accompanying note like
the stop of some titanic organ, whilst the explosions individually formed
a staccato refrain. Some of the guns were still behind us, but the field
batteries had gone up in the night, and as we emerged from the bed of the
Brook Kishon with the mighty advancing host, mighty at least in
numbers, we threaded our way amongst these. Then as we rose higher,
hundreds of kettle drums (machine guns) swelled the orchestra, with the
castanets of the musketry, and at times the flamboyant notes of a myriad
of bullets in the air, cut in like the fiddles in the Overture to Tannhauser.

I am supposed to be the expert on camels and natives, so I was in command of the fifty natives and seventy camels in the Company, and we led on with a number of the Sappers; the horse transport and the rest of the Sappers following.

Many riderless horses were rushing in terror over the plain, a common enough sight by the way, the past fortnight. For some time we were little more than spectators, and a tremendous spectacle it was: Gaza and Ali Muntar blazing and smoking under our intense fire, and enemy shells bursting on our own positions and on hills some distance from us. Only occasionally a shell burst near enough to be dangerous to our party. But soon we were well within the fire zone, and I was rather anxious about my natives, mostly recent recruits. They behaved very well however, they were mostly pallid with fear and walked as in a dream, but obeyed orders implicitly. Poor Gad el-Moula, green to the teeth, kept on though he had assured me he would fall dead with fright at the first shell in his vicinity. Presently we crossed the ridge of Kurd Hill and the sight of the next ridge was truly appalling: a perfect barrage of bursting HE, black and dense, and a curtain of white and yellow shrapnel – and some Infantry of our Brigade were marching through it – or in many cases up to it only. We passed the trough of the valley and a little way up the fiery side we were halted by the OC, Major Rolling (who appeared suddenly from somewhere). It seemed to me none too soon. Most of the shells burst in front of us, or if they cleared the ridge passed over our heads to the ground we had come over, but some took an unhappy mean. Shrapnel cases and noses and half-spent shrapnel bullets whistled over and about us. We dumped the bulk of the transport stuff and some camel loads and then took the cover of a little nullah for selves, horses and camels pending further orders.

Gad el-Moula, who had already dug himself in, sprinted for the new position and had disappeared under the bank before I arrived. He pressed me to take his little burrow, but I had to return and stand by in the open with some RE officers. I can't say I enjoyed it. Out of swank and *pour passer le temps* I botanised, and got some nice little flowers, some of which I enclose and incidentally came across a crested lark's nest with six eggs. I nearly lost hand and flowers once from a jagged lump of metal. I picked it out of the ground and burnt my hand, it was still intensely hot. It was as well I was stooping at the time, as a shrapnel nose struck the ground a few yards off and richocheted over my shoulders.

Lieuts. Steel-Young, Wilson and myself were standing to, with sappers and material (mostly on camels) to follow up the Infantry of the 155th Brigade (52nd Division), and consolidate the trench as soon as they had taken it. As they had found this too rough a job, a tank went out and was followed by more infantry, and we advanced some distance behind them. The fiery ridge when we crossed it, did not seem as bad as it had looked, though quite hot enough. I think it had really slackened somewhat. The

tank leader was knocked out by a bullet through the knee in the first five
minutes, then '*Otazel*'[1] fell into a narrow gully instead of crossing,
wriggled out along the gully, but stuck in the open and had to be
abandoned by the Infantry. We (the sappers) were halted, in view of the
objective trenches and of most of the plain between us and them. The first
attacking party had failed and were in full retreat, but rallied on meeting
the advancing King's Own Scottish Borderers troops and both parties
attacked again. It looked like simple murder for our men. Relatively few
fell to the shrapnel and HE, but the rifle fire and machine guns punished
them terribly. The 53rd Division should have been attacking on the
right, but for some reason they had not come up, and our poor chaps were
exposed to an additional enfilading fire. On making their final charge,
the Turks stood up and received them with hand grenades, fleeing then
to another line of trenches. Our poor chaps occupied the trench for a
time, but under an enfilading fire, and then the Turks attacked with
fixed bayonets, killing or capturing nearly every man. So far from
having new trenches to consolidate, we looked more like assisting at the
liquidation of some of our old ones, and two parties of sappers with
barbed wire on camels went off to wire some of our positions.

I was ordered back to the nullah with the remainder of the camels.
Three had been shelled and quite knocked out and many others were
bleeding. All of my British NCOs had to be handed over to the
ambulance and several of my natives were out of action.

During the afternoon I took advantage of a lull in the Turkish fire to
distribute rations to man and beast: people began to come out of cover
and a number of camels with ammunition and *fantasses* of water came
towards us. I was dividing my attention between a cup of tea and a
vigorous air fight over our heads. A German or Turkish plane,
outnumbered by ours, dropped a smoke bomb. One of two horsemen
riding by remarked that this was a signal for help, but if so, it was
mistaken for an indication of a position and instantly responded to, a HE
shell falling without warning between the two horses. Up to the present
they are lying on the spot back to back, one of the riders, an attached
officer, was killed instantly, the other, who happened to be an
acquaintance of mine, got mild concussion. I was standing with a group
of men about fifteen yards off and was congratulating myself on no one
being hurt, when someone pointed out a man lying on his back about
eighty yards from the nullah in the open. On going up to him, I found a
tiny hole in the middle of his chest, and a little blood on his lips, but he
looked more scared than hurt. The man who spotted him helped me raise
him and a dozen of my natives were rushing forward to help, when
another shell with a hellish crash tore up the ground between them and
us; others came thick and fast in front, behind, everywhere, a whole

---

[1] Not Arabic. By deduction, a driver's name for his tank in the desert: "Ot as 'ell'.

battery had opened on us and it was the hottest minute of my life. I shouted the order to lie down and self and helper threw ourselves down by the injured man, and the others did the same where they were. One only disobeyed, and ran through the hail of shells to where I lay. It was Gad el-Moula!! A part of his scalp was gone, and I had to forcibly hold him down by his bloody head till the storm was partly over, when he helped us carry the wounded man into shelter. We had to put him down twice on the way and to dress him before he would have his own wounds attended to. Poor Shaaba turned out to have a bigger hole in his back where the bit of shell came out, and the only words he spoke were: '*Ashad La illah illa Allah, was Muhammed Rusul Allah* (I bear witness that there is no god but God, and Mohammed is his Prophet)': though he was conscious whilst we dressed him, and seemed comforted by the assurances of his friends that they had 'seen the bastard who had thrown the shell and would have his blood'.

Shaaba died on his way to hospital. Gad was none the worse except that there are some patches on his head where the hair will never grow. He was a great favourite with Major Rolling, my OC, and with all the officers and men before in spite of his atrocious cowardice; now he bids fair to be a sort of mascot to our Company.

We had gained several positions, knocked out a gun or two and downed a couple of Taubes – and lost many thousands of men, our own Division having three thousand casualties and our Brigade, the 155th, being more than half wiped out, but towards sunset another desperate attempt was made to take Gaza. It was fascinating to see our Infantry advance, take, lose, and then retake a redoubt, and they seemed to me to have a more sporting chance as the light faded than the poor slaughtered Battalions of the morning.

Air and earth were vibrant again with tremendous music, flames green, red and white flashed from the guns, the hill of Ali Muntar seemed to be going up in flame and smoked like a disturbed volcano, and star shells threw now one part, now another of the battlefield into vivid prominence.

Night came and found Gaza still in Turkish hands, and our costly attack – though we have gained some ground – a failure. It is the biggest setback we have had, and is for the present an impasse.

We bombarded all night and are doing so now, but I do not think we are likely to make another frontal attack. The Turks have been replying spasmodically, just now at sunset vigorously, and there is a lot of musketry and machine gun fire. A few shells have fallen near us today, and some aeroplane bombs, and a Taube swooped down and turned a machine gun on us, and as I write there is the constant whistle and rush of our own and hostile shells well up over our heads, and at frequent intervals we get a little shower of stuff, aimed at aeroplanes above us, but it was about yesterday, 19 April, that I set out to write, as fast as the fight

At Ajlan near Gaza: 'It was a pretty spot and the bathing was excellent but in full view of the Turks'

came under my practical and personal notice; and so regretting that I cannot describe a triumphant entry into Gaza, and hoping to do so shortly, I will conclude.

At door of dugout, Kurd Hill, Gaza.

The Second Battle of Gaza ended even more disastrously for the British than the First, with casualties after three days of six thousand, five hundred. Over two thousand camels were also killed or wounded. A dangerous stalemate ensued, with both sides strengthening their defences, and maintaining skirmishes and artillery harassments.

McPherson seemed almost exalted by the danger, and at this time wrote a letter which was unusually revealing of his deepest emotions.

How pleasant were the nights. Sometimes I sat late in our subterranean mess carousing with the merry sapper officers: sometimes in the protection of the gloom I took men, camels and horses to the wells in the Wadi for water: sometimes I meandered about alone watching the bursting shells and many coloured flares at the mouths of the cannon, and the rocket-like star shells, and when I turned in at the mouth of my dugout under the sky, its beauty was so great that often I tried to keep awake to enjoy it – and in the silence – for the crash of cannon behind and at the sides, and the whistling of shells overhead did not count – 'all lovely tales that I had heard or read' seemed 'written in starlight on the dark above', and though sleep always came too soon, my dreams were always woven with starlight, till waves of crimson and gold came down the nullah, flooding it with light from the fount of the sun: and I opened my eyes, not on the stars but on myriads of crested larks in the sky and other little songbirds.

I shall always believe that Mother's spirit is at home in the Holy Land, for several times I woke with her voice in my ears, and once I saw her sitting by me smiling approvingly and chatting as naturally as ever I saw and heard her in the flesh. I could not get my voice to reply to her for some time and just as I did so she passed out and disappeared – as I followed her – in a blaze of the glory of the new-risen sun.

12
Farewell to Arms

'So ended my share in the Crusade to my intense
disgust and regret.'

J. W. McP

At the end of April, McPherson was wounded by a sniper's bullet, which
cut a groove in his leg. This was his second wound of the war, and, as well,
he had been savaged by a camel, and taken at least two heavy falls from his
horse at full gallop. He was recommended for a job at Base, and on 9 May,
was ordered back to Cairo, where he was promoted to Major, and
appointed to take charge of political prisoners at Giza. For the rest of his
life he regretted that he was not present to help the 'Crusaders' take Gaza
at their third attempt in October, when, much reinforced and under a new
commander, Sir Edmund Allenby, they broke the Turkish lines, and
swept on to Jerusalem.

He had greatly relished his life of action and danger, which had seemed
to him also a life of freedom. His last letter from Sinai, devoted to his horse
Tammuz, which had been killed some weeks earlier, is both a farewell to
this life, and a celebration of it.

In the last months Tammuz and I had many happy times and merry
picnics in the desert of Sinai . . . Convoy conducting was a pleasure with
Tammuz. He walked demurely at the head of the convoy setting the
pace: carried me back to the rear in no time if a whistle was passed up
that something was wrong, and whirled me to the front again like a flame
of fire in a way that made the natives exclaim: 'Truly by the life of the
Prophet this is an afreet and no horse', and which even excited the
Australian bushmen to strings of adjectives in praise of 'Tammy'.

When we halted he became a rigid statue. When we bivouacked he
could safely be left untethered (provided there was no loose water to
steal), and when our convoy route took us through a narrow pass he often
carried me over the rugged, glittering heights above where we had a
bird's eye view of the convoy, perhaps several miles long, winding snake-
like along. And when our way took us through some recent battlefield he
took me far afield on both flanks to gather loot and note strange and
gruesome spectacles, without losing touch with the convoy.

The last weeks of Tammuz's life, passed at El Arish, were perhaps his
happiest – as they were amongst the pleasantest his master has ever

Tammuz near el Arish, Christmas 1916

known. Neither of us cared a twopenny damn for bombs and other devices of the War which made life ten times sweeter by showing one that it is a glorious gift of the gods, of active, almost infinite enjoyment, and not a mere humdrum matter-of-course, marking time indefinitely.

The water was cold, sweet and abundant, the air like wine, rations for man and beast good and plentiful, and man and beast full of life, good temper and fun. The glittering green wadi, the River of Egypt as the Scriptures call it, flowed as it were between the clear, pure, sparkling sand of the hills, and there in the wadi, Tammuz was welcome to all sorts of green succulent luxuries, whilst his rider chattered with their Bedouin owners, and surprised them by paying for what he or his horse took, unlike their recent Turkish masters; or if that offended them, by an exchange of little presents. The saddle galls of former times were long gone, and the saddle was merely discarded for preference, or used when rations or small arms had to be carried.

It was the end or near the end of a so far perfect day. Never a cloud in the sky, but the cloudlets from the bursting shrapnel of the Archibalds in their attempt to down the audacious Fritz. A gallop at sunrise; a swim in the sea for us both and a good lunch; a pleasant ride to the Intelligence OC and a little roaming about El Arish. A glorious ride in a wonderful sunset then rest in camp. Before turning in pleasantly tired out I saw Tammuz lying in one of his quaint attitudes of abandon, on his side with his legs stretched out. Then after wishing me another goodnight I was soon asleep and Tammuz doubtless in much the same condition.

Suddenly I was half awakened by being dragged on to the sand from my camp bed. I opened my eyes to see a new officer who was sharing my tent and who had been responsible for this manoeuvre throwing himself down at my side. At the same instant a curious pulsating whirr, very loud and very near, ended in a crash that shook the ground and almost stunned us. The tent was shaken as by a terrific wind and several holes appeared in the canvas.

'A beastly near thing, that,' said Lieutenant Kelly, the new officer, 'and there's more coming. Lie down, lie down.' 'Rot,' I replied, 'it's a scientific impossibility for a plane to throw two bombs on the same spot.' 'Granted,' he expostulated, 'but there are a lot more than one plane over us.' 'The camp's big enough for a score of them', I said, but realised from the whirring and crumping going on that this was the biggest bombing any of us had as yet put up with . . ..

The rain of bombs had almost ceased, but the planes swooped down from time to time and sent a hail of machine-gun bullets into the camp. However a few planes had a bomb or two left and one fell about eighty yards from us down towards the Wadi. 'Where did that one drop?' I asked with secret misgivings. 'Bang in the middle of our horse lines,' replied Kelly. 'Good God,' I yelled, 'in the horse lines', and sprinted down to where I had left Tammuz happily asleep.

The camp was flooded with the clear light of a full moon, but here and there a smoke wraith blurred the general glory and marked where a bomb had recently fallen. A blacker pall hung over the horse lines and under it several fine beasts lay already dead and others were in the last agonies, but the moon shone on Tammuz lying much as I had left him, but three of his legs were desperately galloping, the fourth had been almost torn away, and from the severed femoral and other arteries his life's blood was gushing. He stopped galloping as I came up and there was the same old friendly half humourous look in his dimmed eye, and then it glazed over, but as I patted his neck and rubbed his nose and talked to him, his beautiful mane seemed to shake. It may have been a transient breeze, or the gentle breath of the Angel of Death; but in any case it was the last sign of life that ever came from Tammuz . . ..

When I returned to the tent, Kelly was very pale and was sitting on the sand doing something to his leg.

'I can't stop this infernal bleeding,' he said, 'for Christ's sake, jump on old Tammuz's back and gallop for the MO. I know you don't bother about saddles.'

The next day a fatigue party from my men sorrowfully dragged Tammuz's remains down to a green and flowery spot in the wadi and reverently buried him under the grass and flowers and put up a little horse shoe of wood: and under a rough representation of the sun, the symbol of Tammuz, (and a '*Crux Ansata*', which concealed a secret hope for Tammuz like that of the Red Indian for his dog) I wrote (in a scroll of Scarlet Pimpernels)

"*Ἔθανε Ταμῶς, ἔλιπε φιλίαν*"

'My day's delight is past, my horse is gone'.[1]

Erected by Lieut. McPherson in
Memory of his Horse and Comrade, Tammuz
Killed in Action.
19.1.17.

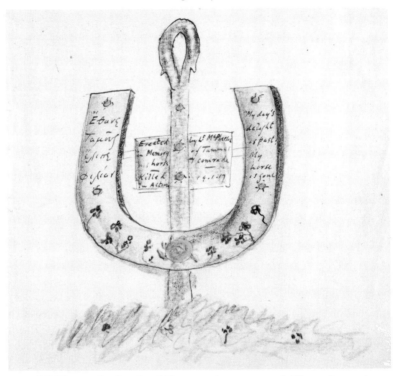

McPherson's sketch of Tammuz's grave and 'Crux Ansata'

---

[1] Adapted from line 930 of Euripides' *Alcestis*. A lament for Admetus's wife:

ἔθανε δάμαρ, ἔλιπε φιλίαν

'(Your) wife is dead, she has left love behind.'

PART THREE

THE LURID GULF
1918-1924

EDITORIAL NOTE

During his years in police and intelligence work, McPherson kept up the Family Letters, which, after the war reports, were now seen by the 'clan' and the writer himself as a unique record. Though often overwhelmed with work, he drafted letters as soon as possible after the dramatic events he described, and expanded them and added postscripts at a later date. He sent or brought back to England a mass of related documentation, e.g. police and intelligence reports, confiscated nationalist propaganda, the wrappings of seized drugs. Sometimes, if he judged the matter sufficiently intriguing, he wrote a letter in the form of a case history, complete with a colourful title. From this material we have selected episodes of historical and personal significance.

Crime and Corruption

'. . . that nightmare full of weird interest and more incident than any other two years of my life, even the preceding years of active service in the field.'

J. W. McP.

The period which Joseph McPherson called the 'lurid gulf' in his life began when he reluctantly left the desert battlefields. He had been retired from active service because it was thought that, because of his wounds and physical wear and tear, he merited a quieter life. In fact, the years immediately ahead of him were to be infinitely more stressful.

In Cairo he was promoted to Major (*Bimbashi*), and put in charge of the political prison at Giza, which contained mainly Egyptian nationalists, out of whom he formed a football team. After a few months, he was appointed to the post of Acting Mamur Zapt, or (approximately) Head of the Political CID and Secret Police in Cairo, where he came under the authority of Russell Pasha, the cool-headed Commandant of Police, whom he much admired.

As Mamur Zapt he was plunged into a world of crime and political intrigue, of unceasing effort and psychological involvement, for which little in his previous career had prepared him. When he left the post for another after two years, he looked back on it with a certain sense of wonderment at how he had coped.

To Ja   *Intelligence Office, Kantara, 5 May 1920*
When in the summer of 1917 I got sniped in the leg at Gaza, and came down to the Base to rest the limb, and take charge of the political prisoners at Giza, there was a *cause célèbre* in the Courts, occupying a remarkable share of nearly everyone's conversation, and of newspaper space.

The Mamur Zapt, Phillipedes Bey, was being tried on a number of charges of corruption, and was ultimately condemned to five years' penal servitude, and his wife, who had a great fancy in valuable jewellery, received a shorter sentence.

Many high police officers were smirched, and in the opinion of many, some of these deserved the same treatment as Phillipedes, some going so far as to think that he suffered as scapegoat for them.

For my part I am quite sure that Phillipedes was guilty up to the hilt,

'Bimbashi'

though I have by no means the same confidence in the innocence of some of those who escaped.

Many of my political prisoners swore that they were interned because they could or would not pay the £5000 or so which Phillipedes demanded to leave them alone, and they informed me of glaring political cases still at large, because they had stumped up, and I have been able since to substantiate a good deal of this.

The post of Mamur Zapt was an anomaly and an anachronism. I know of no existing post with which it compares, but except that it existed for Civil and Political, and not Clerical ends, it was amazingly similar to the office of Chief Inquisitor; I say 'was' and not 'is', because on Phillipedes' downfall it was put on 'memoir' in the Budget of the Ministry of Finance, and was definitely and finally suppressed at the beginning of the current financial year, 1 April 1920.

Prior to Phillipedes, who was a Syrian mongrel, the post had been held by Turks, or Osmanli Egyptians, and mighty fortunes they had made out of it. His immediate predecessor is still living in great style and luxury.

There is not only the chance and temptation of making wealth on the political side, but by compounding civil crimes, and drawing secret fees for approving the promotion of officials; and as the Mamur Zapt is Chief of Secret Police, amongst his functions, he can if so disposed, use his extraordinary secret knowledge to extort blackmail on a colossal scale.

I do not think I was at all interested in this *cause célèbre*, except so far as it threw light on the guilt or comparative innocence of my political internees: but suddenly as I was looking to be sent back to the campaign in Palestine, where I had been supremely happy, I found myself shovelled, willy nilly, into this invidious post of honour, and power.

Political prisoners at Giza: 'Out of these I formed a football XI'

Those who put me in may have looked to an Englishman to break the traditions of corruption and extortion; or they may have intended me as a harmless figurehead who would not in any way interfere with their own plans.

Phillipedes had added genius and an intense zest for his work to a life's training in law, and the methods of police and politics. He was moreover a most subtle detective, whereas I had no liking for the work, and no training nor qualifications except a useful knowledge of languages, and as for detective work, I could never read Sherlock Holmes, and Donovan's[1] and similar detective yarns always bored me to tears; so I feared I should be little but a figurehead, and not a success at that.

I had however two tremendous assets, which he lacked: firstly I was a free lance, and could remain so, not being in need of money, nor having a taste for jewellery, and therefore free and under no obligation to anyone and not liable to be blackmailed by them; and secondly, being a British Officer, at a time of Military occupation, I had the Military as well as the civil power behind me, and incidentally could override the Capitulations.[2]

I was lucky too in having staunch and sound supporters in the Aalim Zapt, my legal adviser and expert, a doctor at law, and in my direct assistant, the Maowen Zapt, and Luga Bey, the Director of Police, and other heads of departments, particularly Major Quartier, my Adjutant

[1] Dick Donovan, pseud. for J. E. Muddock, a prolific writer of detective novels from the 1890s to the 1920s.

[2] The legal privileges and immunities granted under the Ottoman Empire to foreigners, originally for the encouragement of trade.

in the Secret Section, a remarkably straight and nice man, with thirty-seven years' experience in the Egyptian Police.

The Office of Mamur Zapt gave me the right to arrest or imprison anyone on suspicion, and there was cell accommodation under my chamber for a few dozen; also to order anyone to appear at my office, or to search any house or premises, even Harem quarters.

Although working in harmony with Army HQ, and the Commandant of Police, I very rarely consulted either, and all arrests and perquisitions made were on my own authority, without on any single occasion a warrant from Army or Police. I think my chief, Russell Bey, preferred this, because I as a free lance took on stunts for which he would not have cared to take responsibility, and which he would have doubtless repudiated had I failed, but which pleased him well enough, when they came off, which thank goodness they almost invariably did. So little did I trouble him that from July 1918 to January 1919, I only once spoke to him, and that was at a fancy dress ball at Shepheard's. As for A——, the Assistant Commandant, his advice, on the very few occasions on which I did consult him, was so fatuous or impracticable, that after a few lessons I had no more thought of asking his advice than that of the sentry on the gate.

The post carried its privileges: I travelled without payment by train or tram, anywhere in Egypt, though my work confined me more than I liked to Cairo; had free entry to all theatres, concerts or other public places, and a fauteuil always reserved for me at the Opera – which for the short Italian Opera season alone would have cost anyone else £63. Then I had the pick of the horses of the Mounted Troops, with free saddlery, grooming, feed, and fodder, and my cook, Gad, was paid for me, and when I vacated Government Quarters, a house allowance was granted, under the name of a war gratuity.

I had difficulty on several occasions at first in inducing tradesmen and market people to take money for things purchased, as they assured my boy when he went shopping that the late Mamur Zapt had never paid.

Gad, my native Orderly, was inordinately proud of his reflected dignity, and made full use of his similar prerogatives: free trams and trains, free theatres, etc.

My eyes, helped by over a hundred pair, belonging to my detectives, and the farseeing pair of old Major Quartier, were soon conscious of such a vision of crime and corruption, as I had believed not possible out of hell, or hardly in it; and that too where one ought to least expect it, amongst judges and high administrative officials, many of my own officers and agents, in the Australian Pickets, and even amongst British Officers, and in leaders of the Churches, and of Islam: and I realised that I ought to use the mighty sword that had been placed in my hand. I was the more ready to do so as I was being kept away from the fighting line, and the Crusade on which I had set my heart. I lacked the finesse of a

Gad as *askari*

maître d'escrime, and did not attempt to cultivate it, as these subtle fencers would have known how to parry every time: but my crude swordmanship was something quite unknown to and unexpected by them, and my two short years of office did not give them time to learn the proper defence: so as I went for big game from the first, I can claim a very satisfactory bag for a novice.

A prince, two Mudirs (Governors of Provinces), all infernal scoundrels, were downed, a Prelate or two, many of our own officials, who abused their opportunities, the Manager of a bank, and other financial magnates, several groups of army thieves, on two cases of which the Army and the Public were certainly saved a quarter of a million; and later – many of the Revolutionary Leaders, and wire pullers, including some prominent Italians, now deported from Egypt, several gangs of illicit traffickers in arms, a few bomb makers and throwers, and a host of authors, printers, and circulators of seditious papers and circulars, who fell with their presses and products: so that when I left the Governorate, I bequeathed nearly a million sheets of confiscated matter, with type and accessories, and also a small arsenal of revolvers, and other weapons.

His introduction to the job powerfully appealed to the side of his character that loved ritual, ceremony and mystery.

On taking over as Mamur Zapt on 22 January 1918, the Commandant Cairo City Police handed me a couple of keys, explaining that they were the sole keys that opened a box fastened to the wall outside the

BIMBASHI MAC PHERSON BUSY.

Bimbashi Macpherson has seized in a shop for the sale of sweets and cigarettes considerable quantities of chocolate mixed with narcotics and sent them to the chemical laboratory for analysis. A quantity of hashish was also found in this shop.

Bimbashi Macpherson has raided a printing-press in Haret Darb El-Atrak, near the Azhar, and seized 8000 copies of a forbidden publication, as well as some of the type used in this press for printing it.

He also searched an office in Sharia Abdin and seized certain papers, and the house of a student in Helwan for the same purpose.

RAIDING GAMBLING DENS.

The Cairo mamur zabt has raided a house in Sharia Saf El-Din El-Mihrani where gambling was carried on, and confiscated L.E. 95 as well as all the implements of gambling and the furniture of the room. A report was drawn up against the tenant, in which the names of the gamblers were put down. The money confiscated has been divided among the men who raided the house

SMART RAID ON HASHISH DEN

Bimbashi Macpherson, Mamur Zabt of Cairo, while bicycling in Sharia El-Gami ʿEl-Ahmar smelt the odour of hashish, and seeing a boy run at great speed, followed him to a room where he found men smoking the drug. An inspection of the room revealed quantities of hashish, some of which was placed in a tin box hidden in a "zir" (native filter). One man was taken to the caracol.

Bimbashi Macpherson also arrested a foreigner who trafficked in the sale of fire-arms. The man will be brought before a Military Court for trial.

—«O»——

PRINTING PRESS RAIDED.

Bimbshi Macpherson, Mamur Zabt of Cairo, has raided a printing-press in which pamphlets which disturb the minds of the public, have been printed, and seized 4000 copies as well as all the manuscripts found

The Commandant of Police has decided to grant a monetary reward to the civil policeman who discovered this printing-press.

——«O»——

Reports of the Mamur Zapt's operations in the Cairo press, 1919–1920

Governorate, in a rather obscure place, in which from time immemorial had been deposited petitions, denunciations, and all sorts of secret matter, which it was one of the functions of the Mamur Zapt to deal with. At the same time he gave the secret register for these matters, and presented me to the Special Secret Clerk, a highly educated youth, whose two duties were to help me with these documents, and to keep his mouth shut.

This chest is doubtless an anachronism, but unlike the Dogal '*Bocca del Leone*'[1] still plays an important part in secret politics and police work. Very many Egyptians, who would have no idea how to set about getting a letter written, stamped, enveloped, and posted, got a few lines scribbled on a scrap of paper, and the old chest in the dark rather appeals to them.

I have found its contents remarkable: in fact most of my work has

[1] In Venice under the doges, the Bocca del Leone, or Lion's Mouth, was a 'letter-box' decorated with a lion's head, into which Venetians could drop denunciations, to be brought to the attention of the authorities. The missives, however, had to be signed. There were several such boxes in the city-state.

centred round them, especially in times of political unrest. It is rare to find any indications of public spirit; but spite, pique, malice and revenge expose innumerable crimes, family skeletons, and public scandals, and about half the contributions are anonymous.

As a policeman, he was decidedly eccentric, relishing insoluble mysteries ('mare's nests') more than straightforward criminal cases. Thus his letters contained reports on a case of 'spirit rapping', persistent nocturnal knockings in a haunted house; on a clairvoyant who exercised a hypnotic control over a young man to defraud him; on a victim of paranoia whom he dubbed *Heautonotimoroumenos* ('Self-Tormentor', the title of a play by the Roman dramatist, Terence); on an eye-witness report of a double-murder and burial – excavation revealed two skeletons, each two thousand years old! 'A Mystery and a Failure' was his description of the curious case of

THE GOLDEN NEEDLE

To 'Rene   *1918*

Early in 1918, a Captain King, at the base in Cairo, was taken with a mysterious illness. He was found, I think, in a seat in Esbekieh Gardens, in a semi-somnolent condition, as though drugged or bewitched, and taken to bed.

The doctors found no lesions, no indication of a blow, no trace of poisoning, nothing to account for his condition, which persisted, and aggravated. He was in no pain, and all his faculties were normal, except that he seemed unable to rouse himself, or to take the least interest in people or things around him, and when spoken to, he gazed vacantly into space, and replied:

> 'She scratched my eye with a golden
> needle, and gave me second sight.'

Time brought no improvement, and after many days, he became feverish and delirious, repeating the above words, and those only, innumerable times.

One night he beckoned his nurse to his bedside, and said impressively and in a confidential tone:

> 'She scratched my eye, – she scratched
> my eye, with a golden needle, a golden
> needle, – and gave me second sight,
> – and gave me second sight, – and
> gave me –'

and he never spoke again, but quietly died.

The above points were laid before me by Col. Russell, who asked if there were anything in my experience of the East which supplied a clue or a parallel to this mysterious case.

I admitted that there was nothing, but could make careful enquiries as to these words and their possible reference to any Eastern custom or superstition.

I added, 'of course a careful autopsy was made?' and Russell replied, 'Yes, yes, without result, except that the photos of the eyes, both before and after death, as you will see from these enlarged photos, show a mark like a scratch on the corner of one eye and not on the other.'

I took the matter up but my researches were quite negative; so I went to Mr Vandyke, one of the greatest living authorities on such matters. He had already been approached by the Military, but had no more clue than myself: and together we visited clairvoyants, alchemists, spiritualists, Druzes, Chaldeans, Persians, weird people from all sorts of weird places, but never elicited the smallest explanation.

Meanwhile I was attacking the problem in quite another way; by making secret enquiries about the life of the dead Captain and his associates.

He was a normal, pleasant, sporting officer, a moderate drinker, never suspected of drugs, not unduly interested, as far as his friends could judge, in hypnotism, spiritualism, or occult matters. He had a rather conspicuous weakness for women, especially 'Gyppy girls', as his officer friends dubbed them; and he had been seen, several times recently, driving in his dogcart with a lady in Eastern attire – young and beautiful as far as her gauzy white yashmak allowed those who saw her to judge. He had taken a lot of chaff about this 'camarade', good humouredly, but without taking anyone into his confidence.

I made every effort to trace this lady, but all was fruitless, and neither I nor, as far as I know, anyone has obtained the smallest clue to King's mysterious illness and death, nor anything to explain, up to his latest breath, his reiterating:

> 'She scratched my eye with a golden
> needle, and gave me second sight.'[1]

But the intriguing mysteries were only light relief from 'the vision of crime and corruption' that McPherson experienced. He plunged into the grim realities of his job with extraordinary verve. He had inherited a small army of informers, including many street boys, whom he called his 'sleuth hounds', and he recruited more. He believed, however, in personal observation, and often went around in disguise, sometimes as an ordinary Egyptian in a galabieh, sometimes in grimy rags as a 'Cairene carter', sometimes as 'a low-class Greek' or 'an Armenian Jew of means'.

One of his more garish cases concerned an Australian army sergeant who was the lover of a celebrated Madam called Firdus (Persian for

---

[1] This case became part of the anecdotal lore of the British community in Cairo. Lawrence Durrell heard of it twenty years later; transposed to the second world war, it is mentioned by a character in his *Clea* (1960).

'Paradise'), reputed to be the most beautiful woman in Egypt. The sergeant, Johnny Black (not his real name) was in charge of one of the night pickets in Cairo, and with Firdus and a small gang of accomplices assaulted and robbed many of the clients of the brothel. The matter came to McPherson's attention because one of their victims, a British soldier, had died of a fractured skull.

McPherson was intent on getting direct evidence of their association, and sallied out with one of his special agents, a Turkish-speaking Egyptian, to pursue the case.

THE BEAUTIFUL SHE-DEVIL AND HER MATE

To Ja   *1918–1921*

Mustafa knew Firdus, and eagerly fell in with my idea of visiting her. On the way he excited my curiosity by accounts of her almost supernatural beauty and charms, of the numbers of Turkish and Egyptian Officers and others she had ruined, and of rumours he had heard of an Australian lover, and their influence on each other for dark and evil deeds.

We entered No. 14 Sharia el-Genina, in spite of the 'Out of Bounds' notice posted up, and we were dressed as Turkish civilians of position.

Two young boys were on the stairs and sprinted up evidently to give warning of the approach of strangers; for as we reached Firdus' hall door, a portière was being hastily drawn to conceal a very gorgeously furnished saloon opposite the door through which we were invited to enter, but not before I had caught a glimpse of a lot of Beys and Effendis indulging in champagne and other drinks. The apartment into which we were ushered was furnished in a most costly manner, but we had little time to observe details before a queenly and superbly beautiful girl entered and greeted us affably. I had no need to enquire if this were Firdus, except that there was something a little vampire-like in the intense colour of her lips and cheeks, she was as perfectly lovely a creature as could well be imagined.

Though Turkish in origin, she knew little of that tongue, and did not seem pleased when Mustafa and I exchanged remarks in it; but we professed to know no Arabic and Mustafa's French was weak and hers weaker.

Firdus sat with her back to a most gorgeous bed, whose coverlet seemed to me to be of cloth of gold, and its hangings of the most exquisite brocade. I sat almost facing her and Mustafa completed a triangle at the side, and as I glanced beyond her at the fine needle work and lace hanging from her couch, I saw it slightly move, and arranged with Mustafa in Turkish for him to slightly raise the hangings with his stick.

This he did with such skill, that the act was quite unobserved by Firdus: and the threatening teeth and menacing scowl of a huge bull-terrier were revealed to me. It was easy to guess the function of this well-trained canine bully; and later I had plenty of evidence of how 'Risch' backed up his mistress's extortionate demands by guarding the clothes of her guest, and sniffing significantly at his bare legs. In fact on more than one occasion when sufficient gold was not forthcoming, Risch took his pound of flesh.

To Mustafa's disgust I soon took my leave, as it was clear to me that the lady had suspicions. These were confirmed when I pulled out some money and called for a bottle of wine for the three of us.

'I regret', said Firdus, 'that I can only offer you lemonade, and that I could not think of taking money for, as you are my guests. I would be only too happy to offer you champagne, but I hate even the appearance of breaking the police regulations.'

The popping of champagne corks in an adjoining room, and a certain amount of drunken laughter hardly supported this; but no comment was made and, with a few compliments, we took our leave.

The next night, dressed as an Australian Tommy, and accosting a boy of about fourteen at the door, I asked him if he knew my 'cobber' Johnny.

'Oh, yes,' the little lad replied, 'he is in command of the picket, and will be around at 10 o'clock.'

'Well,' said I, 'I want to get on his picket. There's money in the job I'm told, and I won't forget your backsheesh if you point Johnny out to me.'

'Right-ho,' said the kid in English, 'meet me in the arch by No. 14 at 10, and I'll point out Johnny Black, and you will see if he is your old cobber that you are looking for. He is sure to go in there to see Firdus.' The boy gave his name as Mohammad Hussain of Bab el-Shaaria.

I returned rather before ten, and whilst still some distance off, saw Hussein under the arch talking to a thick-set sinister looking Australian, whom I felt sure was the redoubtable Johnny.

> Having marked down the sergeant, McPherson and his agents began 'weaving a web of evidence' which indicated that Firdus and her lover were the centre of a gang which included corrupt Egyptian police askaris, and that the brothel was used 'as a Desertion Bureau for troops, as well as for other highly nefarious purposes'. He heard that Firdus had moved her establishment.

Sharia Huseini, where Firdus and her Australian paramour had taken up their new quarters is a very narrow street, and their windows looked directly into those of the Eden Palace Hotel, closed during the war.

I had seen a petition from the lessee of the Bristol, which is in some way connected with the Eden Palace, begging that the latter hotel might be reopened to a non-enemy person or Company. I therefore dressed as an Armenian Jew of means, in a long greasy black gown, a tarboosh, and silk girdle and shawl, and introducing myself to the lessee of the Bristol, explained that I represented a syndicate willing to take over the hotel if satisfied of its good sanitation, and its general equipment, and that in order to report satisfactorily I should like to pass a few nights there.

The lessee was most obliging, taking me over the Eden Palace, thus giving me an opportunity to select rooms looking directly into those of Firdus. These were fitted up with beds and all that was necessary, also one I selected further back, and which was the only one in which I ever used a light.

I found however that Firdus's bedroom and several little chambers which might be important were at the top, facing rooms for washing clothes and housing native servants. As I had Gad (my orderly) and two detectives with me as 'servants', I endeavoured to obtain the keys of these roof rooms for them, but the lessee, too polite altogether, insisted on fixing them up with chambers near mine. However I soon got them opened by a false key, and got a commanding view at a few yards of Firdus' bedroom.

[On the third night of watching], 21.2.18, leaving Hardie and a detective to watch the very popular salon of Firdus, where Natives, Europeans and Australians were pursuing their orgy excited by illicit drinks, I repaired to my watchtower on the roof.

A message from Hardie brought me down to him. A row had broken out in the salon. Apparently a client who had been 'sitting out' with one of the young ladies, had not produced a satisfactory honorarium to Firdus, and her bullies were coercing, whilst some native and European friends were supporting him. (He appeared to be European or possibly Syrian).

Suddenly, (at 11.30), the bullies commenced using their sticks, lights went out, there was a smashing of glasses and heads, cries of 'MURDER', and shrieks of agony reached us, and then a body fell or was thrown from the window into the street. As well as we could judge from our post, by the light of the street lamp, blood was flowing from the head, and an eye seemed to have been knocked out.

Police Askari No. 486, who had been drinking upstairs, was quickly with the victim. Also some of the poor wretch's friends and Johnny Black with some of his Picket.

Beyond sending one of my detectives to see what was done with the injured man, and secretly putting the regular police in touch, I did not let this side issue divert any of us, especially as Johnny and some of his men went upstairs.

The leader of the picket seemed to be scolding Firdus and the bullies, but after a while, he cheerfully retired with his paramour upstairs, and they undressed. I do not know what happened to alarm him, or with whom he got into communication, but after a few minutes he redressed in great haste, and went downstairs. I descended to the room facing the salon, and in the dark, behind a thin curtain, I saw Johnny emerge from the salon to one of the balconies, and stare into the gloom of the windows in front of him, with the wild terror of a hunted animal in his eyes.

Then he again went upstairs, and pacing about like a caged beast, had a long violent altercation with Firdus.

It was not till about 3.30, that she finally coaxed and cajoled him into a good temper, and he consented to let her undress him and lead him into bed. They neglected to draw the curtains, but I must.

> Eventually, enough evidence was accumulated for the sergeant to be courtmartialled, reduced to the ranks, imprisoned, and sent out of the country. That left 'the beautiful She-Devil' to be dealt with:

As for Firdus herself, she was summoned, in her real name, to the Governorate, where she was arraigned before the Anzac GOC, and Archer and myself.

She came, simply but beautifully robed in fine silk and lace entirely black, with a veil of the same, with the modest quiet air of a vestal virgin. She admitted nothing against herself or any of her party; seemed hardly to know whom we referred to as Johnny Black and suddenly at the moment she deemed propitious, threw her veil aside, and revealed tears of injured innocence flowing from the most lovely eyes one could imagine, down cheeks equally beautiful, but blushing and confused at being thus in the unaccustomed presence of men.

We banished her to a town she expressed a loathing for in the Provinces, where she was kept under police supervision in a circumscribed area, kept for women of her profession. Tanta was the place, but the name was kept secret, for as the OC complained, all his young officers would go there to pass their leave if it were known, and that is the last I know of Firdus.

Postscript dated 17.7.21.

Not quite the last. Three years after penning the account of the doings of Firdus, and her paramour, and their gang of thugs and bullies, during which period not a word reached me concerning her, – happening to take up the paper in the Kantara Officers' Club, my eye fell on the following :–

EGYPTIAN GAZETTE
16.7.21.
TANTA MURDER TRIALS
CHIEF CRIMINAL'S CONFESSION

For the last few days, the Tanta Assizes have been busy hearing the well-known Tanta women murder case. The accused, Mahmoud Allam (there follows the names of eleven other accused), are charged with having during the period between September 1919 and April 1920, at Tanta, wilfully murdered by suffocation and strangulation, Shafika Abdulla, Bahia Ibrahim known as Firdus, Zakia Kamis, Nafousa bint Khalil and Kakia bint el-Sheikh. The criminals are also charged with robbing the victims of their jewels and valuables.

Mahmoud Allam, who was the head of the gang, explained to the Court in detail the crimes he had committed with his accomplices.

Thursday morning the Court concluded the hearing of the case and delivered its judgement referring the documents of the case as far as Mahmoud Allam is concerned, to the Mufti of Tanta – that means the death punishment.

SIC TRANSIT GLORIA demi-MUNDI.

In his work as Mamur Zapt, McPherson confronted powerful and dangerous opponents – much more dangerous than brothel-keepers and pimps. His investigations of massive thefts of British army stores and supplies uncovered conspiracies linking hardened criminals, corrupt police, high officials, important commercial interests, and British officers and NCOs. He made many enemies, and knew that his life was threatened. In one case, which he always referred to as 'The Infamy', involving thefts of grain, he kept a look-out on a flour mill outside Cairo, a known centre of the thieves, from a 'gabel' or nearby hill.

To Jack   *1919–1922*
I was ostensibly engaged in antiquarian research in a lofty spur of the '*gabel*' which almost overhangs the mill in question. Unless specifically recognised, I was not likely to excite suspicion, as this site of an ancient city, probably an annexe of Babylon,[1] which is not far off, attracts many antiquarians, as it is full of well-preserved remains of aqueducts and buildings, ancient drainage systems and kitchen middens of much interest.

At this time there were no genuine Egyptologists about, and except for weird haunters of the '*gabel*' on neighbouring spurs, or smoking hashish in caves and graves, and occasional parties of men and boys fighting not far off with stones, I was quite alone.

On the occasion which gives rise to this letter, I had come rather higher up than was wise to enjoy a very magnificent sunset, and was soon joined by an agent of mine, engaged on the mill business who pointed out that I could be seen from the mill, and advised me not to pass it on my return to the city, as I appeared to be watched by three or four roughs near the main door.

There was no use in running the least risk of being recognised, so I decided to wander right across the '*gabel*', under the Aqueduct of

[1] A very old area of Cairo, supposedly called after a colony of settlers from ancient Babylon in Mesopotamia.

Mohammed Ali, past the old quarries and the mineral springs and baths of Ein el-Sirra, through the Tombs of the Mamelukes, and past the beautiful mosque of Imam el-Shafei, to the Citadel, where I could take a tram. The agent, probably thinking me mad to start on a walk of about six miles, took an intermediate route, and I much enjoyed the stroll alone. Several times I paused to look back at the sunset colours and the afterglow effect and each time I noted three or four men on the sky line, who appeared to be following me.

When nearly across this desert region, I found myself on the brink of the Quarry called Butn el-Baqara, (Cow's Belly), went down in to it and sat for a little while in a comfortable corner, from which an opening framed a quaint old tomb of some great Sheikh not far off and a background of more distant tombs and mosques, just distinguishable in the fading light. Before descending I had carefully scanned the horizon, but saw no trace of pursuers or any life, but suddenly a creepy shivery feeling crept over me. Whether 'someone was walking over my grave', or whether it was the chill of the air which often strikes one after sunset, I was not clear but I got up and went on my way, meeting a man at the entrance, going apparently to the spot I had just vacated and looking at me in great surprise.

Two days later, Quartier brought me a report on the discovery of the body of a man in Butn el-Baqara, with a plan of the place. The body was on the spot I had occupied, and the Report said that after careful investigation by the Mudir of Old Cairo, and the Medico-legal expert, there was no doubt that the death was caused by an accidental fall over the cliff. The deceased was not identified. Quartier, who had been to the spot thought it strange that a man falling seven metres should be found lying the same distance from the foot of the cliff, on sand except for a few large loose stones, with his face smashed beyond recognition, and his chest staved in.

I at once saw the Mudir, and asked him his views. 'Clearly an accident,' said he, 'the cliff was over forty metres high, I have seen it myself', and he turned to his chief agent who had been there, who agreed that it was at least forty, 'nearer sixty metres, he should think'. Asked by me how he explained the body being seven metres from the foot, the Mudir said the man must have been running in the dark. He added that it was certainly not murder as he searched the clothes of the dead man and there was no money in his pockets to steal. Leaving such a consummate ass, I saw Dr Sidney Smith,[1] the Medico-Legal man, and he told me that he had been unable to go himself and that the Report his native assistant gave him had certainly rather puzzled him. Then I took a youngster from a neighbouring quarry, who although he had previously helped me more than once in desert crime cases, had no idea I was in the Police. I was pretty sure that there had been no stones on the sand when I

---

[1] Later, the famous Regius Professor of Forensic Medicine, Edinburgh University.

had sat on it, and the first thing we constated was that the black blocks by the head of the corpse, were of a rock not otherwise existing in the quarry, but abundant up above. Then we examined the blood-soaked sand, and found buried a sharp hard stone like an old axe-head, with blood and hair on the sharp edge. A little way off we found hidden some clothes, beads and cheap trinkets, and many pages of a holy book in ancient Coptic.

I put in a Report to the Commandant declaring my conviction that the Butn el-Baqara was a clear case of Murder: the victim having been killed or injured by large stones thrown on him from above whilst seated near the foot of the cliff. After which death had been ensured by smashing in his head with the sharp stone submitted, and by battering in his chest etc. He had then probably been robbed. Then cloths, papers and other objects useless to the murderers, and the sharp stone had been buried.

I think the Mudir must have had his 'head washed', for he called at my office, and assured me that I was undoubtedly right; in fact, that he had been sure it was a case of murder from the first but that where both murderer and victim were unknown, the recognised police procedure was to bring in a verdict of accident to save trouble, and that he had been unable to state views contradictory to the official report, until as now it was superseded by a higher one. I told him to go and measure the height of the cliff.

McPherson never solved this case, but he had the strongest suspicions that he had been intended as the victim. It put him very much on his guard.

The rocky bit of desert between Babylon and Ein el-Sirra, which was the scene of the last little incident described, 'Butn el-Baqara', has long had a sort of fascination for me. Its ruins of ancient cities, including Original Cairo ('Fostat' itself), its weird and ancient scenery, the few people one meets sporadically, weirder still, and its geological interest all make up a walk or a ride of interest. I might add its murders and mysteries, for these are not lacking. I have had two narrow escapes, long before the Butn el-Baqara affair, one at least of which was duly recorded, I believe, in an old letter. With a view to unravelling some of its mysteries, I made friends, long before I was in the Police, with the workers in the main quarry, a most attractive type, most excellently mannered and physically endowed. They seem all to be of one family, or at least of one clan, and to have inherited this job through the ages, and they bring their babies to learn to carry on almost as soon as they can walk. They live in a village consisting mostly of tombs between the quarries and Imam el-Shafei (Mosque).

Soon after the Butn el-Baqara murder, anonymous letters reached the police, that many of the tombs in this district were used to conceal grain,

to evade the Tariff laws, and that arms were also concealed. Not wanting
to break my incognito, for I have always been known, and still am, to the
quarry people as Signor Martino, a rather erratic amateur of Geology
and Mineralogy, and somewhat liberal in the matter of cigarettes and
piastres, I put on my assistant, Dykes, and some agents, and they made
some hauls of contraband grain, without however involving my friends.
The search for arms being negative, I turned my attention from fossils
and crystals to bones, and with my quarry acquaintances explored many
old graves. One evening after a fruitless but enjoyable hour or two at this
game, on returning I was persistently followed by a stalwart young giant,
who looked strong and fearless enough to be dangerous. Him I tackled,
and he explained: 'I saw you with Rashid and Abu el-Siria, and I hope to
marry their sister, and should not like to see you done in by any *'Gabel'*
brigands, and you scientists are so unsuspecting. I warrant you don't
think to carry a pistol on your rambles.' I did not tell him that at that
moment a revolver was directed at him through my pocket, and my
finger on the trigger, and that I had a useful dagger and knuckleduster
available, but shrugging my shoulders, replied: 'Why should I go about
armed? Who would want to hurt me? You don't carry weapons, do you?'
He grinned, pulled up his galabieh, revealing a dagger strapped to his
leg, and pulling out a loaded pistol, said: 'Come along to our house which
is close by, and I will show you better than this, and lend you one to go
home with, if you will return it, and for God's sake don't let any of the
police see it or hear about our having arms.' I went in with him and his
father and friends plied me with coffee and lacoum and nuts, and showed
me several pistols, mostly old, which they said they needed in this district
'and damn the proclamations'. Murei insisted on seeing me safely to the
tram and begged me to come again, and to keep the subject of the
weapons dark, as there would be a Military Court if it were known; and I
who had come, in my capacity of Head of the Secret Police, in search of
arms could not do otherwise than promise to keep the secret, and this is
the nearest I have come to divulging it.

> After much hard and dangerous work on 'The Infamy' theft conspiracy,
> he accumulated enough evidence for the principals and a number of their
> accomplices to be arrested. Despite the slipperiness underlying the whole
> affair – he himself was offered a substantial bribe to conceal evidence – he
> was confident that they would be found guilty by the military court of
> enquiry which was trying them, and dumbfounded when they were
> acquitted.

A few days after the acquittal, the President of the Court Martial, Major
Something (I forget his rotten name), blundered into a group of officers
and others in the club without spotting me there at first. When he saw

me, he said with a forced laugh: 'Halloo, the Mamur Zapt here, we don't often see you in the Club. I saw our friend Abd el-Raiuf (one of the accused) the other day and he complained that he still suffered from the effects of the beating the Mamur Zapt gave him'. I was too taken aback at such effrontery to be cautious, so I shouted to the Major: 'Tell *your* friend that if I had known there was no justice to be had against him in a British Military Court, I would have broken his damned neck'. Have seen nothing of the Major since.

14

Revolution

The 1919 Revolution failed ... The nation reaped
nothing but a crop of self-suspicion, egoism and
hatred, between individuals and classes alike. The
hopes which the 1919 Revolution was expected to
realise faded. The fact that they faded only and did
not die out is due to the natural resistance of those
hopes which our nation had always entertained. This
resistance was still alive then and preparing for
another trial.

GAMAL ABDUL NASSER: *The Philosophy of the
Revolution* (*1955*)

Many British accounts of the events in Egypt in 1919 refer to them as
'disturbances'. In Egyptian eyes they amounted to an attempted
revolution, which set in motion the slow progression to independence, and
was an inspiration to the successful revolution of 1952.

The first signal that Egypt's wartime resentments were about to
demand political redress came two days after the signing of the Armistice
in November 1918, when Saad Zaghlul Pasha, the leading nationalist
politician, called at the British Residency to advise the High Commissioner, General Wingate, that Egypt wished to be represented at the Peace
Conference, and – putting its faith in President Wilson's tenet of the 'right
to self-determination' – expected to gain its independence. Wingate was
non-committal, but went to London to urge the government to receive an
Egyptian delegation to discuss the matter.

Instead, the British government declared that 'the development of
constitutional reform in Egypt. . .was an imperial and not an international question'. Zaghlul was warned by the acting High Commissioner in
Cairo on 7 March 1919 to cease agitating against the Protectorate, and
reminded that Egypt was still under the martial law introduced in 1914.
Two days later, Zaghlul and others of his party were arrested and exiled to
Malta.

Egypt promptly exploded with riots and demonstrations, not only in the
cities, but throughout the provinces. Trains were derailed, stations
burned, British troops and civilians killed, and Armenians and Greeks also
attacked. The British General Bulfin, arriving post-haste from Syria, took
charge of the situation, sending flying columns into the countryside to put
down the insurrection. By the end of March it was judged to be under

Saad Zaghlul Pasha, nationalist leader twice exiled by the British, elected Prime Minister in 1924

control. The dead included thirty-six British and Indian soldiers and four British civilians, and perhaps as many as a thousand Egyptians.[1]

Meanwhile the British government had appointed Field Marshal Allenby as High Commissioner with special powers. He arrived at the end of March, and took over from General Bulfin. Almost immediately he put pressure on the British government to release Zaghlul and allow him to proceed to London and Paris. The release was announced on 7 April, and was widely regarded, in Britain and, particularly, by Britons in Egypt, as a surrender to violence.

At the Peace Conference, the Egyptian delegation got no satisfaction since the United States had already stated that it recognised Britain's Protectorate. Unrest continued in Egypt, and in December 1919 the British government despatched a Commission of Enquiry headed by the elder statesman, Lord Milner, to investigate the possibilities of constitutional change.

Joseph McPherson had viewed the arrival of Allenby with hope, which changed swiftly to disgust at what he saw as his vacillations of policy. Thereafter he referred to him as 'the jackass' or 'King Log'; among the Family Letters is an invitation to one of Allenby's receptions, on which McPherson has scribbled: 'No damn fear!'

As Mamur Zapt he was close to the centre of operations in Cairo, and his long letter to his brother is a vivid personal record of the upheaval of 1919.

[1] On 4 May 1919, Allenby wrote to Curzon, the Foreign Secretary, that the estimated total number of natives killed during the disturbances was 'under 1000'. (Public Records Office: fo 371/ 3716/24930/68444).

It was, in fact, the basis for the report which he later submitted to the
Milner Commission. He headed it: ANARCHY AND SHAME.

Meidan el-Azhar, No. 11
Dear Dougal,   *Bab el-Luk, Cairo May Day, 1919*

For nearly twenty years now, I have been sending home scraps of
information about the East; and I suppose I ought not to be silent on the
recent events in Egypt, though it is as depressing to write about those
days of shame, as it will be for you to read the unpleasant facts.

I do not know what damned political game may supply a key of sorts to
this interregnum of impotence. Politics is a form of immorality, from
which, thank God, I have kept clean. I assume, however, that as
Roosevelt[1] put it: 'As long as we are in Egypt, we are here to govern it;
otherwise we should clear out'. At present we are doing neither.

That there should have been some unrest was inevitable, Germano-
Turkish plots dating from the beginning of the war, or earlier, had been
put aside, from time to time, and had to be let off like old fireworks, even
when the occasion for which they had been prepared had been lost. But
they might and should have fizzled out harmlessly. The propaganda of
lies, emanating from high places, was as marvellous as the credulity of
the ignorant masses; and these, forgetful of great benefits, were mindful
of little grievances. The work of the propagandists was paved to a great
extent, and rendered more easy, by the arrogance of too many Anglo-
Egyptian officials, the laxity with which we allowed unscrupulous
natives to abuse their powers of recruiting during the war, and foremost I
think among other causes – our miserable kill-joy policy, which has
interfered with innocent picturesque ancient native customs, which has
spoilt the merry Feast meetings (Moulids) for local saints, suppressed
snake charmers, acrobats, wandering conjurors, and suchlike Eastern
accessories, which lend colour and charm to native life, and had made it
an offence to sing at weddings, to weep at funerals, and to dance in native
style at theatres, which has closed bars and cafés at absurdly early hours,
and generally hustled the easy-going and good-tempered native, until he
has become irritated and worried.

Then the refusal to let Zaghlul and party go to Europe, and their
arrest for sedition at the beginning of March – whether justified or not –
formed the immediate pretext for anti-British demonstrations, which
began on 9.3.19 by a rowdy group of students smashing up trains and
lamps.

On 10.3.19 a rowdy mob looted the shops in the Muski, and played the
fool generally. They passed the Governorate, and commenced to smash
the windows there also and I had a lot of fun with Russell Bey, the

[1] Ex-President Theodore Roosevelt, visiting Egypt in 1910, had advised the British: 'Govern – or
get out'.

A political demonstration in Cairo

Commandant of Police and my Assistant Dykes chasing them at the head of bodies of Police troops and men of the guard Company.

We broke a good many heads, and made several arrests, but the mob would never stand, however big numerically, or however big their talk and their sticks and clubs; but their running away pace was really fine.

The show was repeated in the evening, many of the rioters taking refuge in the mosques if pursued.

A brick either from within a mosque, or from a group on the steps struck me without hurting much on the back of the neck, and on turning I just saved my face from another at the expense of my wrist watch.

Many trams had been stopped and damaged in the past couple of days, so I put Secret Agents on the main Depots, and on the Electric Power Station, and applied to the Military authorities for armed guards, at these places, which were granted, none too soon, for on 13.3.19, the big tram depot at Shubra was attacked, and the crowd only beaten off when two or three had been shot.

That day, Thursday, I had a good deal of fun; an imposing procession mainly of Azhar[1] Sheikhs was making for the Citadel Square to demonstrate, but we got a strong body of police on their flanks, and without interfering with the form of the procession, its course was altered, so that they marched into the parade ground of the Governorate. It was difficult to make them realise that they were all prisoners, especially the Standard bearer, who marched proudly into the Spider's parlour, waving an immense banner with the legend:

[1] El-Azhar, the ancient mosque-university in Cairo, the pre-eminent Islamic institution for the study of the religion and religious law. It was a centre of nationalist theory and activism.

Students of el-Azhar
Live FREE Egypt
Down with the Tyrants

As a result of this and other captures, we were full up by the evening;
so the Leaders were sent to the Citadel to be dealt with by the military,
the youngsters summarily caned on the orthodox surface, and the rest
kicked out.

From about 6 p.m. wearing a tarboosh, I sauntered about in the
neighbourhood of the great mosques of Sidna Hussein and el-Azhar. At
the former, groups were openly discussing all sorts of seditious schemes,
and a café I entered in front of the mosque was full of plotters, many of
whose faces were familiar as Government officials, discharged political
prisoners, etc.

Though apparently not recognised I got so many black and suspicious
looks, that I moved on to el-Azhar, where there was less light. I could not
get at the door for the multitude of Sheikhs and others in the open space
in front. One Sheikh of el-Azhar was haranguing an audience of many
hundreds from the top of a pile of stones, telling them that they must
scorn death itself in their efforts to destroy the tyrant, and throw off his
yoke, and promising Paradise to 'Martyrs' in the holy cause. I asked his
name and was told Fath'Allah. In scattered smaller groups money was
being handed over by the Central Revolutionary Committee to stir up
risings in the Provinces, and to cut railways and other communications.
A certain Abu el-Magd (an engineer) was in Cairo from Mit-Qamr in
order to receive funds for cutting the line in that district, and I had
received a report to that effect from a Special Agent in the morning and
had duly handed it in, and now I was getting confirmation of this. I
spotted the very Agent in the crowd looking at me with horror, and
signalling furtively to me to retire.

This I did, and none too soon, as I ascertained afterwards.

Sheikh Fath'Allah's discourse bore fruit the next morning, 14.3.19,
when his audience, excited to such a point that their natural cowardice
was overcome, attacked a patrol in the Muski, firing revolvers into an
armoured car, and attacking it with sticks and stones and smashing and
looting houses and shops. They only desisted when forty of them had
been laid out, twelve of them stone dead.

15.3.19: The ESR (Egyptian State Railway) was on partial strike,
dislocating the train service; and as days went on, riots and murders
increased in Cairo, and sinister rumours came in from the provinces.

Denunciations, mostly anonymous, reached me in shoals, and appeals
for help came in constantly by telephone, or by letter, or by word of
mouth.

16.3.19: An English Bimbashi of Police telephoned to say that he and
his force had been overpowered by rioters at Bulac, and that he had

narrowly escaped, and had taken refuge at the '*Assistance Publique*'. I instantly sent mounted troops who relieved him and scattered the mob, but not before several had been killed.

20.3.19: Hardie of the Ministry of Education came to help me, and stuck pretty much at the telephone whilst I promulgated sentences on students and other rioters. He did not however limit himself to work in the office. He came with me on several outside stunts.

The first of these was the capture of the King of Berberin[1] on 22.3.19 which paralysed a number of Societies, of considerable potential danger, and rendered thousands of domestic servants innocuous.

It was they in 1882 who cut more throats than all the Egyptians. It was a Berberin servant, too, who recently let two others in to murder Mr Davies and his wife, and who succeeded with the first and very nearly with the second, and who has now been sentenced to penal servitude for life.

Then the next day 23.3.19 Hardie's useful voluntary services nearly came to an untimely end. He and I, with Constable Marc of the Secret Police, raided the house of a certain Yussef Abd el-Ghaffar, thinking we might find a few seditious circulars; instead of which we found many hundreds, and Yussef's fellow conspirators, and had in fact got into the lion's lair. (I wrote to one of the brothers telling how we were besieged, and how I had to leave poor Hardie, and Marc to barricade themselves in with the prisoners, and hold the fort, till I got armed forces to their relief. Had I not succeeded in fighting out and through a murderous but cowardly crowd, and had not the Commandant with a force, and a lorry of British troops come quickly to my call, there would have been little left of Hardie.) It is satisfactory to know that Abd el-Ghaffar was sentenced by Court Martial to a long period of penal servitude, seventeen years, I think.

The remainder of the month was full of murders and plots to murder. Mr Walter Davies' murder was followed by that of his next neighbour Dany Bresson, and I got wind of a plot to slaughter Russell Bey, the Commandant of Police, and had a good deal of work to prevent it, and one of my special agents, being suspected to be in my pay, was horribly injured; and meanwhile the Provinces were all ablaze, as in India at the time of the Mutiny. You probably read in the papers of the murder and mutilation of a number of British officers in the Luxor train, and many similar cases.

Now comes the great crime of the civil authorities, to which, I think most subsequent evils have been due:

In the face of strongly worded Proclamations, that any inciting to strikes would be severely punished, the heads of Departments allowed Members of the Society of the Black Hand, and emissaries of the

[1] Berberins: people from Berber, in the Sudan; thousands of them were servants in Cairo. The "king" seems to have been Head of their professional Association.

Revolutionary party of el-Azhar to go round the Government employees, and threaten them with death if they did not sign a promise to go out on a three days' strike, 3–5 April, as a 'protest'.

I had been granted a special fund, to pay extra agents, to look for and arrest anyone advising strikes, or especially those tampering in any way with Government employees; and yet this daylight intimidation, and barefaced insubordination, was connived at by Englishmen, in nearly every Ministry and Department – miserable old women, most of them – good for little but cackling and tippling at the Club, who by their arrogant attitude towards the Natives in the past, their general ignorance and impotence, have done much to bring Egypt into this shameful impasse, and are not likely to do much to get it out of the mess – gutless and invertebrate!

Another insane act of the Civil Authorities (sic) was to beg the Military not to put a guard on the square in front of Abdin Palace, as it would look as if we doubted the loyalty of the Sultanian guard, on duty there.

The strike of Government employees, including some of our own Staff who were allowed to go unpunished – this 'Peaceful Protest' – commenced on 3.3.19, and one of the earliest incidents was the murder of my Assistant, a splendid fellow named Dykes, deliberately shot in the back at short range, by a soldier of this trusted guard, who did the deed with impunity. Men and boys ran up and danced in his blood, shouting ALLAH, ALLAH, and then women came and publicly emptied their bladders in the blood of this unfortunate Englishman; and this went on for days, until the blood was stamped in and washed away, and that under the eyes and auspices of the Sultanian guard, but this and other riots and murders failed to rouse the British Lion. I think I wrote to Cam. on the subject of Dykes' murder.

Another incident of the day was an attack on the Muski Caracol by the mob again, and the British guard had to open fire and kill a few of the attackers.

In these days, Clubs like the 'Black Hand', and the 'Red Eye', which were engineered mainly from el-Azhar, levied blackmail, garrotted, robbed and slaughtered, and committed every imaginable crime themselves and coerced others into doing the same.

We caught one youth of about sixteen with a book of receipt forms, drawing sums of £50 and so from shopkeepers, giving them a receipt in the name of the 'Black Hand', and a sort of Passover badge to exempt them from the 'coming massacre', if, in addition to paying, they obeyed orders. In another letter, I have attached a letter, of the 'Red Eye', or rather a copy of it, blackmailing a Jew, and an account of the action taken.

The humiliation of these days was bad enough; clerks and officials turning up if and as they liked, even here at the Governorate, which

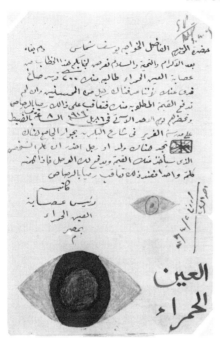

Mr. Yusuf Shammas

Greetings. This letter to you is from the Red Eye group which wants you to pay the sum of 200 piastres as a ransom as we know that you are a generous person. If you do not pay this sum you will be punished by being shot. Bring this sum next Sunday, 16 April 1919 at 8 pm to Friar's school in BAKRI Street near the mosque, where you will see a youth or man. Beware of speaking or saying anything to the person who will receive from you this sum and who will hand you a receipt. If you say just one word to him you will be shot.

The Leader of the
Red Eye Group in Egypt

M.

The 'Red Eye' blackmail letter

ought to be the centre of discipline; and weaklings like A (my acting Chief) put up with it and were alarmed and annoyed when I, for instance, proposed punishing; but the shame awaiting us was beyond all anticipation.

Zaghlul and certain other natives who had risen into prominence on account of their extreme views, and who had not been accepted by the British Government as representatives of the Nation, and who had been arrested for open sedition and sent to Malta, and whom Curzon and others in Parliament had openly condemned and repudiated, had become the idols of a fickle and most ignorant mob, which demanded their release and that they should be the representatives of Egypt at the Peace Conference.

Allenby whose coming, so ardently and hopefully anticipated, had been a bitter disappointment and a failure from the first, undoing much good work which Bulfin [the army commander in Egypt] was achieving, had the inspiration of a madman, and in opposition to his own advisors at the Residency, who were weak enough to agree with him in most things, and in violation of the basic laws of government, and of common sanity, decided as a sop to Cerberus to pay the blackmail demanded and set up Zaghlul and their other false Gods on a pedestal, in opposition to solemn declarations of our statesmen and his own proclamations; so on 7.4.18, the proclamations re these heroes were annulled and an announcement posted up that Zaghlul and Co. were to be released and allowed to proceed to Paris.

I suppose, and am assured by some of themselves, that there was not an Egyptian who attributed this concession to kindness or magnanimity on the part of the British: in it they saw nothing but fear on the English side and strength on their own, and the direct satisfactory reward for their policy of sabotage, truculence and violence; and the contempt that had been growing since the evil day when Bulfin handed over rose to such supreme degree that they did not even want to hurt us for the moment. Their leaders openly shouted, – 'It is a noble trait in the victorious to treat a fallen helpless enemy with mildness so long as he keeps in his place.'

Up to then I had taken my risk and returned alone each day to my quarters, without availing myself of an armoured car, or any sort of guard, but I could not stand the patronising contempt of the rabble, so returned for the first time in an army lorry. The supercilious applause of fools at our folly was worse than bullets...

Banners were displayed everywhere, mostly Turkish, on balconies and housetops, the roofs of trams, and on cars, and in the hands of howling lunatics in the streets, women emancipated for the occasion making stump orations, children and rapscallions of all sorts shouting ribald doggerels in contempt of the fallen tyrants and in the reception porch of the official palace where we are supposed to shield the dignity and honour of the Sultan whom we have set up, were representatives of every crime and vice that the East knows, in brazen naked effrontery, exacting the salutations of the palace chamberlains and officers.

My first act was to put up a mourning card in my office as under:–

IN MEMORY
of BRITISH PRESTIGE
in EGYPT

Died Apr. 7/1919 (Octave of ALL FOOLS)

That day my acting Chief complacently remarked to me, 'Look how friendly the people are, and how joyous.' 'Yes,' I replied, 'at the expense of our honour and prestige.' Then he added, 'How do you feel about it then?' I replied, 'I feel that I envy Dykes.'

The next day, 8.4.19, the mob were allowed to become still further drunk with mad excitement, but naturally the pseudo good-tempered stage wore off, and they began to show their teeth, and showed signs of a desire to commence the extermination of the English which they half-jestingly boasted about the night before.

In the afternoon amongst other acts of fanaticism and violence, they attacked a British officer outside the Continental Hotel, and left him for dead; and a little later, in Abdin Square, under the aegis of the Sultan's guard, still implicitly trusted, several unarmed English Tommies were sacrificed to the rabble in the most brutal and disgusting manner, and after their blood and bodies had been defiled by the women and others, in the same foul way as the remains of Dykes, a Pasha of eminence in the Egyptian Army and in the Sultan's household made a harangue praising the people for their glorious deeds, and advocating a complete and general massacre.

When on the 7th Allenby made the great renunciation of his country's pledged word and honour, I was not surprised at A's [the Acting Chief] attitude, but was amazed to find that my colleague, Bimbashi Ablitt, who had brains, and several others whom I previously credited with a little, actually profess to think that treating our own high decisions as scraps of paper was going to pacify the malcontents, and was a legitimate and real solution to the situation.

If their optimism survived thirty-six hours, I should be surprised, but the eyes of the blindest must soon have been opened, for by the morning of 9 April the lawlessness and anarchy had developed into a complete reign of terror.

My office was besieged with refugees, many bleeding and with clothes rent, bewailing that their houses had been looted, their friends murdered, and that Greeks and Armenians were openly being slaughtered in the main streets.

One very reliable informant Victor Y, a Greek of position, came to complain that some Armenians, whose blood the mob was after having taken refuge in his Baker's shop, the mob had broken in and tortured the fugitives to death, whilst meanwhile our police on that beat had looted the shop, one carrying off a sack of flour whilst the other interested himself at the 'till'.

Agents also came in to report, with every look of terror on their faces, to tell of horrors, and how barricades were being put up all over the city, roads and trams taken up or destroyed to prevent the passage of military cars, and courts and lanes sealed so as to ensure the massacre of the inhabitants, and the pillage of their goods without interruption.

Hardie was hearing similar accounts on the telephone all the time, amongst these a message from a special Syrian agent of mine, Iskandar F_____, whom luckily I had armed, that he had rescued a British soldier from the mob before he was quite finished, by dragging him into the house of a black man. Of course a rescue party was sent and, marvellous to tell, found the soldier still alive, but the poor blackie beaten to death. Several Indian soldiers were found mangled and dead near the same spot.

Then messages came that telegraph and telephone wires were being cut, and communications generally destroyed; and utterly fed up and disgusted Hardie and I invaded the Commandant's office and said strong things about fools who fiddled whilst Rome was burning, and about being ashamed to be Englishmen these times.

The Acting Commandant (for Russell Bey was not there) seemed pretty worried himself especially as he had just discovered that his telephone had been cut, and turning on us savagely said, 'It's no good cursing me, go and talk to Allenby.' So we decided to go to the chief fiddler without delay, but just as we were starting out, a message came from HQ that strong action was to be taken.

In effect I was allowed to go out with a young officer and a few troops, and hardly half a dozen shots had been fired up Muhammad Aly Boulevard, before it was entirely cleared of the thousands of barricade builders; and not only that but the repercussion of those few shots calmed for the time the whole of Cairo, showing, if so well-known a fact requires demonstrating, how the smallest display of firmness quiets this most docile of peoples.

Anyone still in the streets was commandeered to pull down the barricades, and many beys and people of position did their first bit of useful work, to their own intense disgust, and the immense delight of their friends who chaffed them afterwards unmercifully.

Riots the two next days 11 and 12 April culminated on the 13th in a state of things almost as bad as that of the 9th.

I was reminded that it was Palm Sunday, by gangs of blasphemous little youngsters and older canaille rushing about with boughs of the young trees recently planted in the capital, and now almost destroyed. As a matter of fact I did get to the 10 o'clock mass, and though late for the distribution, begged a fragment of Palm from one of the congregation but I was occupied nearly the whole time watching some suspicious-looking Azharists...

Perhaps the most depressing feature of those days was the number of callers of allied nationalities, and of Coptic Prelates, who came to ask why in the name of heaven did we allow such abominable anarchy. 'Did not the British Protectorate extend to friendly Powers and Christians, or only as it seemed to Moslem Revolutionaries?' I had no reply for them.

The rest of the month is one depressing record of disorder and of strikes; pupils, tram employees, printers etc., and even the little road sweepers, who flung down their brooms and played all day long at boarding trams en masse, looting on an apprentice scale, and insulting Tommies, and verily it was better that a millstone should be hung about a man's neck than he should touch one of those little ones. In the evenings they assembled at Khazindar, to receive more than their normal wages from an Azhar representative...

Respectable shopkeepers were blacklisted by the Azharists, and a boycott ordered, and had to close their shops summarily on the orders of the Azhar 'Police', or be attacked and their premises looted if they did not obey and often when they did.

Enormous refugee camps were established, particularly for Armenians, and there was a crowded camp at Bulac for British Refugees. The Sultanian Guard was kept at Abdin, to the exclusion of the British troops, and all loyal and neutral souls abandoned their homes there, or remained in terror of and at the risk of their lives.

I left office work almost entirely to Hardie and Archer and Ablitt, as there was so much to do outside, suppressing riots with the troops, searching houses for bombs, arms and seditious matter; rounding up cafés and restaurants, and after establishing a cordon, searching all present; and frequently I got out of uniform, and into all manner of disguises, and mooned about the mosques and other centres of sedition and in the cafés and native theatres, and as some set-off to the depressing conditions, enjoyed many amusing and exciting incidents. . . . After leaving the Police Station quarters, I took a pretty old-fashioned little flat, in the Bab el-Luk district, and am just concluding this dismal letter in the little garden with Yamani doves making friends, and little birds chirruping round, and palms, oleanders, and orange trees in bloom, all around me – with however a loaded revolver within reach, and a loaded rifle, and good old sword not far off.

Hoping your political conditions at home are better than ours, and with love to all,

Yours,
JOE

When he had the opportunity, he added postscripts to this letter.

Now and again I had a joy ride in front of a lorry or on an armoured car, to break up a dangerous demonstration, my special job being to read the 'Riot Act', as it were, and give the mob a chance of dispersing before we fired. One example, in some detail will suffice. 3.5.19, Secret agents reported to me a monster procession, coming from El-Azhar down the Nahasin towards Mohammed Ali Square. The riotous units had been organised and to some extent armed within the University Mosque, at leisure and with impunity, for that master jackass Allenby still upholds the fiction of its inviolability and sanctity, in spite not merely of my protests, and common sense, but against the urgent prayers of the better-minded sheikhs of the University. In a few minutes I was sitting in front of a lorry of troops, with a young British officer, and proceeding very slowly along the Nahasin to meet the rioters, and another lorry was unobtrusively following them, whilst all side streets were barred by troops. The Azhar leaders had invited Italian and French sympathisers to head the procession, as they said, 'Allenby's soldiers would never fire on Europeans', but these foreign gentlemen preferred to give moral support only within the sacred walls. So when at last we were confronted by the mob, we were disappointed: only a very eminent and well-robed sheikh at their head, swinging a silver cane.

Warned by the murder of my Assistant, Dykes, the shooting of Col. Hazel when he rose to address a mob and similar incidents, I never commenced to harangue, until I had a leader by the scruff of the neck and my revolver against his cheek, or some similar precaution taken. On this occasion I ordered two Tommies to pin the magnificent sheikh gently between their bayonets in full view of his followers, and keep him thus as hostage. I then explained to him and all concerned, that he was a rottenly inadequate hostage, but might do to go on with, and that the smallest aggression against me or any of my party would instantly bring the bayonets together in his vitals. I then made my stock remarks: that they were behaving illegally and foolishly and against the Proclamations, and had been misled by crafty rascals for their own ends, not for their good or that of Egypt, and that I had orders to shoot them down as riotous rebels injurious to their country and the public peace, but that I was their friend and advised them to behave like sheikhs of learning and piety, and go quietly to their homes at once, and to remember in the future that the British were the best friends they had, the British who had made their country rich and upraised their poor, the British who had saved them from the Sudanese when they would have driven them into the sea, and more recently had saved them from the Turks who intended to pillage Cairo, rape their wives and children, and cut their throats, and who were now trying to save them from their worst enemies, their crafty lying leaders and their foolish selves; that, finally, I ordered them in the name of the Army, the Government and the Police to disperse, that I would give them two minutes to obey or disobey, but that on the 120th second I should certainly obey my orders to fire, if mad folly still blinded their judgment. Then holding up my watch, I said in the loudest voice, 'You have one and a half minutes, one minute, half minute, quarter minute, troops prepare to fire (this in English, Arabic and Turkish), five seconds, two seconds, one second. Troops Fire; Advance lorry.'

McPherson added that only this first volley over the heads of the marchers was necessary, since they broke and rushed down the side ways, harried by the police and troops; some, however, were injured by the advancing lorry.

Operating at this level, McPherson had little knowledge of higher policy. He would not have appreciated Allenby's conviction that it was impossible to hold down Egypt by force. Nor was he a political tactician. In his advocacy for 'cleaning out' el-Azhar, he was obviously unaware that his admired Chief, Russell Pasha, had specifically advised Allenby against

To Celebrate His Majesty's Birthday.

His Excellency
The High Commissioner and the Viscountess Allenby

request the honour of

Mr. J. W. Mac Pherson's   Company

at the Residency on June 3rd, 1920, at 9-30 p.m.

Evening Dress with Decorations.

R.S.V.P. to the
Aide de-Camp.

Mr. J. W. Mac Pherson

PLEASE BRING THIS CARD WITH YOU.

No damn fear!

Above: Lord Allenby, British High Commissioner from 1919 to 1925, in
the Residency, Cairo, with his Egyptian attendant, Mohamed. Allenby
forced the British government to grant a (qualified) independence to Egypt.
Below: An invitation to one of Allenby's receptions, and McPherson's
reaction: 'No damn fear'

this, on the grounds that it would mean 8000 more demonstrators on the streets of Cairo.

McPherson's main perception was that the world had been turned upside down; one of the few fixed points was the steadfastness of Gad el-Moula, who was still with him, serving as an askari.

Gad was cursed and beaten, tempted with bribes, threatened with death, forced into a difficult and double game at the expense of his co-religionists and compatriots; but I do not believe ever wavered.

On 3 April, when my assistant Dykes 'Asst. Mamur Zapt' was murdered openly in broad daylight, with perfect impunity, the rumour went round, that it was I, Mamur Zapt, who had been slaughtered, and when I turned in for lunch, for the first time on record, there was none ready, and Gad almost in a state of collapse. He was overjoyed to see me alive, but he soon began groaning with a doleful face, as he was sure that my turn was only delayed. He screened and barricaded the windows and doors – not an unnecessary precaution as things turned out; put my table in the lee of the piano, and did his best to prevent me from going out.

I did so, however, that evening, and on returning at midnight, found him awake, another record – and in the night, thinking I heard a breathing outside my door, on going to look, I found Gad lying across it bristling with weapons, enough to arm a whole attacking party. Before I had gone out that evening he had served up an extravagant and recherché dinner, with the last of a bottle of green Chartreuse, exceeding precious. I knew what was in his mind – that it would be a pity to leave that for anyone else.

On 9 April, when the mob had cut communications, put up barricades everywhere, and were murdering and looting to their heart's content – and as the Sheikhs of el-Azhar put it – 'Allah had smitten the English Chiefs with impotence and imbecility', I saw from my window at the Governorate, a howling threatening mob approaching, with sticks and old weapons of any sort, and to my amazement in the thick of it, shouting the revolutionary war cries with the worst of them, and smashing glass and other property right and left, Gad, positively, Gad. Had our troops opened fire, and happened to shoot him, I should never have known what to make of it. As it was, a few minutes later, he appeared in my room, very dishevelled and rather bloody – and blurted out: 'Name of God, you shall not come without a strong guard of soldiers, you would be surely murdered; the streets are running with blood. They commandeered me to help build a barricade on my way here, and I only got off to warn you by swearing I was off to kill someone, and then I had to howl with the rest to avoid being suspected'.

'Yes, you scoundrel,' I said, 'I saw you breaking up the town, and heard you shouting. What were you saying?' 'Oh, nothing,' replied Gad, 'just the old whoops – "Down with the Sultan – Down with the Government –

In the Secret Service.

A wonderful Londoner over the week-end has been Colonel McPherson, who knows more about secret service work in Egypt than you or I. He told me a delicious story about his work in Cairo. It appears that just as he was sitting down to a midday meal one Sunday —a meal that had been prepared with great care by his wonderful Egyptian cook—a terrific disturbance arose outside. Leaving his meal, and going out to investigate, he found that a mob of Cairenes was maltreating some wretched Armenians. He took steps to rescue the victims from their persecutors and went back again. But there was a sequel.

Giving Notice.

That evening his cook, with tears in his eyes, gave notice. Naturally the cause was inquired, for nobody will let go, without a struggle, a chef de cuisine so artistic as Colonel McPherson's. The cook explained with dignified sorrow that he had no alternative but to leave the colonel's service. He had taken much pains and a long time to prepare a meal worthy of appreciation, but the colonel had chosen to disregard it in order to save the lives of a miserable Armenian or two. These artists! They are so temperamental!

A diary entry in a London newspaper, 1920

Death to the English Tyrants".' 'And', I added, 'I suppose you would have killed a few Greeks or Jews, rather than turn back.' 'Of course,' said Gad, with a grin, and a look of surprise at the simplicity of the question, 'I had to come and warn you somehow . . . .'

As head of the secret police, I was often glad to use Gad as secret agent in special cases, and generally with success. Dressed as a simple countryman, the part was so natural, and he looked so simple, that he was never suspected as being a police agent, and came off where my most finished sleuth-hounds had failed; and moreover he never accepted a bribe, as, unfortunately so many agents do, or if he did he brought it to me at once.

He smelt out, and put me on my guard against more than one neat little murder plot against myself. For instance, at one time there was a strong combination against me and it was important, but difficult to know the leaders. One morning my horse had been brought round, as usual by a soldier of the mounted troops. Gad took it over from him and awaited me at the door. There was a spot of dust on the saddle, so calling Gad a son of a dog, I put my whip across his shoulders; and rode off leaving him, to all appearance, very sullen and resentful. As I did so, I remarked a look of sinister satisfaction on a suspected face, and was not surprised to hear from Gad when next I saw him, that the owner of the face, deceived by the 'Camouflagellation' had at once approached Gad and said: 'Are you then so base as to allow him to beat and abuse you, when within ten days, there will not be an English dog alive in Egypt'. And on Gad professing great resentment at the treatment, the other added, 'Work in with us and you shall soon be avenged, and be well paid too by those who will be glad to reward you' – and so on, until Gad had obtained much of the information we wanted.

McPherson had made many enemies, and as time went on, threats against his life mounted. In a memorandum to Russell Pasha on 25 March 1920, he listed some of the reports from his informants.

24.2.20: Azhar *Fiqi* reported verbally and very secretly: 'indignation at el-Azhar against Bimbashi McPherson, Mamur Zapt, greatly revived lately on account chiefly of his raiding so many presses, and seizing so many circulars, and interfering with propaganda. They said he must be killed.'

25.2.20: A Copt . . . brought following report: 'I went since some days ago to Mosque El-Azhar, there I have heard that Mr McPherson, the Mamur Zapt, makes for getting out leads, guns and revolvers from houses of Egyptian men . . . also he does not give the newspaper to speak free . . . Thus they try now to kill him and they know that he goes at street of Gheit Edda riding a bicycle.'

26.2.20: Hussein K_____, Temporary Special Agent with me for arms cases reports: 'In a café last night I overhead Mohammed Sharaf plotting to murder the Mamur Zapt, Bimbashi McPherson, because he raided his house and seized papers. He is very murderous and has bad friends.'

26.2.20: Capt. Clayton reports: 'With regard to the verbal information I have given you of reports of threats against you . . . I send you this note . . . "A sheikh told me he had heard a student, seeing you pass, say to another 'Who is that?'; the other answered 'That is the Mamur Zapt, McPherson, we are going to attack him'".'

28.2.20: Special Police Agent Osman F_____ reports that the assassination of Mamur Zapt was advocated at the Club at 56 Gama el Qaid.

3.3.20: SPA Osman F_____ and etc., reported Sheikhs and others in Sharia Gheit el Edda whom they gathered to be an ambuscade for me. I posted agents near – armed – and passed the group in order to draw fire, but had no luck. I heard one say to the others '*Da Hoa* (that's he)'.

When, after two years, he was transferred to another post, he wrote:

I have bid anything but a reluctant farewell to the Governorate, and to my office of 'Chief Inquisitor', and it is well that I am out of it. I could not have gone on indefinitely. Plots against me were thickening, Plots, however, which were known ceased to have much importance. It was the chance of the existence of other more subtle hidden conspiracies: and not so much those 'Who will kill the body', as schemes to destroy my reputation, and position, and such would certainly have been devised, if more direct methods had failed for long – for here in Egypt a little money will procure any number of false witnesses, who will swear to any accusation in the most solemn and convincing manner.

In spite of the panache of his performance, McPherson was not one of nature's policemen, and had been deeply stressed by his two years as

Mamur Zapt. The 'vision of crime and corruption' had shocked him; the compromises and obliquities essential in managing Britain's ambiguous role in Egypt grated on him. Hence, perhaps, his scorn of colleagues who seemed to him to lack zeal and energy. As well, his temperamental need for periods of solitude and reflection, so evident in his pre-war life, was totally at odds with the unremitting strain and labours of his job. Russell Pasha valued his services (he later recalled him for further duties) and on occasion wrote him a soothing letter, but he probably decided that it was time to give McPherson a rest from the 'front line' of Cairo. Perhaps he had noted a sentence in one of McPherson's last reports to him, about the multiple calls – political and criminal – on his attention:

I often feel as I did in Gallipoli when there were so many desperate cases to be passed up to the skilled surgeons that I was in despair to know which most needed any field dressings.

McPherson's reactions to Egyptian nationalism before the war had already shown that, for all his rapport with Egyptians, he was politically a conventional Victorian imperialist, in so far as he gave much thought to the matter. As Mamur Zapt, he had been forced to act on his convictions. Some years later, in happy retirement in Egypt, he wrote an article setting out his ideas on Egyptian nationalism. It is a credo of classic paternalism, which explains much of his bewildered rage at the events of 1919.

Egyptian acquaintances have often said to me: 'How is it that you, our Friend, almost an Egyptian in many ways, would hesitate to give us complete independence?' 'Because', I reply, 'I love you too well to give you what would harm you, on the same principle that I should hesitate to lend you my sailing boat, without someone on board to manage her, lest you should come to grief.'

Egypt is as much the land of paradox today as it was in the days of Herodotus. This is most unhappily true in the realm of politics, where Independence of Egypt means servitude for the Fellah. Lovers of liberty and of Egypt should pause before they, in the pursuance of their ideals, help to thrust back these worthy people into the abyss of oppression and misery, in which they agonised for some six thousand years, until by the instrumentality of our country they were raised to their place in the sun.

Next to Father Nile, it is the Fellah who matters. He is to all intents and purposes voiceless in the Nation, and there are many in the noisy minority who would fain batten on him again as in the past. By such he has been misled, and at times even excited to compromising action, but there is something pyramidal in his solidity and simplicity of character, and happily he still remains what he has been through the ages. His ideals are perhaps not high, but they are natural and peace-loving; he loves to employ his wonderful physical strength in tilling the land, and is contented if he may keep a modest share of what he produces for his own simple needs: a share sufficient to enable him to marry, to keep up a mud hut for his family and domestic animals, and to supply himself and them with food; and he likes after working from dawn till sundown, a little leisure for his evening prayers and his evening meal, and to linger in a café, and listen to some raconteur, or a few musicians. Almost above all he loves to talk...

It is difficult to realise that before we entered into their lives, these admirable beings had never known social liberty. Through the ages they had exchanged one servitude for another: in recent historical times the oppression of the Mamelukes for the tyranny of the Pashas, and the extortion of the otherwise unpaid officials. Fifty years ago they were compelled to work in '*corvées*' for the government, naked under the lash, without pay and without rations; and it is impossible to overestimate the good done by early British officials in conjunction with a few of the most enlightened and humane natives, in abolishing the *corvée*, and in obtaining for them some tenure of security for their lowly persons, and their modest possessions and earnings.

McPherson could not know that, at the time he wrote this, the ultimate liberator of the fellahin from feudalism was already developing political consciousness. Gamal Abdul Nasser, as President of Egypt, recalled:

'When I was a little child every time I saw aeroplanes flying overhead I used to shout: "O Almighty God, may disaster take the English!" Later I came to know that that phrase had come down to us from the days of the Mamelukes. Our forebears of that day had not used it against the English, but they used a similar one against the Turk: "O God, the Self-Revealing! Annihilate the Turk!" My use of it was but an adaptation of an old form to express a new feeling. The underlying constant continued the same, never changing. Only the name of the oppressor was different.'

15

Zzarr

The Ginn are said to be of pre-adamite origin, and, in their general properties, an intermediate class of beings between angels and men, but inferior in dignity to both, created of fire, and capable of assuming the forms and material fabric of men, brutes and monsters, and of becoming invisible at pleasure.

E. W. LANE: *Modern Egyptians*, 1836

Throughout his 45 years in Egypt, Joseph McPherson was intensely interested in traditional rituals and ceremonies, and in spite of his many cares as Mamur Zapt, he maintained his interest. In fact, he was not averse to using the powers of his office to fathom the deeper Egyptian mysteries.

To Brenda   *Cairo, 1920*

Most visitors to Egypt, or residents who have explored the outlying native quarters, will have heard women's voices raised in bacchanalian chorus, and will have been informed by their guide or donkey boy, or people in the vicinity, that a Zzarr, or casting out of devils from some woman or girl, is proceeding.

They will have received little information on the ceremony, except that certain animals are sacrificed by an Aalima, or witch, in the presence of the patient and certain initiated women.

At least that was my experience, and reference to Egyptian friends, communicative on most topics, and to European authorities on Eastern customs elicited little more; then I turned to Lane's *Modern Egyptians*[1], which had never before failed me, but this time it was silent.

A surreptitious peep which I contrived to get at a Zzarr at the village of Zenin, where I saw wild looking women dabbling their hands in blood rendered me more *intrigué* than ever, so that when my official position gave me the right to enter any house, or inspect any assembly that might possibly have political or criminal objects, I resolved for once to push my authority to its limit if I were lucky to get wind of a Zzarr in time.

Consequently, when in February of this year, 1920, one of my secret

[1] *Modern Egyptians* E. W. Lane, pub. Charles Knight & Co. 1836.

agents reported that a Zzarr was in progress on the outskirts of Cairo, I lost no time in making for the scene.

In the dark, Osman, the agent, was not too clear of the route through the devious complicated streets, so we approached from the mountainous rubbish heaps, which divide the Gamalia district from the tombs of the Khalifes. It was easy to locate a patch of brilliant light, and guided by it, we soon reached a once pretentious mansion, now most decrepit, and passing through the riven walls, and over crumbling debris, we reached a door closed on the other side by a wooden bolt.

Through a gaping crack, we saw a number of men drinking coffee in an outer court, and we both recognised the host as a certain Mustafa, who had once brought me some useful information about a gang of army thieves, and whose life had been attempted in consequence.

On my ordering him to open the door, he did so at once, but implored me not to introduce the troops which he thought were doubtless behind me.

I thereupon gave bogus orders to an imaginary body of men, to retire a hundred and fifty paces, and await a signal, and without waiting for any explanation, crossed instantly to an inner court, full of girls and very young boys, and beheld on one side of this court an inner chamber, through the windows and doors of which came a flood of light and sound.

The indignant eyes of a figure, clad seemingly in a white shroud, met mine: a cry which was at once a shriek of dismay and a command, was uttered, and in an instant all was dark.

I thought with some trepidation of Tam O'Shanter and Meg wi' the cutty sark, but stood my ground.

It was a case of eclipse rather than total obscurity. The door had been almost slammed to, but there being neither shutters nor blinds to the windows, a number of women assisting at the rite, had sprung on the ledges, and formed a living screen, and from over their heads poured the light of sixty-six candles, as I afterwards learned.

My moment's glance had revealed more than the shrouded witch. I had seen some fifteen or twenty women, many with tambourines above their heads, circulating in a weird dance around some object erected in the centre.

The male guests were now crowded in the doorway which communicated between the outer and inner courts, and Osman discreetly with them; Mustafa had advanced a little into the inner court, asserting with solemn oaths, that what was proceeding was of a most innocent and religious nature, and beseeching me to depart out of their coasts.

Assuming all the severity I could muster, I said: 'For myself, Mustafa, knowing your good character, I am convinced that all is as innocent as you declare, but you have put yourselves under suspicion, by convening such an assembly in these times of disorder and sedition, without first obtaining the consent of the authorities, and now the best course of all, is that I should remain, and bear witness in my report that there has been no intention to contravene the laws and proclamations. Bring me a chair at once, and I will stay in the inner court, and undertake not to enter the ritual chamber.'

'But, Excellence,' said Mustafa, greatly perturbed, 'no man may behold these sacred offices, not even I may remain. This is a Zzarr. My sister Munira, whom you have seen, for once you condescended to notify her of my being wounded when those sons of dogs shot me, has for sometime been ridden by a child of *Eblis*, yea, perchance, by many devils; and the Aalima who is possessed of a Sheikh's spirit, and endowed with the gifts of prophecy and clairvoyance, is convinced that she can free Munira's poor body of these evil tenants. Oh my Lord, we implore thee to allow the rites to proceed.'

'Certainly,' I rejoined, 'that is my wish, and if it is not right as you affirm, that I should behold the rites, place my chair if you will with its back to the windows, but go I shall not, unless accompanied by you, the Aalima, and all concerned, all under arrest.' And pulling out my whistle, I made as though I would blow it.

'Stop, stop,' cried Mustafa, 'I will consult the Aalima: if she will but consent,' and the Aalima emerging, some angry words passed between her and Mustafa. Then she stood before me, like a Medusa who would turn me to stone by her glance.

My idea of a witch had been something 'wrinkled, sand-blind, toothless, and deformed,' with nut-cracker jaws, clad in foul tatters and a pointed hat, or a mutch and riding a broomstick, but this presiding genius was young, and of a singular, classic, though hard and repelling beauty, and of remarkable dignity.

My surprise elicited a genuine exclamation of admiration:'*Maa sha Allah*' (what marvels God has willed), I exclaimed, and the look of fury and antagonism faded somewhat from the witch's face, for after all she was human and a woman; and almost a smile flickered over her chiselled, marble-like features.

Of course I followed up my advantage with all the blarney I could attain to, mingled with pious citations from the Koran, intended mainly for the sheikhs in the doorway, and with many platitudes and Platonisms. An unexpected ally burst on the scene from the inner chamber. It was Munira. She seized and kissed my hand, thanked me for avenging her brother on his would-be murderers, and turning to the witch, declared, that if I did not remain, she would not part with one of her devils, no, not for sixty Aalima.

She was savagely rebuked, slapped, and driven back to her corner within and the witch continued to raise objections, but in the end a chair was brought, placed in the position I had undertaken to occupy, and the prophetess retired to her disciples.

A few timbrel notes rose undecidedly, and died down to silence again, and I sat waiting in vain for the music and dancing which my coming had interrupted: the increased light indicated that the human barrage had taken itself down, but I dared not look round.

In truth there was much to console me for my reversed position, for the court was full of beautiful faces, on which the light fell: faces of maidens from about twelve to seventeen years, with a sprinkling of little lads, all cleanly and prettily dressed, most robed in keeping with the initiates within.

One shone out from her fellows, like the moon amongst the stars. She was dressed rather more elaborately than the rest, in Cleopatra mode, and carried herself like a queen, though acting as servitor for the others, bringing water to the door of the inner chamber, and offering it to the company outside. Her face in spite of big black eyes, and long dark lashes beamed fair in the light, and when she moved in the shadows, it seemed to glow of itself like the charcoal embers in the corner, on which a little boy was constantly brewing coffee.

There was a twinkle in her beautiful eyes, when occasionally they caught mine, as though intensely amused at my untoward irruption. In fact all my companions in the court seemed friendly disposed, in contrast to the sheikhs without who were obviously displeased.

After about ten minutes, occupied in admiring Cleopatra and her companions, the Aalima came out and told me she regretted it, but the women refused to proceed with the Zzarr, and had resolved on a silence strike.

I told her that I could not believe that her disciples had dared to disobey her orders, and trusted her to enforce them, but there was no hurry: that I was quite comfortable for an indefinite time. In point of fact I was little disturbed by the intelligence.

St John's account of 'silence in heaven for half an hour' has caused many to doubt his inspiration and veracity, or to suggest that the fair sex are excluded from the paradisal zone, so that I felt confident a score of unredeemed women would not be able to maintain a silence strike for very long.

And so it was, for the beating of cymbals, dubertas and timbrels was soon renewed, and a curious song arose, from a few throats at first, and then with great zest from all.

The singers and minstrels were apparently still sitting, for there was no sound of feet, nor any movement, and the words and the rites came all the clearer. It was nothing Koranic, Islamic or religious.

I had heard nothing like it previously in Egypt, and from the repeated reference to the sacrifice of a beautiful youth whose blood became a flower, I was reminded of the half mundane vision of Ezekiel in the Temple:

'Et ecce ibi mulieres sedebant plangentes ADONIDEM'.[1]

I feel sure that the Zzarr must be an imported institution, dating back to the Grecian mysteries, or to the cults of Baal and Tammuz.

Many Persian words were in this hymn, and in the refrain came the Greek word *ORKOS.*[2]

As excitement waxed higher, one by one, they rose to their feet, and the circular dance resumed.

The moon in her course peeped down on me, through the space where once had been a palace roof, and as imperceptibly as she turned round the heavens – and as surely, my chair revolved – until through the window I saw women, holding the ends of long plaits of hair, except those who held musical instruments, circling round what now I clearly recognised as an altar.

It bore its office lights, and a number of small candelabra, and near one end burnt a painted candle quite four feet long, suggestive of a Pastoral Taper.

Pyramids of white and red cakes, sweets, and wafers on the altar blended with flowers in these colours, and with little leaf baskets of nuts and fruit.

I had noticed when the Aalima first addressed me, that her shroud-like garb was in reality made up of vestments strangely sacerdotal in their form, alb, amice and girdle, and now I noticed that when engaged on altar ceremonies, she raised the amice, cowl-wise above her head, like a Capucine or Dominican monk. Her Deaconess too bore simple vestments, and a maniple, at once Grecian and sacerdotal in their form.

Success emboldened sin, and curiosity overcame caution, for I suppose I revolved faster than the moon, and several hecates gave warning of my perfidy by shrill cries of alarm, but my eyes closed instantly, and my head nodded listlessly, and the dance went on.

The afflatus was wafted to my company in the court: girls and boys a-dancing and a-spinning. Only Cleopatra pursued her functions of a female Ganymede, and I, hoping that I am typhoid proof by now, received many cups of dubious nectar at her hands, and chatted with her as I sipped, feigning a deep and recurring thirst. She proved a sceptic and a cynic, in a virginal sort of way: explained that Mustafa had been egged on to this expense by the Aalima, who not only received a very considerable fee from him, and half of the flesh of the immolated animals, but presents from most of those taking part, and that she had been supported by many of the others, who looked forward to a Zzarr for its excitement. She did not think Munira possessed more devils than some others present, and doubted the efficacy of the rites to exorcise them;

---

[1] 'Behold, there sat women weeping for Tammuz.' Ezekiel 8.14 A.V.

[2] Ὄρχος: the object by which one swears, an oath; also a divinity who punishes the false and perjured.

indeed she was of the opinion that most women had a few, even the Aalima, who professed to turn them out; that one indication of this was the mad lead the Aalima gave to the dancing, which she regarded as a mark of drunkenness or insanity.

How like Horace's Satire, I thought:

'Omnes insanire, etiam STOICOS ipsos, qui hoc dicunt.'[1]

and Cicero's dictum:

'Nemo fere saltat sobrius, nisi forte insanit.'[2]

When the orgy was at its height, there was, without apparent cause except exhaustion of the performers, a dramatic apotheosis; every sound was hushed, but the panting of women who had fallen, utterly spent, upon the floor; so to relieve the tension, I passed out to the outer yard, and asked to see the animals doomed to bleed at the altar, and enquired with some anxiety (for it was already past midnight) when the crowning rite was to take place.

'Normally,' I was told, 'the beasts were sacrificed two hours after midnight, but that it was allowable when midnight had passed, and might be expedited if the Excellence wished.'

Osman who looked very ill at ease, begged me to come away, and reminded me of the many fanatics in the district (for we were near el-Azhar), who were out for my blood, and the chance there was of some of the unfriendly sheikhs going to them to betray me; but I was bent on witnessing the sacrifice.

First they paraded before me a very beautiful young horned ram, covered completely with jet black curly locks, except for a white blaze (stained red now with Henna) between the horns. Mustafa told me the fabulous sum he had paid for this, and the long search before they had been able to find a ram with all the necessary markings. Then two white ganders were shown me, two red doves, and two rabbits.

An 'old mysterious man', whom they declared was more than a centenarian, with eyelids like scales, and on whom I looked at first with some misgivings, for he was sharpening a long knife on a little hone, was presently led by the deaconess to the altar, on which a very large basin was placed, and with considerable ceremony, the burning of incense, and chanting of incantations, the ram first, and then the other birds and beasts were immolated.

The blood all remained in the basin, and the witch, raising her amice, and receiving from a young woman acolyte, a sort of Humeral veil of white sheeny material, she thrust arms and hands into the blood, muttering as she mixed it. Then she signed herself with it on her robes, and the patient Munira on the face, and all the initiates marked

---

[1] 'All men are mad, even the Stoics themselves, who say so.'

[2] 'For almost no one dances when sober, unless perhaps he is mad.' (Cicero: Pro Murena 6.13)

themselves in turn. It seemed to have a magic effect, for their previous frenzy had been cold compared with the mad fury which now possessed them. Their hair was torn down by bloody fingers, and their gestures and cries were frantic. My companions caught the infection, and danced and howled as wildly as the initiates. Sometimes they bent their bodies back, till they formed a vibrating and writhing bow, resting on the ground by the heels and back of the head, whilst the muscles of their bodies carried on the dance with unbelievable contortions.

Only the Aalima showed some restraint, and Cleopatra refrained altogether and even took advantage of the intensely rapt condition of the others to give me scraps of information. The Aalima she informed me was not married, and did not wish to be, she was indifferent to men, except now and again, though she was never indifferent to their respect and admiration, she was intensely attached to some of her disciples, particularly the Deaconess, and the two young acolytes (I had already in my mind given these three the names of Gyrinna, Anactoria, and Atthis,[1] and that of Lesbia to the witch herself); on my asking Cleopatra if the initiates were all virgins, she replied elliptically: 'Virgins born, my Lord'.

I was distracted from the fascination of Cleopatra's conversation by observing that many of the women in their Bacchanalian frenzy were pulling from their bosoms, and holding carefully concealed in their hands as they danced, some little objects which I in vain tried to get an adequate glimpse of.

The words they had sung immediately after the sacrifice had been for the most part Koranic, or at least Islamic and of a religious nature, with invocations of the Prophet, Sidna Hassan, Sidna Hussein, the Hidden Imam, and Saida Zenab, but once more the words became erotic, and in keeping their dancing became indecent, and I was reminded of the scene in Petronius, where Encolpe and his friends trespassed in the Temple of Priapus, and stole a view of the sacred rites, and the dancing Priestesses:

'Bacchantium instar mulieres vidimus.'[2]

The thought filled me with misgivings. Perhaps the Aalima had a Tertian fever like Quartilla. Quite possibly these ladies like Petronius' heroines would lose all reason and control, if indeed they had any left, so I walked out to secure the moral and physical support of Osman. But Osman and most of the Sheikhs had disappeared.

It was unthinkable that the trusty Osman could have abandoned me, and whilst I was still wondering at his absence, he reappeared looking extremely scared.

'For God's sake come away,' he said. 'It is not these beldames I am

[1] Intimates of Sappho of Lesbos.

[2] 'We saw women looking like Bacchantes.' A scene referred to in Petronius's *Satyricon* (Penguin edn. Section 16).

afraid of though they are bad enough. Look at their mad antics and listen to their shrieking jargon' – and Osman stole a glance at the forbidden chamber without attracting their attention. 'But do you know where the Sheikhs are gone? Some are looking for our supposed military guard in the '*gabel*', to see if it really is there and of what strength. These I have followed; but the others I expect are gone to betray us to the Azharites. All is not well, I am certain from the angry altercations they have had with Mustafa, who I can see is greatly alarmed for your safety, and from the care they have taken that I should hear nothing.'

'But,' I protested, somewhat feebly, 'let us see the end.'

'The end!,' he exclaimed, 'The Zzarr lasts twenty-four hours, from sunset to sunset, and the feast is not till the afternoon. Come, come along, or there may be an end of us.'

'One moment then,' I said, and turned to say goodbye to Cleopatra, but she also had been caught up in the divine or infernal aura, and was dancing wildly, with strange ejaculations and contortions, that seemed scarcely human.

I could not find Mustafa, to say goodbye to him, and to thank him for the unique entertainment, and the scene was ear piercing, eye racking and brain bewildering, so we passed silently into the night, and skirting the desert by a devious route, we entered Cairo by Bab-Nasr and made for our homes.

The next morning but one following, at a very early hour, I was visited by two relatives of Mustafa – an old man and a little girl of about ten. They had brought greetings from my host, and a goose and some cakes and nuts, because as they said. 'I had not remained to the feast, and having seen the sacrifice, must partake of the meats' – so loading the old man with tobacco and the little maid with chocolates, and a pretty bottle of sweets of many colours for Munira, and greetings to Mustafa, and Cleopatra, and perfunctorily to the Aalima, I let them depart, and never heard if Munira was successfully released from the incubus of the children of Eblis.

16
Entr'acte

'I had a lot of fun.'
J. W. McP. in the Family Letters, frequently.

In August 1920, Joseph McPherson sailed for England on three months' leave. On the return journey he paused in Paris, where the Peace Conference was in session. Saad Zaghlul Pasha and his delegation were there on their fruitless mission. It is characteristic of McPherson that, as he relates in the following letter, he called on them at their hotel. Zaghlul's nationalist goals were anathema to him, but nevertheless he wished to pay his respects to his old chief at the Ministry of Education. It's equally characteristic that he says nothing about the delegation, but veers off onto some enjoyable Parisian hi-jinks.

Dear Ja   *On board the* Milano. *Off Candia. 9 December 1920*
It was about 4 a.m. when I turned in, but thanks to that inexplicable machine which winds us up, even when our clocks go wrong, I woke at the time I hoped, – 7 o'clock to the minute and duly caught the train to Newhaven, lunched on board, woke up at Dieppe and again at Paris.

Wortham[1] had kindly seen me off at Victoria, and intended joining me in Paris, if his duties on King Feisal's suite permitted: so I went to the Hotel he proposed using, the Oxford and Cambridge: quite against my principles, as it is one of Cook's hotels, which to me are all on the *Index Expurgatorius*.

They offered me a room at 23 francs, (exclusive of food, bath, and everything, all of which was proportionately dear,) and the stuffy little place was full of Americans, and no room to move, so the *lendemain* I repaired to my old pub, which you know in the *Boul. Mich.*, (No. 31, *Gd. Hot. de Suez*,), but it was absolutely *complet*.

That day passed in hunting for an old lady, Mme. Harispe, for whom I had been entrusted with little presents, and messages from Egypt. She had changed her address, and it was night before I hunted her down in the Rue Bouille, near the Bastille, and got quit of the commission I had rather rashly taken on.

The next and last day, Thursday, No. 25, I went in the morning to the

---

[1] H. E. Wortham (1884–1959): journalist; foreign correspondent in Egypt 1901–1919; tutor to King Fuad; attached to the suite of the newly-created King of Iraq for the Peace Conference; *Peterborough* in the *Daily Telegraph* 1934–1959; mentioned elsewhere by McPherson as a 'chum'.

McPherson with his great-nephew Kenn on the beach at Port Eynon,
Wales, 1920 'Home'

'Grand', on the hunt for Zaghlul's party. Harari Pasha[1] and some other
people I had met in Cairo were there, and I got fixed up, rather to my
regret, for dinner.

So after an early lunch at the Duval, which you know, near the statue
of St Jeanne d'Arc, cheap and good, as I have always found it during the
last thirty years, I walked in the blazing sun of a perfect summer-like day
through the gardens of the Tuileries and Champs Elysees, to the Bois de
Boulogne, hoping to find, or to get tidings of our old friend Guzman,
from his sister, the Duchesse de Morny. Guzman was believed to be at
Monte Carlo. I was well received, but left about 4, carred to L'Étoile, and
deciding to make a detour, took a Clichy tram.

There was much gaiety in the Champs and the Bois, owing to the
double fête of St Catherine, and the great national Loan of 25.11.20, but
when the tram crossed the Faubourg Montmartre, there was so much
noise and excitement in the Boulevards that I got off and joined the
throng. I was in uniform and my medals up, (acquired a few days ago in
town) in continental fashion, and whether it was the French cut of my
Gaberdine tunic and breeches, or a temporary expansiveness of the
French towards Khaki, I cannot say, but I became instantly and
immensely popular. Blue-coated soldiers and officers were embracing
ladies of position and rank in the streets, and no objection raised, as
apparently it was the *mot d'ordre* of the day, and I was soon asked why I
did not avail myself of my '*Droit du Militaire*'. There was only one thing to
do, and I wished some of you, and especially a near neighbour of yours

[1] Sir Victor Harari Pasha, a Jewish notable in Cairo.

had been with me to relieve the pressure; but after an uncertain amount of promiscuous embraces, I was rather glad to get attached to a party of young officers, with one or two older ones, and also some military cadets, from, I think, St Cyr; with also a following of the fair sex; and in a band we invaded the cafés, hotels, theatres, etc., in the Boulevard des Italiens, and were received in an enthusiastic, if somewhat *bruyant* manner everywhere.

It was the time of my rendezvous, when we reached and raided the Café de la Paix, and other places in the Place de l'Opera, so, as I was being almost kissed to death, I was not sorry to take refuge in the Grand.

My host was ready, and exclaimed: '*Allons, mes amis, au Prunier*'; and off we went to the Rue Cambon. I had never heard of Prunier and had a vague expectation of French plums.

The locale was a blaze of light and illuminations, and the Rue blocked with cars; so that I was surprised to find that the attraction was oysters and '*crustaceans*'.

After champagne and oysters, or in my particular case, lobsters' claws, we moved on to the Ritz Hotel, and had a good, but rather dull dinner. My host, and the guests, with the exception of one young chap, Paolo de Broglie, were of the type of dyspeptic millionaires, and very blasé; but they cheered up, a little at my expense, when they heard of my reception in the Boulevard des Italiens. Paolo was frightfully annoyed, as he had only just arrived in Paris, after many years, and knew nothing of St Catherine, and the *Emprunte*. He was mad on my going out with him after dinner, and not being in uniform, nor having any decorations with him, he borrowed the latter shamelessly. I was not sorry to escape Poker, which was the vice selected for the evening, and my host was quite willing that we should try our luck, so we bolted out.

The streets were as full and lively as ever, and more rowdy than ever, but the whole character of the festivities had changed miserably. In place of the ladies of the beau monde, who had shown such gaiety and *empressement* at their temporary patriotic emancipation in the afternoon, all sorts of people had come out; so Paul and I slipped into the Café Cardinal for a quiet time.

Numerous noisy bands passed by and occasionally entered; and suddenly the old original St Cyr crowd of officers and girls burst in.

There was no escape: I was tried by summary Court Martial for desertion, condemned to be shot, reprieved on condition that I kissed the girls present all round, and swore not to again desert, and Paul and I were marched off, first to a swell dance in an Italian place, in an arcade just off the Italiens, of which I forget the name, then to a theatre or two and then all made for the Montmartre quarter, passing up the Rue de N.D. de Lorette.

In this *rue*, a short call was made at a most extraordinary tavern, with a double name, American and Belgian. It was past the *limite* even for Paris,

McPherson with a prolific branch of the 'clan' at Port Eynon, Wales,
1920 'Church Parade – Sunday Morning'

and I could not have believed that such a place could exist out of Berlin.
(Particulars on application).

The officer who assumed the lead of our little band, gave right about
turn, and shouted: '*A l'enfer, a l'enfer*', and to *enfer* we went in the
Boulevard Clichy. You may know the place, where a red glare shines
lurid across the street, from over a group of devils busy with pitchforks.

Without paying the customary obole (fr. 3 in French money) we were
enthusiastically received by Satan and his imps, most of whom were of
the gentler sex. When however we visited '*Le Ciel*', next door, though the
'*Glorieuses*' rejoiced over us, *Le Bon Dieu*, as he styled himself, was very
wroth.

Then the party patronised the booths in the middle of the Boulevard,
rode pigs, and swings, fired at *poupées*, bought whistles and trumpets, and
then after a flying visit to the '*Chat Noir*' and the *Cabaret de Néant*, a dance
or two, and the celebrated Café de la Place Blanche, we settled down for a
bit at a *bal masqué* at the Tabarin in the Rue Perelle.

When at about 3.30 Paul and I doffed our dominos, and turned out to
go to our hotels, leaving most of the party still dancing, it had
commenced raining torrentially, and there were no cars to be had, and
the '*Métropolitain*' had long ceased running; so we took a double bedded
room in the nearest good-looking hotel – the Hotel de Paris. I saw
nothing wrong with it. It was clean, well furnished, with hot and cold

water, and even a telephone, and to my surprise the bill for an excellent room only fr.15; but I was chaffed about going there after, as it seems it has some curious notoriety, in some way connected with Mrs. Asquith.

..., Well, hoping life will be as smooth for you all as this sea, and serene as today's sky,

With love to all,
JOE

17

Back to Duty

Lord Allenby came to Egypt in the midst of a fierce
storm. He leaves it in a calm which is striking in its
contrast and full of good augury. British prestige in
Egypt stands higher today than it has done since Lord
Kitchener left the country in 1914 ... His personality alone did much to restore the name and word
of an Englishman to the high pinnacle on which they
stood in the East before the war.

(*The Times*, July 1925)

'. . . that jackass Allenby'.
J. W. McP.

When Joseph McPherson returned to Egypt from leave at the end of 1920,
he still had several years of public service ahead of him. They were also
years of momentous developments in the relationship between Egypt and
Britain.

The Milner Commission which had been sent to Egypt to study the
possibilities of constitutional reform had produced a recommendation: it
was for a form of independence so qualified with rights and powers
reserved to Britain that no Egyptian politician dared agree to it. Zaghlul,
who had returned in April 1921, mounted a fiery campaign against it, and
against the sitting Egyptian government which was trying to negotiate
some of the qualifications. 'Not a single British soldier must remain on
Egyptian soil,' he declared, 'if negotiation fails, Egypt will fight like
Ireland.' There followed outbreaks of violence in Cairo, Alexandria and
other centres, in which Britons and other Europeans, mainly Greeks, were
attacked. At the end of 1921, the High Commissioner, Lord Allenby,
ordered the arrest and deportation of Zaghlul and some of his followers,
who were sent to the Seychelles. Immediately after, Allenby took the
initiative himself. Using the threat of his resignation, he forced the British
government to grant independence unilaterally to Egypt, while reserving
some powers to itself for future negotiation. He had pushed the British
government further than it wished to go, and Lloyd George exclaimed
about him to King George V: 'I know now why he is called the Bull; he
has got into our Eastern china-shop and is breaking everything up.'

On February 28, 1922 the formal declaration was published: 'The
British protectorate over Egypt is terminated, and Egypt is declared to be

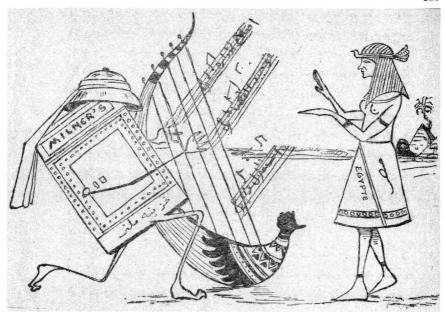

'Lord Milner woos a reluctant Egypt with his report'. A cartoon in a nationalist journal confiscated by McPherson

an independent sovereign state.' The powers reserved to Britain covered the security of the communications of the British Empire in Egypt; the defence of Egypt against aggression; the protection of foreign interests and minorities in Egypt; and the control over the Sudan.

A new Egyptian government was formed prepared to work within this imposed limited independence, and the Sultan Fuad assumed the title of King.

However, the running fire of violence could not be stamped out. Murder gangs operated, attacking British soldiers and civilians and Egyptian cabinet ministers. Among the British community there was strong criticism of Allenby for his 'leniency'.

In September 1923, Zaghlul was allowed to return from exile; after elections, he became Prime Minister, and launched a vigorous campaign against the reserved clauses. Attacks on Britons continued, and on 19 November 1924, Sir Lee Stack, the Sirdar of the Egyptian Army, and Governor-General of the Sudan, was assassinated in a Cairo street by a group who escaped in a taxi. Only a few days before, Zaghlul had denounced the system whereby an Englishman could hold both these offices.

On the day of Stack's funeral, Allenby drove with an escort of cavalry to the Egyptian Parliament. Marching into Zaghlul's office, he delivered an ultimatum, demanding an apology for the murder, the apprehension of the murderers, a ban on political demonstrations, the payment of a fine of half-a-million pounds, the withdrawal of Egyptian troops from the Sudan, and the releasing to the Sudan of Nile water for irrigation.

PUNCH, OR THE LONDON CHARIVARI.—December 3, 1924.

TO ALL WHOM IT CONCERNS.

Britannia (*to Egypt*). "I GAVE YOU LIBERTY. SEE TO IT THAT THE THINGS DONE
BY YOU IN HER NAME DO NOT MAKE ME REPENT MY GIFT."

Punch's view on 3 December, 1924 of the murder of
the Sirdar, Sir Lee Stack

Six months later, Allenby resigned, and was succeeded by Lord Lloyd,
an autocratic personality with a brief from the British government to rule
with a firm hand. For McPherson, it was good riddance to the vacillating
'jackass' and do-nothing 'King Log'. But the Egyptians gave Allenby a
respectful, indeed affectionate farewell. Perhaps it was because they
realised that, in his six years in office, as his biographer Lord Wavell
wrote: 'Allenby had recognised in Egypt the awakened spirit of a people.'

At the beginning of these years of political fluctuations, McPherson was
not as intimately involved as he had been as Mamur Zapt. His new post on
his return to Egypt in 1920 was Intelligence Officer and Passport Control
Officer at Kantara on the east bank of the Suez Canal. He embraced it
with relief.

I am now once more breathing the purer air of camp; and feel as though I
had awakened from the long gruesome but often amusing nightmare....
There, (in Cairo as Mamur Zapt) there was always some plot to foil,
some villain to thwart, and any recreation or rest seemed like robbing the
public, and when the body rested, there was little chance for the brain to

do so. Here in Kantara there is rest and recreation for body and brain –
plenty of leisure for reading, writing, and typing and other occupations
and I get plenty of tennis, riding, wolf-hunting, fishing and swimming.

> In the confused state of the Middle East after the Great War, there were
> many travellers who were officially unwelcome in Egypt. Their numbers
> had recently been increased by the conflicts between Jews and Arabs in
> May 1921 in Jaffa, after which the British authorities in Palestine tried
> and deported a number of Jews. McPherson listed among his detainees
> travellers he suspected of being involved in the Jaffa disturbances, along
> with a miscellany of others, suspected spies, deserters and political and
> religious agitators.

At one time my ordinary Black List of persons wishing to enter Egypt
and forbidden contained over three thousand names, besides the special
Jaffa lists, Foreign and Home Office names and special cases notified by
telegram, so that in the rush between arrival and departure of trains
there was not much time for minute questioning of each and detailed
examination of Passports, and even if this technical control could have
been exercised perfectly some of the worst cases, which had spared
neither time nor money to get their papers technically above reproach
would have escaped.

I was happily allowed a very free hand, and had full authority to stop
anyone on suspicion, even if his papers were perfect, or to pass anyone
who was technically without valid authority, if I believed him to be
harmless and his error unintentional so that I came to run my control
almost entirely on impression . . . .

As no complaint was ever substantiated against me, I must either have
had the most marvellous luck, or actually possess a peculiar instinctive
faculty for penetrating instantly and easily through the veil of
appearance. Often where I could detect no technical flaws, and had
actually signed the visa to proceed, a sigh of relief, a too hasty retirement
from the office, an exchange of glances, or an obvious desire to keep the
face in the shade, were enough to recall the person and put him under
arrest.

> The work was not demanding compared with his earlier post, and the
> letters turned to more personal matters, rather in the vein of his pre-war
> descriptions of his household. Gad el-Moula was still with him (indeed was
> to stay with him for another twenty-five years), and one of the letters gave
> a résumé of his fortunes, since they had left the desert in 1917.

Gad was heartbroken at first at leaving Cairo and his beloved Saida
Zenab [the shrine of his favourite saint]: and particularly at no longer
being able to describe himself as *Murasla* to the Mamur Zapt, which two
words expressed for him almost the last limit of power and dignity,

objects so worshipped by the Oriental mind; but he is comforted to find that I can still arrest a man, and hand him over to him as prisoner, or bundle him back to the place he came from, and he is very proud of our quarters here, and pleased with the freedom.

He has developed the rudiments of a moustache, and has to shave his chin about once a month, has lost his timidity and gained great bodily strength, but he is the same old Galumph, and has still the same fixed idea that his mission in life is to look after me, and still does idiotic things with the best intentions.

Yesterday I gave him a telegram just received from GS 'I', to take to the APM at Kantara Station West, to ask him to arrest a suspect believed to be on the coming train, and told Gad to leave some job he was busy with at the time lest the bridge [a pontoon bridge] should be 'broken' before he reached it. He was a bit slow in getting away, and was dismayed at finding the bridge actually 'broken', so feeling that he would be rightly blamed if the message were too late, he ran down to the British bathing place, whipped off his uniform, asked the first bather, who for all he knew might have been the Base Commandant, to keep an eye on the same, and swam across, and handed in the telegram. Judging from the wet and chewed and half-intelligible chit he brought me back in reply, I have my doubts whether the telegram was much good to the APM when he got it . . .

When transferred to Cairo in 1917 I made some enquiries about Gad's few paternal acres, but found them to be hopelessly alienated, and that the *Gamusa* (buffalo) on which his brother and sister now depended entirely for their food, drink and living generally, was mortgaged to the extent of £10. The mortgagor was about to distrain, and as he claimed the legs as his share, the milk-giver would soon have walked off, but I got that move stopped pending enquiries.

At the same time letters came from a Sheikh of Qoft, reminding Gad that he had undertaken to be his son-in-law, and that the fair maiden had consented to wait for her soldier lover, but that now it was for him to claim her hand.

I had heard him talk of the *Gamusa* scores of times, but never of his inamorata. Now however, he waxed flowery in praise of her charms and accomplishments: eyes, form and gait like a gazelle, and a voice like the crested larks of Palestine. Her chief charm seemingly to Gad, however, was her subtle skill at the milk pail – she could extract from the *Gamusa* far more milk than could Gad's sister, Rabia, and turn out a maximum of butter and cheese.

But the *dot* required for her was £10, and the wedding would cost at least another £10, and he had barely £20 in the world; and the *Gamusa* was in peril. He thought long and deeply over the alternatives, the maiden pulling one way, and the *Gamusa* the other; and I was curious to see which would win in this tug of war.

I had decided to save the *Gamusa* from being distrained on, in the case of his deciding to marry, but did not tell him so, as I did not wish to get him into the habit of borrowing, or receiving gifts of value, if avoidable.

As his heart remained torn between his two loves, and he was visibly pining, I gave him a railway pass to his distant home and a month's holiday.

Having spent about £5 on presents, which I supplemented with unheard-of delights, such as toffee, chocolates, jam, honey and curry, and rice – unknown in his part of the world – and which he astonished his friends by making into curried chicken and rice puddings, he sewed his remaining £15, and a month's salary in his shirt and departed, happy in a promise from me to send what more he required.

He did not draw on me, but wrote to say the *Gamusa* had gained the day, that he had cleared the mortgage by paying £15 cash, and had paid a retaining fee to the girl's father. This was repeated in 1918, but as the father insisted that his daughter was now sixteen, and getting old and past marriageable age, Gad married her in his holiday last October, 1919, and left her to look after his young brother and the *Gamusa*.

This young brother, by the way, had been rather a care to Gad, as he had long suffered from acute anaemia, and attacks of jaundice, in spite of medicine Gad had induced me to send per the MO of the Political Prisoners, and in spite of the treatment of local practitioners, who had sedulously cauterised him with hot irons, and cupped the back of his head. His case had become so serious that in 1918 Gad brought him back with him, in the hope of his life being saved. I diagnosed Ankylostomiasis, a disease which readily yields to specific skilled treatment, but which otherwise goes on inevitably to the bitter end; so avoiding the big Government Hospital, which like most institutions in Egypt is as corrupt as anything could be, out of hell, I sent Gad el-Kerim to the CMS Hospital, where I know the doctor, and to which I sent a small subscription, and the boy was radically cured, and has become a healthy youth.

> During the War, McPherson recalled, Gad had sworn to light candles at the shrine of his favourite saint, Saida Zenab, if she diverted bombs and shells away from him and McPherson. The number of candles pledged had reached several hundred, and though Gad had reduced the sum because of the shrapnel that had nearly scalped him, it still had taken him much trouble to accumulate and offer them to her shrine in Cairo.

Gad's dilemma, having promised Saida Zenab more candles than he could possibly pay, reminds me of the similar fix Miltiades found himself in after the battle of Marathon. He had vowed to Artemis as many goats as enemies slain in the battle. The number was so enormous that it was impossible to find the goats. He compounded by offering up five hundred goats on every anniversary of the victory, in the month of Boëdromion.

At the Church of the Nativity in Bethlehem

Had Gad's vow been to Artemis, and in goats, he would probably have recollected that the Goddess of the Moon loved candles. The Altar cakes in her honour at Munychia had lights all round – *lumen Artemidis* – to solemnise her aid – as the full moon – at Cyprian Salamis.

> Away from Cairo, McPherson was beginning to purge himself of the Mamur Zapt's 'vision of crime and corruption'. He renewed his spirit by periods of meditation and solitude, sometimes camping in the desert at night, once by a stay at a Franciscan monastery in Jerusalem.

Opening the door at the far end (of the library) I was surprised to find myself in the Chapel, quite dark but for one tiny red lamp near the Epistle side of the altar. One almost invisible figure was kneeling when I entered, but quickly passed out.

I often think it is a pity that people are quite so gregarious and spend virtually their whole lives in the glare of social intercourse and company. They would enjoy and appreciate much better if they varied it by a few hours occasionally in utter solitude; in the silent lifelessness of the desert, or the mountains, or the darkness of an empty church. They would find that there is no such thing as an empty solitude, and discover new companions, and new beauties and wonders, as invisible in the day-glow of social life, as the stars would be to anyone who never looked at the sky except in the light of the sun. Many hours must have passed unnoticed for the night was far spent when at last I turned in, but the Chapel without lamps or human creatures was to me anything but lonely and dark.

Late in 1921 he was transferred from his agreeable billet in Kantara back to Cairo, to the Special Section of the Department of Public Security, War Office, where, to his disgust, he found himself desk-bound. He was there during the riots that erupted after Zaghlul was exiled for the second time, and – perhaps because he had no responsibility for controlling them – in his comments let the boyish anarchist show through the Police Bimbashi.

All attempts to enforce order were hampered as usual, by Allenby's asininity, and gutter urchins had commandeered the trams, and with the help of bigger roughs were overturning and burning them, when tired of riding on the tops. Others were tearing up the suburban lines and of course plate glass windows were being smashed all over the place, partly for fun, but mainly to create a diversion, whilst the looters cleared the till, etc. There was one thing that kids had discovered which quite took my fancy: they broke off the tops of the street gas lamps, and lit what remained, obtaining glorious torch flames a yard or two long.

He was not happy in the 'Dossier Garden', as he called it. There are a couple of references to feeling 'beastly ill', and for nearly a year he had a recurrent fever, and was only intermittently at work. The experiences of the war and the Mamur Zapt period were still affecting him. However, desk work was intolerable, and he welcomed an invitation from Russell Pasha to return to his cloak-and-dagger operations, directed at uncovering the assassination plots. He headed his letter-report on this period Café Maraschino.

CAFÉ MARASCHINO

Near the end of 1922 I was dug up to my joy, and put on to my old Secret Police Work; for assassinations of Englishmen, bombings and all sorts of outrages were becoming of common occurrence, in spite of Allenby's '*bruta fulmina*'[1], posted up everywhere, that any unauthorised person in possession of arms or trading in them would suffer the pain of death.

I was not reinstated as Head of Secret Police as in 1918–20: Bimbashi

---

[1] *Pliny: Natural History*, Book 11, xliv (*Loeb* edition): '*bruta fulmina et vana*' (senseless and ineffectual thunder-claps).

B. occupied that chair, from which he never budged, and though he was a nice chap, and had been a fine officer in the war, he was without imagination, originality, or genius and no match for the criminals, who like the Scarlet Pimpernel, were working in broad daylight in populous thoroughfares under the very eyes of the authorities. Russell Pasha, the Commandant, a fine chap, had too much to do looking after a disaffected police force and a captious public to specialise in this direction, and the Special Criminal Investigation Committee sitting in the War Office had no-one in it with brains or method, except Colonel R——, who was far too selfish to let anything substantiate that would not redound to his own glory, and Kaimakan I——, a highly capable and shrewd man, who would have done well if not so topweighted by nincompoops, and handicapped by petty jealousies.

I, to my great joy, was to be a free lance. I took up the work on 26 December 1922, and by the New Year, had fixed up an 'office' in a sous-sol with windows looking on to the Boulevard Abbas on one side, and Sharia Zaki on the other. I had located it on the 27th, but it was days before I could find anyone there to open the door, a great advantage ultimately, as it proved to be very private. The windows and door were ornamented with coloured pictorial advertisements for 'Ollandia Milk'. 'Olia di Lucca', and some Italian wines. The district was excellent, neither a native quarter nor an Engish quarter, but a region of Italians, Greeks, etc. At last I had found the proprietor, Sig. Maroncini, an importer of the luxuries specified above, and he willingly gave up the rooms I wanted, his offices, as he rarely used them, the place being rather his store than his bureau. I was a Sig. Martino, of Italian father and American mother (oh, horrible thought): discharged soldier, who had to carry on a little business to supplement a meagre pension. I had no objection to the advertisements remaining at the doors and windows, and a few shelves of milk and wine might remain, and his notices on the walls. His name might remain on the door and would do for both of us, and if he would allow me to use it sometimes, I might get him orders now and again, and would try to sell the things on the shelves (I may mention that enough wine and cognac was disposed of during my occupation to more than justify my promise, and people who really took me for the Fratelli Maroncini, gave me several orders for milk and other things which I transmitted to the real Maroncini).

Domenico, my fratello, delicately refrained from asking particulars of my business, which I know he suspected to be more or less illicit. This was a great point. I have found that when in secret police work, I have been masquerading, suspicions will come, and it is a necessary trick of the trade to encourage very covertly a false one: and keep the hounds off the real scent. The subtle odour of hashish which some of my villainous clients left behind them kept Domenico on the trail he had chosen.

I may mention that no inkling of the truth ever leaked out, until, when nearly a year later I gave up the place for my present office at Abdin, I appeared in full police uniform, with Gad, the 'café boy', in Askari's rig, and thanked Domenico on behalf of the Commandant of Police and the Ministry for the use of his rooms. He had the shock of his life, and declared he had never suspected me of anything worse than of being in with a few smugglers, and doing a little trade not approved of by the police, but as I had never compromised him, and kept in every way to my contract, he had considered it none of his business: and was only afraid sometimes that the police might raid me, when night customers of dubious looks and cognac were about.

You will wonder with me that they never did, when I explain my plan of campaign, and the function of my 'Café Maraschino', as it came to be called by the 'select' few who frequented it. I started with my old agent Mustafa N—— , who looms largely in my Mamur Zapt records, under the new name of 'Hasan Ali'. He brought me an old Army secret agent, A——, who had retired to a little farm commanding a view of the house where he had every reason to believe the main conspirators met from time to time. He changed his name to 'Yassin'. With their help I got two criminals, whom I had watched since 1919, and against whom I had hanging evidence. These were lured by 'Hasan' and 'Yassin' into my café and found the drinks so cheap though strong which the disreputable attendant Gad served them, and the other customers, an Italian anarchist (myself) such a sympathetic listener, that they blabbed and hopelessly committed themselves before my only respectable agent, L——, an ex-schoolmaster came out from behind the wooden partition, with a revolver in one hand and all they had said taken down in writing in the other, and passed the latter to them to sign. They demurred of course, but as I politely explained, they had no option, and had moreover to choose between hanging and helping. They wisely chose the latter, and were useful helpers, and though I cheated the convict prisons and perhaps the gallows it was only of a scoundrel who robbed or killed individuals to earn a livelihood, and another a highly respected and well-to-do Bedouin who did the same for sport, in order to enrich both cells and gallows with wretches who wreck communities, and under the aegis of political liberty, and the guise of patriotism do infinitely more harm.

These two in their turn brought other flies into our parlour: all people who would never have been lured into the Governorate or Ministry, and if taken by force would have told nothing but lies.

Before his retirement in 1924, he was asked for one more service by Russell the Commandant of Police, who was beginning his campaign against narcotic trafficking which was to bring him to world fame as the Head of the League of Nations anti-Narcotics Bureau. Some of the gravest problems arose because most of the drug traffickers were non-Egyptians and therefore under the protection of the Capitulations, the legal

Trademark on wrapping of
drugs confiscated by McPherson

immunities granted to foreigners under which they could be arrested only
by their own consular police and tried only by their own courts. Russell
Pasha in his memoirs *Egyptian Service* wrote: 'It is hardly possible for
anyone who has not had actual experience of them to appreciate the
enormous difficulties that the Capitulations put in the way of the police
generally, and particularly in the fight against the drug trade. Writing
now in 1946 with the Capitulations abolished, I say advisedly that had it
not been for the protection that the foreign trafficker derived from them,
the narcotic problem in Egypt would never have reached the magnitude it
did and the ninety per cent improvement today could have been achieved
in a quarter of the time with a quarter of the expenditure of police time,
funds and energy.' McPherson's experience confirms this.

COCAINE

My Chief, now Brigadier (Lewa) Russell Pasha was keen on my helping
him in the terrible problem of cocaine, to which I gladly agreed. I
thought I knew something about its traffic and its ravages, but the
statistics he gave me were appalling. 'It is literally ruining the race,
physically and morally,' he declared, 'and as I am always rubbing it into
the Government, we Police are practically powerless, as long as its use
and traffic is barely an offence legally. Thank God, they are at last
formulating stringent laws against drugs, and my idea is for you and
your dope squad to raid enough to keep the public satisfied, and to take

advantage of the present relative openness with which the drugmongers ply their traffic, to register and card them, and that when the law makes it a crime and gives us the power to deal with them severely and effectively, we can mobilise all our forces and round them up *en masse.*'

Russell gave me as second in command an ex-NCO, Berry, who was keen, shrewd and intelligent and had a natural flair for this kind of game, and best and rarest of all, was loyal and straight; and a few police agents, all experts in that line. To these we added sundry 'confidants' drawn from the ranks of dope fiends, and dope dealers. I gave up Café Maraschino, and was authorised to take a five-roomed flat in Abdin . . . .

The twenty names or so registered at the Governorate in this connection I was able to more than double at once from my old records happily not destroyed, and before I gave up the quest they had increased to over two hundred. The public that wrote to us, and the papers trying to put us wise on this subject, would have been surprised to see our Register, almost as explicit as a trade directory. It contains the firms which manufacture cocaine and other drugs, the shippers who bring them to Egypt, chief of whom is an old political prisoner of mine, a Greek; the wholesale importers, nearly all wealthy Armenians, the doctors and chemists who abuse their special opportunities, and the cafetiers, pastry-cooks, restaurant keepers: the gamins, camelots and old women who hawk it in the streets, the police officials and sanitary inspectors who connive the traffic for gain, and the judges and boys who are dotty for its use. I regretted that the 'Grand Ingomboco',[1] which Russell looked for, could not take place in my time.

However, without forgetting or endangering the main issue, we got much fun and sport out of the raids we organised once or twice a week, and incidentally kept our dope hounds busy and content, and hugely pleased the public, or at least that portion of it which was interested but not addicted.

It was an easy game after the hunting of arms, and the field was vast, so that I only remember drawing blank once, when we were let down and our quarry warned by a confidant.

One of the first raids was a general round up of the shops in the Wagh el-Birka, the Boulevard Clichy of Cairo. At about ten in the morning, Berry and I simply strolled down the street, with a large party of agents, confidants, and ordinary police in plain clothes, and dropped a couple of each at each shop to immobilise the occupants. Then when our force was exhausted we walked back and searched shops and owners one by one, and found cocaine, hashish or other drugs in every one, in varying quantities, with one exception. That we were about to search like the rest, when a handsome well-dressed young Tripolitan objected on the ground that he was an Italian subject, and could only be legally searched by his

---

[1] The Zulu witch-hunt or 'smelling-out', as described by H. Rider Haggard in *Nada the Lily* (1892).

own Consul. 'As it is', he said, 'I shall prosecute the police for your trespass and that of your spies.'

Had it been a case of arms or a more important matter, I should have professed to disbelieve him, treated him as a local subject, gone ahead, and wriggled out later. As it was, I said, 'Are you dotty to treat your customers as trespassers? All I want, and doubtless what these gentlemen want, is a packet of cigarettes, if you have any which are not doped' – and I tendered the money.

'I'll be damned if I supply you', he said.

'*Tanto meglio*,' I rejoined, 'please note that, Mr Berry; he refuses to supply the public with the goods he professes to sell, in itself a misdemeanour which will justify us taking steps to have his licence taken away and his shop closed, but there is in addition a serious presumption in his case, for in refusing to supply undoped cigarettes he indicates that all his stock is doped.'

He did not know how far this was bluff and how far it was sound law, and was obviously very uncomfortable, and became correspondingly polite. 'I did not mean that,' he said, 'of course I am only too delighted to supply you, only I do not want money. Take these and these, I won't be paid.'

'Note this also, Mr Berry: a clear attempt at bribing the Police. Come along! We will not perquisition. We will report him to his Consul.'

The last threat rather relieved him, for the Consul, though a charming man and the best dressed at social functions was a bad rascal and protected worse scoundrels than Tarabulsi (the Tripolitan) for a share in their plunder.

We left the sealing of the shops, the marching of the prisoners to the Caracol, and the opening of the *procès verbal* against them to our subordinates, and my service car being at hand loaded it up with the loot, and left the lot with the Mamur at Ezbekieh, on our way to the Consul, for that was the course we decided to take.

Signor Sachioni was at his toilet, but received us in a dream of a dressing gown, and though he knew I had long suspected him of importing arms for the natives, and divers irregularities, nothing could have exceeded the cordiality of his manner. 'Who was this wretch who abused the protection of Italy, and where was he to be found?' We both regretted that we had foolishly omitted to remark his name, or that of the street, but we had clear proof that he dealt in cocaine, and only asked the Consul to send his representative with us, for we could find the place.

'Gladly,' said the Consul, 'I would come myself but I am suffering from an exhausting night, for I confess I have been on the "bummel", and unhappily my *kawass* (consular policeman) is away, but get me particulars and I will arrest him tomorrow, and *corpo di Bacco*, he shall pay dearly.'

As we went down the stairs feeling that the game was up, by luck we

met the *kawass*, and told him we had the Consul's authority to take him
with us. 'But I can only take my orders from the Consul. Let me go up to
him.' 'No, he is unwell, we will telephone up.' And Berry phoned up the
stairs that the Signor would be glad to hear we had found the *kawass*, and
availed ourselves of his kind permission to use him, and without waiting
for a response, we half carried the *kawass* into the car, sword and all, and
in a few more minutes hustled him into Tarabulsi's shop, where Berry
was relieved for a further raid by the Maowen Zapt of the district, who
searched the shop with me in the unwilling presence of the Italian
representative. Tarabulsi's case was far more serious than that of the
local subjects, as he would be tried by Italian law, which holds the traffic
in drugs as a high offence. I was called at his trial at the Italian Consulate,
but was not asked to give evidence. I understand he was convicted – his
shop has never been reopened. His hope in Sachioni was baffled, as that
gentleman disappeared suddenly and mysteriously in a night. It was long
after, that I heard from my 'fratello', Domenico Marocini, that he had
denounced the Consul as a traitor to Mussolini, when in Rome, and that
he had been arrested by the agents of the latter in Cairo and was taken
before the Dictator, and disappeared, believed to have been shot for high
treason. Such a nice man too!

> McPherson lists other cases, but retirement came upon him too soon to be
> in at Russell's great round-up. Nevertheless he had notably contributed to
> the list of suspects. Russell wrote: 'It was not till 1925 that the first effective
> narcotic law was passed ... We had not been idle during the previous
> years. We had been collecting information and forming an index of local
> traffickers, with the result that within twelve months of the publication of
> the new law we had made 5,600 prosecutions under it in Cairo City alone.'

> Late in 1924 there is a final glimpse of McPherson the public official,
> involved in political preoccupations. It was just after Allenby's ultimatum
> to Zaghlul following the murder of Sir Lee Stack. McPherson was writing
> to a friend, who had been a colleague at the Agricultural College before
> the war.

Dear Base

On Sunday 24.11.24, when Zaghlul refused most of the conditions of
the British ultimatum, the club was very full and I had an opportunity of
expressing my views on the responsibilities for the Egyptian imbroglio
... and of revealing a few cogent facts, and startled some of the members
not a little. When the news came in that the refusal had been overridden
and that orders had been sent to turn Egyptian units out of the Sudan,
and etc., a loafer who never ought to be in any decent club and would not
be in the 'Turf' if I revealed a very nasty secret dossier I compiled about
him in the course of police work, a man to whom I had never spoken and

never wished to, came over to the group in which I was sitting and said: 'Now, you fellows, I propose that we all go to the Residency and congratulate Allenby.'

While I was yet speechless, one of my party said: 'Well, if he had let us down in the past, he seems to be showing firmness at last and to be trying to make good.'

The club members were thick about us when I recovered my voice, but not my disgust and indignation, and I said: 'If anyone is such an ass as to go and flatter the master jackass for being at last kicked into the track, after fouling our pitch and the Gyppies' for years, trampling on our prestige and every sane basis of government, and committing every asininity, let him go. I, for one, would rather shake hands with old Zaghlul. He has been treated like a mouse by a very cruel and silly cat: allowed again and again to run as he liked and then clawed back. He at least has remembered his friends and consistently suppressed his enemies, whereas Allenby has let down his supporters, Egyptian and English, and encouraged their enemies . . . . If he is showing firmness today, he will show weakness tomorrow, as ever, and undo any good that is done. There is no hope for us or the natives as long as that fool is here. Go to him by all means and tell him if he wants to benefit England and Egypt, for God's sake to clear out.'

That is almost the last reference to politics in the Family Letters, which continued for another twenty years. Though the appellation of 'The Bimbashi' clung to him, he returned to his private concerns, and the first letter of his retirement is headed 'Free as the Sea'.

PART FOUR

FREE AS THE SEA
1925-1946

EDITORIAL NOTE

During the years of McPherson's long retirement, the flow of Family Letters slackened. Some of the older members of the 'clan' died; his favourite correspondent among the younger generation, his nephew Campbell, lived in Egypt for some years. Nevertheless, there were seven volumes of letters from which to choose extracts for the following two chapters.

18

Retirement

'When of late I retired from active service and public life, I wedded the Lady Idleness, and am truly attached to her, though I seem to betray her every day.'

J. W. McP.

'Free as the Sea!' Joseph McPherson wrote at the head of his first letter after his retirement. Unshackled from duty, he applied himself immediately with energy to his true interests – 'vagabondage', scholarship, and making a home. He retained a small flat in the centre of Cairo, near the Abdin Palace, but he was, he wrote, 'fed up' with the city.

My thoughts turned at once to a sweet old place, not far from Giza, which I have visited from time to time when walking or riding, during the past twenty years. Often in a gallop over the desert, I have reined up in this little oasis of rich greenery and roses and rested under the fine Lebbeck trees or in the vine-covered verandah. I had always found it empty except for an old man who acted as gardener and caretaker.

This derelict villa belonged to the Franciscan Order of monks, and when McPherson bought it, he named it *'Porziuncula'* – 'A Little Portion', an expression from the *Fioretti* or *Legends of St Francis*. The house was perfect for him, not far from the desert, near the farming village of Bein el-Saryat, and bordering on fields. It was set in a walled garden, filled with flowers and fruit trees – mangoes, guavas, figs and oranges. The sounds that came to him when he rested on his flat rooftop, where he mostly lived and slept, were of birdsong, the creaking of a waterwheel, and the flutes of bedouin shepherd boys outside his walls. Soon he established what he called his 'little farm': on an adjoining field he grew maize and cauliflowers, and inside his enclosure he kept a cow, donkeys, ducks, geese, goats, rabbits, doves and chickens. The family was informed of his farming successes:

To Dougal   *'Porziuncula', 17 July 1925*
I have beaten you as regards eggs as far as numbers are concerned. In the half year, 1.1.25 to 30.6.25, mine laid 3560 eggs, of which I sold 2555 for Piastres 814, and used the rest in the house (1005), with the willing help

McPherson's household at 'Porziuncula' with his brother, Jack who visited
him in September 1935. Gad is behind Jack; Gad's daughter, Warda 'Rose',
has her arm around his shoulder

of the staff. About 100 of these, picked English and Fayoumi eggs, were
put under broody hens, and 23 fine chicks survived from them. You are
lucky in losing only one. The rats ate nine prize chicks in one night and
six others died, and two fine hens. One of these today without any
warning. They do not usually have the chance of dying, as, with such a
lot of fowls, rabbits, pigeons, etc., all together, the smallest symptom of
being unwell means throat cutting at once, when they are promptly
cooked and eaten. We killed two on suspicion today, of which I gave the
gardener one, and the other I hope to eat tomorrow. I have now only
eighty-seven fowls including cocks and chicks, about fifty bunnies, and
about a hundred pigeons, besides four goats, a lamb and a donkey; all as
friendly and sensible as if they considered themselves part of the family.

> He had also a handsome tribe of dogs, known to the villagers as the
> 'Golden Hounds'; they were of a breed called 'Armant', and had gold
> streaks in their coats, and golden locks about their eyes. Three of them he
> named 'Gold', in Arabic, Turkish, and Persian.
>   He installed Gad el-Moula as majordomo, and Gad's wife as chief
> dairymaid in charge of all milking and butter- and cheese-making. Other
> servants were recruited, nearly all from the 'Tribe of Gad', that is, from
> Gad's family in his village in the Thebaid. Their names constantly appear

in his letters – Mousa, Sayed, Noos, Murid – the cook, the gardener, the groom, the waiter, and so on – with details of their characters and deeds. In time, his household expanded by natural increase and in the mid-1930s a photograph showed a smiling group of a round dozen of servants and their wives and children and babes in arms.

In 1924 he was visited at 'Porziuncula' by his nephew Campbell, with his wife and two young daughters, Hilary and Christine. Later on, Campbell's wife sent a gift of baby clothes to Gad's wife, who was expecting a child. Gad wrote a letter of thanks, which was translated by McPherson.

Bein el-Saryat
To the honourable lady, Mrs McPherson the Noble *1 January 1925*
Thank you very much for this precious present, which will be most useful to the Bimbo, and my Sitt thanks you very much and says, 'The things are all very very nice, real wool all, and I am delighted with them, and so is Bimbo, although he is not yet born, and the first thing he shall do when he comes down, shall be to thank you and Hilary and Christine', and I, Gad, thank you more than all of them, and tell the Sitt she must hurry up a bit . . . and I hope you will give my greetings to Hilary by hand and by a kiss for by God I love her with a strong love, and our Salaams to H.E. Mr Campbell, and to the people who honoured us by their presence, and all the bunnies and the little pigeons, and the kids and Lucy the donkey send greetings to Hilary, and long for a kiss from her, and H.E. the Pasha greets you all, and the Christmas picture reached us and by God it was sweet, live for ever.

Signed: Gad el-Moula Abd el-Rahim Abu Domo.

In fact, Gad's 'bimbo' was a girl, as McPherson's letter to a niece two weeks later revealed:

Dear Irene *'Porziuncula' Bein el-Saryat, 2 February 1925*
Sunday here though a day of perfect rest is not a day of sleep: Friday supplies that weekly want, and then the staff are allowed to sleep on as long as they can or wish: they are not expected to bring me early tea, and I lie in bed reading if I cannot sleep till they are about and bring me my breakfast.

On Septuagesima, when Sayed brought me tea and biscuits a bit before 6 o'clock, the crystal clear sky was still star spangled, but the 'dawn came up like thunder' whilst I was dressing and the Eastern horizon seemed to burst into flame. The hunter of the East, too, caught Sultan Hussein's turrets in a noose of light, and as I was biking in to early Mass, 'nor dim nor red, like God's own head, the glorious sun uprist'.

What is more rare here, the trees and fields were covered with hoar frost, and when after leaving the convent, I rode through the Giza

gardens, the lightly frozen paths crunched beneath me. The still crisp air was full of the scent of many flowers.

On returning I noticed beneath the two great Lebbeck trees at the entrance to the garden, great dishes of hot rice and other luxuries spread, and bowls of tea and milk, and remembered that this was the seventh day from the birth of a little girl to Gad's wife, and felt rather curious to observe the traditional ceremonies that would inevitably be observed.

In reply to my asking Gad whom he had invited: 'Nobody,' he said, 'Allah will send his poor'. Though this is an act of faith which exacts little grace and is liable to be superabundantly fulfilled, I rather wondered how it would come about before the rice pudding, and *full muqdamis* (buttered beans) were cold, but just then an old man passed through the fields on his donkey, and was constrained to dismount and come in. A few well-to-do farmers and effendis were allowed to pass, but all poor men and lads were hailed in. Yet there was room for one, and a mischievous-looking boy passing, Gad bade him to the feast. Perhaps he had something on his conscience, or was a sceptic, for he incontinently bolted: but Hafiz the gardener pursued him and led him in by the ear.

Then all fell to, and when they were well filled, praised the Prophet, and blessed Gad and his offspring. The proud mother and the gardener's young wife sat near by but hidden by a fence of palm fronds, and with them the old Beldame who had acted in place of a doctor at the birth, and who was not likely to get her fee out of Gad until the seven days were fulfilled – for about ten months ago, his first little boy died on the morn of the *Saboa.* No other women were admitted, as the risk of the evil eye would have been too great. Men are not credited to anything like the same extent with that invidious power.

Meanwhile I had breakfasted in a bed of violets, whose exquisite scent struggled with that of the honeysuckle overhead, and had retired to read on the verandah. But presently the men guests were replaced by a number of tiny boys and girls, carrying flowers, and the 'Hakima' appeared with a bowl containing a mixture of salt, wheat, maize, and other fruits of the earth: accompanied by Khudra the gardener's girl wife, bearing a censer. First the thresholds and outbuildings were incensed and sprinkled, and then a procession forming up, a complete tour of the garden round the house was made, the Hakima leading a curious chant, interrupted by prayers, blessings, and incantations. The childen took up the chant, and walking backwards scattered roses and other flowers, over which walked the mother bearing the baby, who up to then had been concealed, almost from her own father even. They did not come upstairs, but thoroughly sprinkled everything in the *rez de chaussée*, including the billiard table – and the procession terminated at the bed chamber, where the Hakima intoned a sort of Epithalamium. There was a long ritual both before and after the procession, but of too intimate or secret a nature for me to be informed. One point however was the naming of the baby, and I was invited by the father to give her a name. I at once named the kiddy 'Warda', which means a rose, and as Gad had vowed to dedicate her to Saida Zenab, as he did the candles in the war, she is named Zenab Warda Gad el-Moula. The point that struck me about the whole ritual, as in the case of the Zzarr described in earlier letters, was the pagan nature of the rites. The names of God and the Prophet, which are brought into almost every sentence of an ordinary conversation amongst Egyptian Moslems, were almost entirely absent . . .. I think, like the Zzarr, this ceremony dates back to long before Christ or the Prophet, and though I have not the smallest support for this view, I cannot help suspecting a connection between this ceremony and ancient rites of the Eleusinian type. The Hakima, with her cornucopia of the fruits of the earth was very suggestive of Demeter, and her acolyte of Proserpine. A Jewish element entered also, for when Gad paid his fee for services at birth and during the week and at the *Saboa*, eighty piastres I believe, the Hakima demanded also a brace of pigeons, '. . . *par turturum aut duos pullos columbarum*.'[1]

A Christian custom also came in, for I, on naming the child, involved myself in the obligation of giving it a present. Gad explained that this was best in the form of coins which could be hung round the baby's neck, or attached to the forelock, when sufficiently developed, to keep off the evil eye, and asked for two milliemes (one half-penny). As he had not asked me to subscribe to the ceremony, I gave him a lot of little coins, Turkish, Italian, Greek, etc., for the baby. These however greatly aroused the cupidity of the old Beldame, and filled the mother with alarm as she knew an old woman of this type would have as little hesitation as Atropos in cutting the thread of the baby's days, if rubbed the wrong way, so I appeased her with a shilling and some beads Duncan gave me years ago. I also supplemented the nuts and sweets Gad scattered for the kiddies, by figs, almonds, etc, left over from Christmas.

After getting a keen appetite by trying the young Arab horse of a neighbour and enjoying lunch in the garden, I found siesta spread on the little tiled platform, outside the South door of the house. This with its little parapet of old bricks is quite a suntrap, and in the shade of passion flowers and honeysuckle, all in bloom, the thermometer recorded over eighty degrees and in the sun well over a hundred degrees.

I used to go to St Mark's at Shoubra to Vespers, but have so often been let down by Holy Rosary, or one of those substitutes for the good old liturgical 'Hours', and I know of no other church where either Vespers or Compline is sung, that I shirk the journey of five or six miles . . ..

Therefore, rightly or wrongly on the Sunday I am describing, instead of going to church in the afternoon, I tackled your last budget you sent me and when the sun set in great glory, and the chilly air drove me for a

[1] Luke 2,24: '. . . A sacrifice according to that which is said in the law of the Lord, *A pair of turtle doves or two young pigeons.*' (A.V.)

long walk and then in to a huge log fire, I continued to enjoy the *Franciscan Monthly and Calendar*, and the copies of the *Universe*.

My reading was not unpleasantly interrupted by a recherché little dinner, for Gad who never forgets Friday, always remembers Sunday as a feast. Also when I returned to the fireside, I noticed that he had laid a havana by the side of my café and cognac, instead of the usual Indian cheroot.

A perfect day fittingly ended with a perfect night (*gratias Deo ago*) when at last I abandoned fire and books.

Apologies for this long screed, and much love to both,

JOE.

The life at 'Porziuncula' was idyllic, but McPherson had too much physical and mental energy to give himself up to settled lotus-eating. Future years found him touring strenuously in Libya and Tunisia, and around the Red sea. In the first year of his retirement, 1925, he went on a trip quite worthy of his 'vagabondage' before the war. It was a long meander through the Isles of Greece, following the voyage of the Argonauts. His letter describing this is sprinkled liberally with quotations from the classics and Shelley, and glints with happy observations, as when he sights in the phosphorescent bay where the Argo was built a dolphin 'like a Catherine wheel revolving and sparking in the water'. He decided to climb Mount Pelion (5090 feet) in the steps of Jason, and disdaining mule and guide, set out with 'a mountain staff, cheese and bread in my pockets and a flask, and box of bugpowder and a map of Thessaly'. At the summit he 'drank to the health of the Clan under the eyes of the Olympians', and descending partway, bedded down for the night.

The sun was down and the moon up, so I found a nest of heather and wild thyme for the night, by the flowing water a little further down the glen. It seemed too lovely a spot and too sweet a night for sleep. 'The heavens were telling and the bright-eyed stars looked as though they would like to speak.' I began to trace the Argo and the Argonauts in the sky, as they endure after their apotheosis, Orpheus and Butes, Castor and Polydeuces, but sleep overwhelmed me like a wave of the sea . . .

I know now, almost as well as Jason could have, the vineyard with choicest grapes and figs, the little hollows in the bed of Anauros where ripe pomegranates lurk, and the apples hang red and the pears golden. I know the softest beds of Thyme and Basil under sheltering Planes and Olives, the sweet spot above the little village of Almeria where green tree frogs and baby tortoises watch one quaff the icy water as it springs from the ground like Arethusa to meet one's lips.

Returning to Egypt, he embarked on the study of a subject in which he was to become a noted authority – the liturgies of the Eastern Christian churches. His interest had been aroused by his nephew Campbell, who,

On the Red Sea Cruise in 1930. With his nephew Campbell (in the tarboosh) at the lighthouse on the Daedalus Reef. Campbell was at the time Senior Engineer with the Egyptian Ports and Lights Administration

improbably, combined a career as a mechanical engineer (he was for some years in the Egyptian Ports and Lights Administration) with a private passion for church rituals. McPherson had always had a general interest in the subject, and now focused this more precisely

Cairo, *facile Princeps* amongst the cities of the East, though exulting in as many mosques as there are days in the Moslem year, can boast at least as many churches as there are Sundays in the Christian year, and these, though lacking in external magnificence, and in fact often camouflaged and hidden away, are, I feel sure, richer in cosmopolitan interest than the churches of any town in the world, from the point of view of Church History. They are a very palimpsest of apostolic, patristic and mediaeval lore.

During Christmastide in 1926, he noted that he heard masses in Armenian, in Greek mixed with Arabic (at the Melkite church), in Latin (with the Jesuits), in Chaldaean, Coptic, Syrian, Syrian Arabic and Egyptian Arabic, and in Slavonic (with announcements in Maltese). The letter glows with descriptions of vestments, ikons, candlelit altars and processions, joyous chants as 'the baby saviour reigned from his manger, Death was flying into the night, and Sin was hurtling back into the Pit'. But the sacred merged easily into the profane:

To 'Rene   *Feast of St Stephen (Orthodox) 26.12.25–8.1.26*
The chanting of the Christmas lessons, in Greek and Arabic, was so

interminable, and I so footsore and sleepy, that I reluctantly left, and bee-
lined towards my rooms across a rather disreputable bit of Cairo; but
finding I had a thirst and was hungry withal, I deviated through a worse
towards the beer gardens of the capital. Dogs and cats and nightwatchmen were squabbling over the contents of the rubbish bins, a few
revellers were singing arm in arm, and a few girls behind locked doors
and iron-grilled windows, like animals in a menagerie were taking the
air by swinging their bare legs through the bars. A little light burned
here and there at the tomb of a holy sheikh, and a face or two might be
seen watching at the Judas windows of some gambling dens, and in one
narrow *Haret*, shrieks from a window seemed to indicate that a difference
of opinion had arisen between the sexes within. And the moon threw her
virgin rays over all. When nearly out of this picturesque region, and
passing the door of a well-lighted bar, a Greek at the door suddenly
greeted me effusively, and begged me to come in. I returned his
Christmas greetings but declined his invitation, whereupon he shouted to
one Panagiotis within to bring chair, beer and maza outside. A smiling
ruffian, who also seemed to recognise me, and who, I observed had lost
half an ear, brought a wobbly chair, but sound good beer at once, and
soon followed it up with grilled kidneys, cutlets, etc, and excellent mixed
grill. After trying in vain to recall my entertainer, I put a leading
question or two, and he said: '*Christe kai Panagia*, seven years ago tonight,
what a night that was, when you and your police rounded us up, just
when the fight was getting a bit sultry. Our old friend Panagiotis here
had just had his ear bitten off, and I had a bullet in my arm from 'Mitry's
revolver, and, by God, Sir, if you had not come when you did the next
would have been in my heart, for 'Mitry was a devil and could shoot.'
Not being able to disentangle the incident in my memory, I evaded by
asking what had become of 'Mitry. 'That, *Kyrie*, you ought to know better
than I; he jumped out of the window and escaped at the time, but I heard
you got him and deported him to Crete; anyway he has never appeared
since, I have still got his wife, whom all the trouble was about; and she
has dreamt, God bless her, three times that she saw the crows picking his
bones, so I don't think he will trouble us again. Eh! Sir, God is good, and
here's luck and a good Christmas to you. Panagio, you old *Poustis*, fill the
Excellency's glass.'

I went my way, refreshed, vaguely recalling having sent a very bloody
object, presumably my host Spirides, to the Police Prison, about the time
he referred to. *Où là gratitude va-t-elle se nicher?*[1]

During the following Easter he enjoyed a similar profusion of liturgical
splendours, followed by a reminder of the 'lurid nightmare' of past years.

[1] An echo of Molière's comment on a beggar who tried to give him back an accidentally
over-lavish donation: '*Où la vertu va-t-elle se nicher?*' (*Vie de Molière*, in Voltaire's *Mélanges
littéraires*)

To Campbell   Feria Tertia post Pasqua. *6 April 1926*
I had intended sleeping in Cairo, but the slightly de-crescent moon and
the general beauty of the night and atmosphere tempted me to ride out to
Bein el-Saryat. Though long after midnight, the innumerable cafés in
town and in the village of Dukki, and in my own little *esba*, were full of
life and music, and crowded with people who had professed to keep the
Fast of Ramadan in the day, and made up for it at night. My own staff
were lying about in the garden when I arrived, listening to Mousa, Gad's
little brother-in-law, singing the Koran. He had been right through it
once during Ramadan, and was back on the Surat el-Baqara, the *sura* I
sang in the gates of el-Azhar during the anarchy and the bloodshed, with
revolver under my Sheikh's robes, and armed Sudani in hiding outside to
help me immobilise the mighty sheikh who was preaching massacre, if
and when he emerged.

Entering quietly by my private doors, no one observed me but the
dogs, so I sat in the *'propylaea'*, in front of the south door, only a few yards
from the group, but so hidden by a maze of honeysuckle and passion
flowers in bloom, that still no one saw or heard me and the plaintive
cadence of Mousa's clear young voice, and the general repose and
atmosphere, were not interrupted for a moment. I was not really
listening to the words of the Prophet, but thinking of the Sheikh Mustafa
Obeid, referred to above, the 'Lion of el-Azhar', how after deciding on
the assassination of the Premier, and other members of the government,
and the utter extermination of 'all English vermin', and after
reproaching them for cowardice in allowing the Mamur Zapt (me), a
few nights before, to arrest the good Omar Bey, with sacred secret papers
of el-Azhar, instead of killing him and setting the Bey free – and that in
the very door of the mosque of Hussein; how after this and more he
emerged with his disciples, like a lion amongst jackals, the jackals
praying for the honour of the lion's sojourn with them, as his own house
was watched by police; and how I cut in with a still more pressing
invitation for the night, and the disciples fled, and after vain appeals for a
rally the lion fled too, and was caught and handed over to Gad, whilst I
dealt with the one man, 'Gunna', who really showed fight and stabbed
one of my agents; how the armed Sudanese kept the mob off as we
marched the 'Prophet' to the cells under my office; how – but here I was
brought back to the words of the greater Prophet which Mousa was
reciting: 'Oh, sons of Israel, remember the blessings wherewith I blessed
ye!' for they reminded me of the Reproaches of our Lord to *'Popule meus'*
which I had heard at church in the morning.

Soon after this, he fell seriously ill, from the relapsing fever which had
plagued him for several years. His eldest brother, Ja, sent a message of
thanks to Gad for the care he was taking of him, and Gad replied, for, as
McPherson noted: 'Gad was extraordinarily bucked by the appreciative

remark in your letter, and this letter is entirely off his own bat. He got
Mousa to write it at his dictation in Arabic and implored me to turn it into
English. I am doing so as literally as possible':

5 Shaaban, 1345, 2 February 1927

Oh, my Father,
most respected and beloved, the Bey,
Chief of the Tribe of McPherson

Accept my *salaama*, Oh, my father, and the Peace of God, and His
Blessing. Since a small space of time, His Excellence the Major, read me
from your letter, that you (and your tribe) thank me for looking after the
Major, and he very ill. By Allah, I thank you and your noble daughter,
and the Tribe. It is true that I have helped him in his illness as ever and
done all I know to tend towards his good health, but how could not this
be: was not I with him in the war? Did not Allah spare us both, when
thousands were killed, even when the shell fell in his dugout and burnt
his blankets, and we lived the rabbits' life and I, the little rabbit, made
burrows for the Excellent big rabbit, and afterwards, for me: and the
shells said whurrrrr whurrrrr boom. And your brother the Major found
me little and poor, for my father had died and my uncles and relations
took our land and our cattle, for they said father owed them money, and
my uncle Khalifa paid money to the Omda to send me to the war instead
of him: and when the war was over he did not forsake me, but made me
his special Orderly, with good pay and Oh my God what rations;
especially at Kantara for I ate too much and sent sand-bags full of tea and
sugar, and other things to my sister and brother at el-Awadat. And he
saved my money which would have gone in air, and I was rich then, over
£10 a month with allowances, and helped me to redeem our *gamus*, and
save the house from going with the land.

Now, thank Allah and the Major, I am rich. I have two acres of land,
which my brother, Gad el-Kerim looks after, three *gamus*, a camel, sheep
and a wife and baby, and the house rebuilt and increased. And all the
people of our village are afraid of me because of the Major, for he is very
great in the Ministry of Interior, and was Mamur Zapt, and Head of all
Secret Police. By God, if I served him all day and all night, I could never
pay him for his goodness. With words I cannot thank him and only a
little by my deeds. At Kantara I was ill to death, and he tended me and
saved me. Now when he is very ill I am ill too, and when they said he was
going to die, I felt I should die too. When father died, the Omda and my
uncles and relations treated us like mud 'Gad, you dirty son of a dog, do
this!' 'Gad, you lousy bastard, clean up this!' Now when the pasha gives
me leave to my village they meet me at the station: the Omda brings me
his best donkey to ride, worth fifty ginehs. '*Gad effendi*, you must honour
us tonight by coming to dinner, there will be music and dancing girls to
celebrate your blessed arrival!' 'Sir Gad, the village is bereaved when

you go away and take the light from us!' 'Welcome, my Gad, son of the crescent moon, the village prays for naught but your precious health, and long life to the noble pasha!' Thank God, in spite of their prayers, he is better now, and I am well and strong because he is nearer well. And we went to Cairo, and he was weighed and had improved seven lbs. And I do not thank the doctors. What have they done? But I thank Io the cow, whom God bless. She gives five litres of milk every day, and cream and rice puddings and cheese and *liban zibadi*, and butter, and prawn custards, and fish pâtés, and *egflibs*. And the hens lay twenty eggs a day, and the *Zagluls* (young pigeons) are good in soup, and the young rabbits and chickens are good every way : and in the garden there are vegetables, so I go little to the markets, and all is good and like medicine to his health. And this morning Lucy the donkey had a baby boy, and his name is Shaaban: and he rides Lucy nearly every day, and sometimes Shindawi, Lucy's brother. And I and my wife and baby Zenab ask the Lord always to take from the Pasha this cursed illness, and I think little by little it will go, for we say ' *Ya Rob, Ya Rob*, there are many you could better give it to'. And in conclusion my *salaama*; and to you and the noble daughter and all the family of your house we ask our God when you are coming with an honoured visit, and I shall be much blessed if you come to my village, which is close to el-Aqsar and King Tut-ankh-Amun, and when we were building up my house we dug up an old stone full of pictures and old Egyptian writing and we buried it again for you. On the morning of the great feast of the Nebi Jesus, at dawn all the dogs broke into the pasha's bedroom, and sang to him a hymn. And last Sunday all the eggs under the Goose hatched, and her children are very beautiful. And God's Peace on you and His Blessing, my Lord.

GAD

Note – Gad's ideas become less connected as he proceeds, as you will perceive, so that it is not always easy to determine whether he is referring to me or Allah or the donkey. I fear you will find it as hard to follow as I have to read and translate. The dogs' carol singing on Christmas morn, is quite true, but Gad's remembering the incident and introducing it into his letter strengthens my suspicion that he engineered the entry into my room.

Salaam alekum,
JOE

Another Christmas was the occasion of a letter to McPherson's young great-niece, the daughter of Campbell. He had a gift of making friends with children, and was known to a whole generation of great-nephews and great-nieces as 'Uncle Quack', for his spirited imitation of a duck. He is here seen at his most charming and playful.

Left: McPherson as Father Christmas at a children's party. *Right:* In the garden at Porziuncula with two monks from the Carmelite church at Shoubra

My dear Hilary

What news I have is in my letter to your dad, which I expect you will read, so this is just to tell you that all the little birds and beasties here, including Gad's kids, send kisses, and wish me to say how much they missed yours when you left.

Which reminds me that a few days ago we had another little Xmas party at Porziuncula, in which many of the pets took part in a way: for when we were sitting by the fire after lunch, some of the guests wanted to go round and see them all, but were too full and lazy: so the Staff arranged a procession through the room, entering by the balcony door, and exiting by that on the S. side of the room. Io's little calf whom the boys declare is my foster-sister, because we are being brought up on the same milk, was restive and had to be carried through, and Meroë and Fotis, the goats, wanted to pull crackers, and the moke Lucy to eat the marron glacés, but the geese marched through in perfect military order, and the turkey cock was majestic, and so on.

Two monks were of the guests, and were the jolliest of a jolly party. They had blessed the yule log, over which we sat and drank toasts in DOM, and we watched that it should not burn right out, like the log of Meleager, which would have been a shocking tragedy.

Your dad in his letter told me that you still sing 'Daddy wouldn't buy me a bow-wow.', and that you remember our singing it as we crossed the Nile. Are these the right words?

'DADDY WOULDN'T BUY ME A BOW-WOW'
wowowowowowowowowowowowowowowowowowowo

1 Daddy wouldn't buy me a bow-wow wow-wow –
I've got a little cat, but she does things on the mat,
I'd much rather have a bow-wow-wow.

2 Daddy &c. as before
I've got a little kitten, one of Marmy's latest sittin',
But I'd rather &c.

3 Daddy &c.
I've got a cockatoo, but she talks like auntie Loo,
So I'd rather &c.

4 Daddy &c.
I've got a little pig, whose tail's all curly wig,
I'd rather &c.

5 Daddy &c.
I've got a wallaby, but she pockets buns at tea,
I'd rather &c.

6 Daddy &c.
My silly little hen, only lays eggs now and then,
So I'd rather &c.

7 Daddy &c.
I've got a little cock, but he crows too soon o'clock,
I'd rather &c.

8 Daddy &c.
I've got *un petit singe*, who holds views like Canon Inge,
I'd much rather &c.

9 Daddy &c.
I've an ornithornyncnus paradoxus, but he winks at us and mocks us,
So I'd rather &c.

10 Daddy &c.
I've got a Teddy Bear, but he's much the worse for wear,
I'd rather &c.

11 Daddy &c.
I've got a baby calf, but can never make him laugh,
I'd rather &c.

12 Daddy &c.
It's but a little while, when again we'll cross the Nile,
Singing, 'DADDY'S BOUGHT A BOW-WOW-WOW'.

To supplement his pension, McPherson turned to writing articles for various well known magazines of the day, including *John o' London's Weekly*, and *Wide World*.

His subjects ranged from the ancient Coptic monasteries of Egypt to the Belief in the Evil eye, from Egyptian folk medicine to the theory that Egyptian Arabic contained elements of Ancient Punic. But his main interest then and for years ahead was the study of the 'Moulids' or religious festivals of Egypt, on which he was to publish a comprehensive book. He was encouraged in this study by a close friend, one of the greatest anthropologists of his time, E. E. Evans-Pritchard, later Professor of Social Anthropology at Oxford, but in the 1930s for some years Professor of Sociology at the Egyptian University in Cairo. A brief note to Evans-Pritchard shows the idea for the book taking shape.

Dear Bakurëmi[1]   *'Porziuncula' Bein el-Saryat 18 July 1934*
Moulids: There has been an almost continuous succession of excellent moulids, of which Sheikh Farag, and Sheikh Nasr are quite new to me, and if your gentle urging ever overcomes my lazy inertia, and I write my book, there will be a good deal of new matter, (though the behaviour of *'Qara Goz'* in the Punch and Judy shows, and the Phallic and Lesbian dancings and much else will have to be left in Arabic, as English versions of Boccaccio and Petronius leave passages in Italian, and Latin.) At the moulid of Fatma el-Newawiya, there were several booths of a type new to me, but probably you met with them in more southern Africa. Jet-black boys and girls danced to strange instruments – the *Ringa*, in a sort of shrine, which was like a small piano with the jumps, the *Mugrizan*, a sort of zither, *shackshackas*, like cocktail slings, and a barrel-shaped *tabla* which at times made a noise like guns firing; the whole a kind of jazz in its primitive *désinvolture. Booza* was passed round in bowls, and some got very merry.
Music: After a couple of little dinners here recently in the garden, the boys and little Zenab Warda, and Antar, have given alfresco displays of quarter-staff, dancing, mummery, and music, and elicited considerable applause from the guests, but when Sencourt's[2] boy has danced in with *Sigat*, or *Tarr*, or led with the *Darabuka*, he has brought down the house, and I have handed castanets to the English ladies and they have danced in too.

[1] 'Blood-brother' in the language of the Zande people of the southern Sudan. In *The Zande Trickster* (Oxford at the Clarendon Press 1967), Evans-Pritchard writes that 'Zande men, because they are friends ... make blood-brotherhood between them by consuming each other's blood.' Another authority on Zande states that *Bakurëmi* is often used in a general sense of chum.

[2] Robert Sencourt (1890–1969): critic, biographer, historian. A resident of Cairo at this time, and Professor of English Literature in the University of Egypt, 1935–36.

Vale: All here deeply lament your departure. All the villagers, including my own boys, particularly love you because of the hearty way you return their salaams, and the human way you laugh and wrestle with them. If you disappear again into the heart of Africa, as seems imminent, this must be a most valuable asset, and help in research, and a powerful weapon to ward off dangers from savage primitives.

Vale, si possis cito veni!
Yours,
MAC.

Among his many interests, politics and public affairs ranked low, perhaps because the modulations in the relationship between Egypt and Britain in these years seemed rather humdrum in comparison with the dramas of 1919 and the early 1920s. After the 1922 declaration of independence, with its massive reservation of powers to Britain, the political situation had become more complex, and more confused. There were now three protagonists on the stage – the British High Commissioner, the Wafd (the nationalist party), and King Fuad. The king detested the parliamentary constitution that had been imposed upon him, and hankered for a more autocratic role; the Wafd manoeuvred to check the king's ambitions, and aspired to abolish the powers reserved to the British; the High Commissioner's brief from the British government was to encourage a stable, moderate, Egyptian government and obtain from it formal consent to the reserved powers.

In the many manoeuvrings inside this triangle of power, there were two constants – the determination of the British to protect their imperial interests, particularly the Suez Canal, the corridor to India; and the desire of Egyptians of all classes to end the British occupation. In 1936, a treaty was signed by the two countries; it was for a twenty-year military alliance, and it formally ended the British occupation. Britain undertook to defend Egypt against attack, and promised to use her best endeavours to induce the various European powers to give up their legal privileges under the Capitulations; British troops were limited to ten thousand in peacetime, and confined to the Canal Zone; the RAF would have airfields and fly-over rights; the Royal Navy could use Alexandria Harbour for eight years. Egypt, on her part, was to provide roads, and services and the necessary buildings in the Canal Zone for the British troops. In fact, this last provision lagged behind, so that by the outbreak of war in 1939, the British troops were mostly where they had always been – in barracks in Cairo and elsewhere in Egypt.

During this whole period there was sporadic violence against Britons living in Egypt. McPherson himself once beat off an intruder at Porziuncula. However, it is a remarkable testimony to the tolerant and forgiving nature of the Egyptians that the ex-Mamur Zapt lived out his retirement, not only in peace, but also surrounded with respect and affection.

19

Swansong

Give me my scallop-shell of quiet,
My staff of faith to walk upon,
My scrip of joy, immortal diet,
My bottle of salvation,
My gown of glory, hope's true gage;
And thus I'll take my pilgrimage.

Sir Walter Raleigh: *The Passionate Man's Pilgrimage*
(quoted by J. W. McP.)

On the outbreak of war, the Egyptian government fulfilled their obligations under the 1936 treaty. Though they did not declare war on Germany, they broke off diplomatic relations. The British exercised their full rights and turned Egypt into an armed camp crammed with British and Imperial troops. In late 1940, the Italians invaded from Libya, and advanced to Sidi Barrani, a hundred miles into Egyptian territory. Within a few months they had been briskly evicted by the British forces under Wavell, and driven back another five hundred miles.

At this stage the mood in Cairo, as many observers have testified, was of an extraordinary detachment from the military drama in the Western Desert. Cairo had seen so many wars in her two thousand years of history. Alan Moorehead, the Australian war correspondent, wrote in his *African Trilogy*:

'. . . if towns have a gender, Cairo is a lady. It was meant by the High Command to be a basic fortress in the Middle East, as Spartan as Gibraltar, as grim as Malta. But something in the climate thwarted the design . . . Swollen to nearly two millions by the influx of troops, artificial and dirty, filled with rickety noisy streets and tumbledown buildings, the city sprawled over the lush mud-flats at the apex of the Nile Delta. Its mood was gay, rather flashily romantic in the evening, shrill and ugly in the morning. By instinct, I am afraid, the lady was a prostitute.'

In this frenetic city, Joseph McPherson was sometimes to be seen threading his way through the traffic on his white donkey, usually accompanied by his syce. He owned no car, and rarely travelled in one, regarding them as one of the great banes of modern times. Well into his seventies, he was restless at the restrictions of age, and wrote to his nephew Campbell, now a Brigadier in the Royal Electrical & Mechanical Engineers:

To Campbell   *'Porziuncula' 2 April, 1941*
What I should love would be to have the command of a little company of
natives in the heart of Abyssinia: a job which Evans-Pritchard is now
enjoying, and for which I think he is eminently suited, or failing that a
War correspondent's post on one of our battleships; but unhappily age
and health, particularly a major aneurism of the aorta, makes it
impossible to take up anything which I may not drop instantly on feeling
the warning, for long and complete rest, the only cure. So I have to try to
make myself believe that the pen is mightier than the sword, and be
content with a bit of writing, propaganda, and such like.

1942 was the year of crisis in Egypt, both for the relationship between
Egypt and Britain, and the war. When the Germans made their
formidable entrance into the North African campaign, immediately after
their triumphs in Greece, important elements in Egypt began to display
their pro-Axis leanings. Both King Farouk (who had succeeded his father
Fuad in 1936), and his Prime Minister Aly Maher were prepared to
intrigue against the British. As Rommel's Afrika Korps scored more
successes against the British army, student processions in the streets of
Cairo chanted 'We are Rommel's soldiers'. The masterful British
Ambassador, Sir Miles Lampson (six feet five inches in height, and
weighing twenty stone, with a personality to match), went to the Palace
escorted with armoured cars, and presented an ultimatum to the king –
either he must abdicate or appoint a Prime Minister more sympathetic to
the British cause. Farouk submitted to the demand. (Incidentally, the news
of his humiliation convinced a young officer in the Egyptian Army,
Lieutenant Nasser, that Egypt's only hope for national regeneration lay in
a revolution.)

   In the summer of 1942, Rommel's Afrika Korps pushed the British
forces back to the Alamein line only sixty miles from Alexandria. If that
line broke, the Axis troops could be at the gates of Egypt's two principal
cities within hours. In Cairo, the legendary panic known as the 'flap'
ensued, as a mass exodus of, mainly, European residents began.
McPherson described it as 'the darkest night of my life'.

On Friday, 3 July 1942, enemy occupation (anyway for a time) seemed
inevitable. Our fleet had gone East, 'fled', it was said, GHQ was doing
the same. Their bonfire of papers and that of the Embassy were imitated
by civilians, self included. Up to then the chief fear for people like myself
was compulsory evacuation, but on 2 July, a man in GHQ assured me in
confidence that there was no time to apply the scheme drawn up two
years before, that civilians could stew in their own juice, for the army
would evacuate entirely, and that I might know when the Boche had
actually broken through at el-Alamein, by the British Guards in the
village decamping. This they did about 2 o'clock that night. A new
guard, or the same, returned at about 3, were declared by my neighbours

'Porziuncula' in the mid-1930s

to be enemies; and crowds of colonial troops which cumbered the road near here were entirely believed to have fled from the broken front.

The Vth Column is immensely strong in this land of Quislings, German-paid agitators, and a marvellous almost uncontradicted enemy propaganda, radio and the rest, swallowed whole by even friendly Egyptians. It's wonderful how well they behaved, but there is no doubt the Germans, had they got in, would have followed up their propaganda by every urge to massacre, and to loot anything they did not loot themselves.

Towards dawn Mousa came to me on the roof, in great agitation, with a complete Egyptian rig-out, and implored me to put it on and to come away at once. 'Sayed and I,' he added, 'have been burying arms and treasures, yours and our own, all the night, in the hope that we get back, but come along now.' Sayed came and backed Mousa up, – in vain, – and they argued, – 'you have kept us and fed us the last twenty years, and now it would be a privilege and pleasure, to return it a little, so come away to our quiet village'.

I thanked them, but asked Sayed to go on with the burials, under my guidance a little, whilst Mousa helped me pack and hide my Twenty-five Books of Family Letters, my stamps (catalogued a lot over £1000) and many little treasures, which my *neutral* (Swiss) neighbours, the Jägers, nobly took over at great risk to themselves, as well as £100 in loose cash, – and later my piano, wine, statue of St Michael, and much else . . .

To recall such instances of loyal friendship makes this crisis almost a joy to look back on. Some of my other friends offered me a place in their car, if, as they then contemplated, they motored south, including Col. F——, quite a new acquaintance, with special sources of information. A note came from him early that day, – 'In my opinion there is not a minute to lose'. He told me also where I could join him in a country place of his near Luxor, where he proposed waiting to see which way the wind blew. Omar Bey Wahby, the Sub-Governor of Cairo, an old friend whom I have seen only two or three times in the last forty years, offered me a home in his country house, permanently if I lost my own. For true friends, for the passing of a horror, and for innumerable blessings, '*El Hamd Lillah*', God be praised.

The tension was much relieved when I ascertained for certain that the new troops in my old fields were British, not German, – for me, that is, – not for the villagers I fear, whose relations with our men were deplorable, making my position most difficult. It was an immense relief when later, they did go . . .

That same morning, 3.7.42, Mr B—— a Palace official, whom I have known for many years, dashed in with his car, shouting, – 'Mac., you have not five minutes to lose'. He is a man who professes inner knowledge of everything, and usually bursting with secrets. For the first time in history, he would not stop for a drink; and I hurried to town, not in his car, but in one the Jägers had kindly put at my disposal, with a chauffeur, and found it impossible to get money out of the PO where I had a deposit, or from the Bank: both were thronged and the streets outside . . .

Anyway I had decided to sit tight: to parley with the Italians if they came, and to let my revolver do the parleying as long as it could in the case of the Germans, whom I have always loathed too profoundly for any dealings, even long before the other war.

The 'flap' subsided as General Auchinleck took personal charge at the front, and the British line held. Four months later, with Montgomery's victory at Alamein, the 'Battle of Egypt' (as Churchill called it in his message of congratulations) was over, and the Axis forces were pursued ever further westward to their defeat in Tunisia in May 1943.

McPherson meanwhile had published in Cairo his book, *The Moulids of Egypt*. This study of the religious feasts of Egypt (126 of them) was the product of forty years of fascinated observation. He dedicated it to 'H.Em. the Sayed Ahmad Morad el-Bakri, Grand Sheikh of the Sufi Orders', and in his introduction paid tribute to the friends of his early days in Egypt who had set him on the path of knowledge, notably Dr Ibrahim Zaky, and Hamid Mahmoud, now Minister for Hygiene in the Egyptian Government, and also the late Grand Mufti, the Sheikh Mohammed Bikhit. He began with the words: 'The writer has spent more than half of a long life in Egypt and thanks Allah that such has been his privilege'. The anthropologist, E. E. Evans-Pritchard, at that time on active service in the

Middle East, wrote the preface in which he declared himself to be, in this
field, McPherson's pupil, and added: 'It is a contribution to our knowledge
of Egyptian life, a worthy supplement to the immortal writings of Lane.
Major McPherson has paid to the people of Egypt the debt which he freely
acknowledges he owes them for the hospitality and kindness he has
enjoyed at their hands for close on half a century.'

McPherson surveyed the beliefs and practices of Sufism, Moslem
mysticism, and the sacred aspects of the Moulids. But he reserved his most
detailed descriptions for the secular side, the carnival celebrations. In this
book is preserved a record of Egyptian diversions, many of which go back
to mediaeval times, or in some cases (he would contend) to the Pharaohs:
processions, whirling dances, chants, traditional music on many curious
instruments, conjurors, dwarfs, giants, strong men, muscle dancers, fire-
eaters, snake charmers, dancing horses, games of chance and tests of
strength, sugar figurines marvellously arrayed in tinsel, gorgeous booths
hung with lanterns – an endless list of popular delights. McPherson
lamented that many of these pleasures were being quashed by the
authorities, apparently on the grounds that large crowds led to disorder.

Those who are divorcing games from the worship of our modern moulids
are leaving the Sacrifice, but a sacrifice which is not for the people, but a
sacrifice of the people, of their inherited rights, of their joys, and with
these, of their religion.

The monks and anchorites of Islam, especially the Sufis, have
preached love and joy in earthly matters as leading up to rapture in
heavenly things; and the Christian church is superlatively hedonistic in
the right way. The Church which has bred an army of martyrs, and a
host of eremites, ascetics and contemplatives, uses a liturgy which is full
of calls to joy and song: the Introits to its masses begin frequently with
such exhortations as *'Gaudete, Laetare!'*. . . .

Surely no Pope, Khalif, Monarch, Prince, Potentate, Ruler, or
Teacher, no Man who ruthlessly or unnecessarily wipes the smile instead
of the tear from the face of the people, can hope for God to smile on him
or wipe away his tears.

He had another project in hand, a sequence of family letters of a different
sort from the preceding ones. He called it 'Swansong', and divided it into
two parts, the first entitled 'An Ethical Odyssey or The Tao Quest', and
the second 'Down the Arches of the Years'. He had intended a brief outline
to fill in his life story up to the age of thirty-five, when he came to Egypt
and began the family letters, but as he wrote, memories crowded in upon
him and it turned into a substantial work.

The 'Ethical Odyssey' exhibited his profound interest in philosophy and
comparative religion. Though its argument was primarily concerned with
his firm adherence to Catholicism, he paid his respects to pagan

McPherson mounted these two photos together,
showing Gad as the 'honoured Rentier' after he
had acquired some land nearby; and (inset) the young
Gad as the raw recruit or 'lousy bastard'

philosophers, and to the Islamic faith he had observed for so many years –
with a personal aside.

As I write on the twenty-first day of November (Mother's birthday) . . . I
can hear the voice of my old batman Gad el-Moula, so wrapt in prayer
that he is oblivious to all around him even to the smell of a steaming flesh-
pot of Egypt round which the other servants are already sitting; yet he is
a gluttonous rascal and has tasted nothing since before dawn this
morning, for this is the month of fasting. Though he is fat and lazy, it is
the great desire of his life to perform the pilgrimage (i.e. to Mecca),
regardless of a wretched diet, and all sorts of hardships and fatigue.
There are multitudes like him! How many Christians conform to their
religion to the same extent – anyway in outward observances – I wonder.

'Down the Arches of the Years' traced his life up to the age of thirty-five
from his childhood. He recalled the happy days at 'The Rookery' with his
five brothers, his uneasy relationship with his father, his devotion to his
mother, and his exhilarating years at Oxford (when, it seems, he might
have first earned his nickname of 'The Wild One'). He exhumed an old
unhappy love affair from fifty years before: he and his best friend had

The Water wheel at Porziuncula. McPherson is behind the buffalo

fallen in love with the same girl; she had rejected McPherson and married the friend. The marriage proved disastrous: 'She turned out a slatternly, lazy, useless hussy', who neglected her baby so that it sickened and died. The friend disappeared to Australia, never to be heard of again.

In a rare mood of self-analysis, he pinpointed the moment in his adolescence when, reading Keats, he came across the lines:

'I can see
Nought earthly worth my compassing.'

and realised that he was devoid of ambition for wealth, power and position. He added: 'I most earnestly wish it to be understood, especially by any youthful members of the family who read this, that I am not advocating this or that. This is a record of my own life-scheme, not advice to follow it, or the reverse. Call this an admission, a confession if you like.'

Part of that confession was a description of the determined, even desperate, way he had clung to boyhood. He called his graduation day at Oxford his *Dies Irae*.

I know not what misgivings assailed the Roman youth when he assumed the *toga virilis*. Perhaps he saw further and more truly than I, for I as an adolescent was obsessed with a horror, not only of old age but of manhood, for men seemed to me (as to Grahame's little boy of *The Golden Age*), to reject all that made life light and joyous, and to accept all manner of yokes and loads. Like Lear's pelicans, 'I think so then and I thought so still', but I have learnt that the rain which soaks through the fledgeling down bringing chill to the heart of the young bird, flows off the feathers of the grown-up bird: that adolescence exaggerates its pains in its moods which regard impressions and ills as permanent and irremediable, that youth by nature is *heauton-timoroumenos.*

How as a school boy I pitied the masters, and as an undergrad, the dons, wondering what they had kept of life that was worthwhile! I think my attitude to grown-ups was that of the tadpole to the frog, hating the idea of losing his tail and his free swimming existence, to sit and croak and seemingly pass dull hours. I liked men well enough, and immensely admired their learning and knowledge, but not their wisdom, which I early realised is a very different matter.

The reiterated dictum of Lucretius that all change is the death of what went before, is I think a striking truth, when taken with his contextual implication, that death need be neither an end nor an evil.

The change of the crawling grub into an immobile pupa, then of the chrysalis into the imago, perhaps a beautiful free flying creature, may savour more of resurrection than of death, yet it is death to the grub, and death to the pupa *per se*; and it is death to the tadpole *per se*, when he loses his tail and gills, and assumes the batrachian imago. So it is Death to the boy, *per se*, when he advances to man.

When his mother died, he wrote, it was again a sort of death of boyhood.

I could no longer cling to boyhood's ways: a son is always a boy to his mother, but dying she had taken with her that vision to realms of eternal youth.

His cure for the accidie that followed this loss of a cherished image of himself was to leave England and go to Egypt.

Horace's assertion that people who run away over the seas change only their climate, but not their state of minds, is nailed to the counter as false and dangerous currency by my forty years of practically unclouded happiness, and undiminished interest in my changed life. In some way the change did supply the something essential lacking in my rather curious make-up. The depression which followed mother's death has never returned, though I think constantly of her, and dream of her frequently. . .

I never pray, and hope I shall never be tempted to, for I have been given so much without begging, that I should be ashamed to ask, and I so detest beggars and begging myself; and naturally I feel the more love and gratitude to Him who has not waited to be asked, and certainly, whatever may happen to me in the future, I could have no complaints. I fear indeed that the impulse to return thanks leads me to do so quite naturally when I have brought off something for which it would be so much more appropriate to ask pardon. I so seldom omit doing so after a meal at home, and very audibly, that if I forget to do so, the *suffragi* reports me to the cook, who comes to say that he fears I found the dinner rotten as I omitted ejaculating '*El-hamd lillah*' – 'Praise be to God'. (I then reassure him by shouting '*El-hamd lillah*', or if the dinner has not been a success, I use the Arab expression after bereavement or great affliction '*El-Hamd lillah ala kul hal*' – 'Praise be to God, under ALL circumstances'. Then the cook retires with his tail between his legs, more utterly crushed than if he had been between the upper and the nether millstone.)

When out, I do so mentally, or *submissa voce* in a Christian language, but sometimes forget and startle the assembly by '*EL-HAMD LILLAH*'.

As the war drew to an end, Joseph McPherson's letters, mainly to his Brigadier nephew Campbell, mentioned that his health has been showing signs of worsening with some 'nasty turns'. Nevertheless he was leading a lively social life, citing a couple of parties he had attended. At one there had been a group of 'Khuderi dervishes, who danced wonderfully, ate snakes, and impaled themselves on long '*dababis*''; at another 'towards midnight turkeys and sheep cooked whole and much else came on, and whisky, etc, flowed ad lib. I rode home across country about 2 a.m.' There was also news of Gad's children: 'Little Rose' had been married, and the *Aris* (bridegroom) had favourably impressed him; another daughter and a son were coming along well. He was planning 'a bit of a change at the Lake of Crocodiles'; Mousa would come with him. He asked Campbell, who was in Italy: 'When at Rome, enquire if there is any truth in the ghastly rumour that HH is contemplating an aerodrome in the Vatican gardens (if so, don't give him my love)'.

In the autumn of 1945 Campbell visited him at 'Porziuncula' and later wrote: 'It was a delight to meet Gad, Mousa and Sayed again, and witness their sheer love and devotion to you, and their happiness at seeing me'.

On 26 December, McPherson blithely responded.

The boys and all here send affectionate greetings with mine and shared my joy at having you here once again for a bit. Sayed has just brought me a pot of foaming beer in which I drink deeply to you and yours – with love and all fond wishes,

JOE

He had recently, in his eightieth year, completed a final chapter of his Swansong, which he entrusted to Campbell, with the instruction that no one should read it until after his death. It is the last of his family letters.

The war has given me many more guests than usual, including I am glad to say, some of our own young heroes. At present, Evans-Pritchard is up from Cyrene and making this place and the Abdin flat his HQ, whilst in Cairo for ten days or so. It's delightful having him.

The fire with immense logs from the garden trees was a great attraction during the long dry but cold winter, as the garden and balconies are now, and the billiard table and piano add to the amenities

'Bimbashi and Askari'

at all seasons; but however pleasant the days and merry the evenings here or in Cairo, the crowning delight to a lazy old person like myself is settling down to rest on my roof bed. So far it seems from the world, and so near the starry heavens, and the 'drowsy morphean amulets' of peace and repose transmute material dross into stardust, nebular but golden, and blend the microcosmos, and the cosmos and what is beyond and above the cosmos in some sixth dimension where man and nature and God are old acquaintances, never alien, where the *'flammantia moenia mundi'*[1] consume and disappear.

With them too dissolve the boundaries of life and sleep and death. Yet when the voice of the muezzin, or the call of the birds, or the glory of the rising sun, wake you to a new day, and you try in vain to grasp the elusive secrets of your visions, and wanderings of the night, you know that the Ego was never lost, and feel that it never will be. Nirvana is not its annihilation: nor is the goal of its evolution its mergence 'as a drop in the sea of Oman', as the Sufis express it. Rather, it seems to me, the individual is the asymptote[1] of the eternal hyperbola, ever approaching, but never merging.

This though expressed in pagan wise, and by a geometrical figure, is, I

[1] 'The blazing walls of the world' (Lucretius: *De Rerum Natura*, 1 : 73).
[1] Asymptote: A line which continually approaches a given curve, but does not meet it within a finite distance.

'Bill Sykes and his dogs'

believe, what has been revealed to and is taught by the Church, touching the mystery of individual existence.

And if the human spirit is so vagabond in sleep, 'twin brother of Death', it is a great thing to have the sacramental send-off of the Church, and Her spiritual ration of the Viaticum for the journey, even though when separated abruptly from the body – its guardian angels guiding – it may come safely into the hands of the Prince of Archangels, whose *métier* it is to receive it, and to present it in the Holy Light.

And so, if and when some morning, the 'Swan' has sung his last note, and seems deaf to the *ALLAH AKBAR* of the muezzin, blind to the glory of the rising sun, and dumbly irresponsive to Mousa's greeting when he brings the morning tea, tasteless now, and to grow cold as his body; and the doves and bulbuls and other bird friends try in vain to rouse him, and wait too in vain for their morning portion, and the hoopoe wags his head and flickers off, and the carawans, self-appointed guardians of the night stand by on their long legs like mutes, gazing with wonder in their great eyes like the herons of Diomedes, and the flowers have lost their colour and their perfume, – when it is

'Sunrise and morning star, and one clear call,'

then 'let there be no moaning at the bar!' – not even the moaning of friends, – but a flower-lined resting place, and flowers above. If friends wish to place anything more enduring than flowers, let it be engraved with the old greeting of Farewell – the one word, –

XAIPE

and should anything further be added, it might be, –

Sancte Michael, represente animam ejus in lucem sanctam.

Love enduring to all relatives and friends, and warm greetings to all who have the patience to read the 'Swan Song'.

JOSEPH MICHAEL VENANTIUS, BEN DOUGAL,
OF THE TRIBE OF CHATTAN.

On 18 January, 1946, the Eve of the Coptic Epiphany, he went into Cairo for the 'Blessing of the Waters'. He contracted a slight chill, and rested at home. Four days later as his servant Sayed handed him a hot drink to sip, he suddenly fell back dead. He is buried in Cairo, and his tombstone bears the inscription he wished:

XAIPE

Hail and Farewell.

Bibliography

Ahmed, J. M.: *The Intellectual Origins of Egyptian Nationalism*, London 1960
Aldridge, James: *Cairo, Biography of a City*, London 1969
Baedeker, Karl: *Egypt – A Handbook for Travellers*, London 1902
Berque, Jacques: *Egypt – Imperialism and Revolution*, London 1972
Blunt, W. S.: *The Secret History of the English Occupation of Egypt*, London 1907
Bowman, Humphrey: *Middle-East Window*, London 1942
Burgoyne, Elizabeth: *Gertrude Bell 1889–1914*, London 1958
Cecil, Lord Edward: *The Leisure of an Egyptian Official*, London 1921
Cromer, Earl of: *Modern Egypt*, London 1908
Elgood P. G.: *Transit of Egypt*, London 1928
Flower, Raymond: *Napoleon to Nasser, The Story of Modern Egypt*, London 1972
Gardner, Brian: *Allenby*, London 1965
Grafftey-Smith, Laurence Sir: *Bright Levant*, London 1970
Jarvis, C. S.: *The Back Garden of Allah*, London 1939
James, Robert Rhodes: *Gallipoli*, London 1965
Lane, E. W.: *Manners and Customs of the Modern Egyptians*, London 1836
Little, Tom: *Egypt*, London 1958
Lloyd, Lord: *Egypt since Cromer*, 2 Vols., London 1933–4
Lutfi al-Sayyid, Afaf: *Egypt and Cromer, A Study in Anglo-Egyptian Relations*, London 1968
Mansfield, Peter: *The British in Egypt*, London 1971
Marlowe, John: *Anglo-Egyptian Relations, 1800–1953*, London 1954
Massey, W. T.: *The Desert Campaigns*, London 1918
Milner, A.: *England in Egypt*, London 1901
Moorehead, Alan: *Gallipoli*, London 1956: *African Trilogy*, London 1944
McPherson, J. W.: *The Moulids of Egypt*, Cairo 1941
Nasser, Gamal Abdel: *The Philosophy of the Revolution*, Cairo 1955
Newman, E. Polson: *Great Britain in Egypt*, London 1928
Official History of the War: Military Operations Egypt and Palestine, 1930, Gallipoli, 1932
Richmond, J. C. B.: *Egypt 1798–1952*, London 1977
Rowlatt, Mary: *A Family in Egypt*, London 1956
Russell Pasha: *Egyptian Service*, 1902–1946, London 1949
Seth, R.: *Russell Pasha*, London 1966
Storrs, Ronald: *Orientations*, London 1943
Vatikiotis, P. J.: *The History of Egypt* (from Muhamad Ali to Sadat), London 1969

Wavell, Viscount: *Allenby in Egypt*, London 1943
Willcocks, William: *In Egypt During the Forty Years of the British Occupation*,
    London 1926
Young, George: *Egypt*, New York 1927

Glossary

Aalim (Ulama): a learned person(s)

Aalima: generally applied to a professional woman expert, e.g. the leader of a Zzarr

Arabieh: carriage; cab (horse-drawn)

Aris: bridegroom

Arusa: bride

Asha: dinner

Bab: a city gate

Balad: locality

Bairam: a short period of fasting after Ramadan

Barak (a): to kneel (of a camel)

Berseem: a kind of clover

Bey: Turkish title, often associated with official post; lower than Pasha

Bimbo: baby

Booza: fermented barley drink

Borkah (correctly, *burqu'*): veil

Caracol: police station

Corvée: system of forced labour

Dababis: pins

Dabour: wasp

Dahabieh: large felucca with a cabin

Darabuka: large musical instrument of earthenware, open at one end, but covered at the other, and larger end, by skin

Dervish: an initiate into one of the Islamic 'orders'

Dhura (or *Dourah*): Indian corn, maize

Dyb (pr. *deeb*): wolf

Effendi: mister

Esba: country dwelling outside a village

Fantass: metal water tank carried by camels (capacity 15 gallons)

Farsi: Persian

Fatiha (or *Fattah*): little opening chapter of the Koran

Fatur: breakfast; the sunset meal of Ramadan after the day's fast

Fellah (fellahin): peasant(s)

Ferash (*ferasheen*): servant(s)
Fikhy (or *Fiqi*): a professional singer of the Koran

Gabel: rocky hill
Galabieh: a man's robe
Gamuz (or *Gamuza*): water buffalo
Gamos: water buffaloes
Ghafir: guard; watchman

Hakima: wise woman
Harba: Sudanese spear
Haret: lane or small street
Harim: women's quarters; the women folk in a household
Hazam: sash around waist

Ifrangi: European

Kaimakan: Turkish title, equivalent to Lieutenant-Colonel; sometimes
    associated with official posts, e.g. city governor
Kassaba: metal ornament attached to the veil, and fixed between the
    eyebrows and the nose
Kawass: consular policeman
Khalifa: 'Commander of the Faithful – a title of the Ottoman Sultan; the
    rider in a zeffa representing the sheikh who is being honoured
Khamsin: desert wind
Khan: inn; caravanserai
Khoaga: European gentlemen settled in Egypt
Khoga: teacher
Khutba: sermon
Koran: the sacred book of Islam
Kurbag: whip
Kutab: school

Lacoum: Turkish delight
Liban Zibadi: yoghourt
Lokanda: hotel; inn

Machzan: shop
Madna: minaret
Magnun: in the power of the Djin; crazed
Mamour: district officer
Maulavi: Sufi dervish
Maza: mixed hors-d'oeuvres
Mihrab: niche in the wall of a mosque, indicating the direction of Mecca
Moulid: a popular religious feast in honour of a saint

Mudir: governor of a province

Mufti: Chief Doctor of the Law, with considerable ecclesiastical and civil jurisdiction

Mughrebi: Moorish head-gear

Murasla: messenger

Muski: district of Cairo

Mutasarrif: Lieutenant-Governor (Turkish)

Namuseyeh: mosquito net

Narghileh: hookah

Nebi: prophet

Omda: mayor, headman

Padisha: a title of the Ottoman Sultan

Pasha: A Turkish rank, often associated with an official post

Pir: spiritual father (Persian)

Porte: The Turkish government (from the residence of the Grand Vizier in Istanbul in the eighteenth century: Bab ulAly – in French *La Porte Sublime*)

Qibleh: praying niche of a mosque

Rakaa (or *rikaa*): the bending of the body in prayer

Ramadan: the ninth month of the Arabic year: the month of fasting (or Ramazan)

Riees: foreman

Ruhbat Laqaom: Turkish Delight

Saboa: the day a week after a birth of a child when certain ceremonies are performed

Sai: chain-man (in surveying)

Salamlek: public *levée* of the Sultan or his representative

Samaa: whirling dance of the dervishes

Sanjak: sub-division of a province

Saqqieh: water wheel

Sarraf: money-payer

Shakhshakha: rattle; sistrum

Shanta: case

Sharia: street

Shawish: policeman

Sheikh: master, head, learned or holy person

Sheshkama (Turkish: *şeşhane*): rifle

Sigat: brass castanets

Sitt: wife; lady

Suffragi: waiter, steward
Sufi: Persian dervish sect, particularly associated with Jalal el-Din
Suq: Market
Sura: chapter of the Koran
Syce: groom, running footman

Tabla: drum
Taliani: Italian
Tarr : tambourine
Tekieh: monastery
Turuq: sects; orders of Dervishes

Ulema: leading sheikhs (e.g. of el-Azhar)

Walad: boy
Warena: monitor lizard
Wizier (or *Wazir*) : Chief Minister

Ya!: Oh!
Ya hafeez!: Oh Protector! (said when frightened, or when seeing
   something unpleasant)
Ya Rob!: Oh God!
Ya salaam: How wonderful!

Zabadi: curds
Zaptieh: mounted soldier (Turkish)
Z'b: wolf
Zeffa: Dervish procession, the great feature of a complete Moulid
Zikr: a religious observance, whose essential is the repeated utterance of
   'Allah'; those who are devotees of this observance

Chronological Table of Events

1879 Khedive Tewfik succeeds Khedive Ismail.

1882 Nationalist Revolt by Arabi Pasha ends with defeat by Sir Garnett Wolseley at the Battle of Tel-el-Kebir.

1883 Sir Evelyn Baring (later Lord Cromer) becomes British Agent and Consul-General.

1892 Death of Khedive Tewfik, succession of Khedive Abbas Hilmi II

1906 Denshawai Incident.

1907 Sir Eldon Gorst succeeds Lord Cromer as Consul-General.

1911 Lord Kitchener becomes Consul-General on the death of Gorst.

1914 Break with Ottoman Empire: Abbas Hilmi II remains in Istanbul on outbreak of War.
Egypt declared a British Protectorate.
Hussein Kamel appointed Sultan by British.
Sir Henry McMahon replaces Kitchener as High Commissioner.

1915 *March – October*, Gallipoli Campaign.
February – Turks attack and are repulsed at Suez Canal.

1916 Sinai Desert Campaign – Turks driven back as far as Gaza.
Sir Reginald Wingate succeeds Sir Henry McMahon as High Commissioner.

1917 General Allenby ocupies Gaza and drives Turks from Palestine.
Sultan Hussein Kamel dies and is succeeded by Sultan Fuad.

1918 End of War – In November the Nationalist Leader Saad Zaghlul Pasha demands independence for Egypt.

1919 Revolution in Egypt: *March* – Zaghlul exiled to Malta.
April – Field-Marshal Allenby replaces Wingate as High Commissioner.
December – Milner Mission arrives in Egypt. Zaghlul now released from exile boycotts the Milner inquiry and remains in Paris.

1920 Milner Mission completes inquiry.

1921 Zaghlul returns to Egypt but refuses to accept Milner recommendations.
In December Zaghlul is deported to the Seychelles.

1922 Egypt is declared a sovereign independent state by the British government but with important powers reserved to Britain.
Sultan Fuad becomes King.

1923 In April Zaghlul's banishment ends and he returns to Egypt.
In September elections are held.

1924 In March, Zaghlul becomes Prime Minister with a Nationalist Majority Government.

In November, the Sirdar (Commander-in-Chief of the Egyptian Army) Sir Lee Stack is murdered.

1925 Egyptian Parliament dissolved.

In May a Coalition Government is formed in which Zaghlul declines office.

Allenby resigns and is replaced by Lord Lloyd.

1929 Sir Percy Lorraine replaces Lord Lloyd.

1933 Sir Miles Lampson replaces Sir Percy Lorraine.

1936 In April, King Fuad dies and is succeeded by his son Farouk.

In August, a treaty of mutual defence and alliance is signed by Egypt and Britain.

1939 Egyptian Government decides on policy of Non-Belligerency.

1940 Egypt invaded by Italian forces.

1941 *Jan–Feb*: Successful British counter-offensive.

March–April: German troops arrive in North Africa. Axis offensive under Rommel's command.

1942 *May 30*: Fall of Tobruk.

July 5: Rommel's forces at El Alamein, 60 miles from Alexandria.

Oct. 23–Nov. 4: Montgomery's Eighth Army defeats Rommel's Afrika Korps in Battle of El Alamein.

1945 End of War.

1952 King Farouk abdicates.

1953 Monarchy finally abolished by the Revolutionary Command Council.

1956 Prime Minister Nasser became President of the Arab Republic of Egypt.

1956 Suez Crisis.

Picture Credits

BBC HULTON PICTURE LIBRARY pages 77 (left) & 221; MANSELL COLLECTION pages 76, 120 & 254; POPPERFOTO pages 43, 121, 151, 223 & back cover; TOPICAL PRESS page 233. All other illustrations belong to the McPherson family.

Maps drawn by Line and Line.

Index